MOTOCROSS ON AIR!

*The BBC Grandstand Trophy
1963 to 1970*

Ian Berry

Forewords by
Dave Bickers
Murray Walker

Panther Publishing

Published by Panther Publishing Ltd in 2013
Panther Publishing Ltd
10 Lime Avenue
High Wycombe
Buckinghamshire HP11 1DP
www.panther-publishing.com
info@panther-publishing.com

© Ian Berry
The rights of the authors have been asserted in accordance with the Copyright Designs and Patents Act 1988

All rights reserved, no part of this publication may be reproduced, stored in a retrieval system or transmitted, in any form or by any means, electronic or mechanical, including photocopying, digital copying, and recording without the prior permission of the publisher and/or the copyright owner.

ISBN 978-1-909213-13-5

Cover photo. *The star of the show; Dave Bickers, pictured at West Stow Heath, Suffolk (BH)*

Dedication

I would like to dedicate this book to two special families. The first is the family I grew up with; my mother, Daphne, father, Roy, and sister, Jackie, all of whom revelled in watching the Grandstand Trophy races on TV with me, though not always at the same time. The second is the family that has endured the process of me writing this book, sharing the ups and downs (far more of the former than the latter) and supporting me throughout the process. They are my wife, Xana, and my children, Thomas and Lauryn.

I would also like to dedicate the book to the memory of John Done, who sadly passed away in December 2011. I had the great pleasure of meeting John whilst researching this book and found him to be a charming man, who looked back on his days in the sport with great warmth and affection.

Acknowledgements

Firstly I would like to thank 'the cast' of the Grandstand Trophy Moto-Cross series, for providing me with such a wonderful topic to write about. This includes all the riders who graced our TV screens throughout the 1960s (too numerous to mention, though one way or another many of them feature on the pages of this book), the ACU officials, organising clubs and club members who all worked tirelessly so these meetings could be broadcast, and last but by no means least, the BBC engineers and technicians who also performed heroically in such adverse conditions.

I would especially like to pay tribute to former BBC Producer, Brian Johnson, as without him the Grandstand Trophy Moto-Cross series would almost certainly never have happened. That would have denied millions of sports fans the opportunity to watch the sport on TV, and one obsessive writer the occasion to create this work.

I am also grateful to all of those who so gladly gave me their time and delved deep into their memory banks! They are: Jim Aim, Jimmy Aird, Les Archer, Robbie and Vic Allan, Arthur Browning, John Burton, Chris Carter, Terry Challinor, Barry and Roger Chaplin, Marge Clarke, Dick Clayton, David Cordle, Dave Curtis, Tony Davis, John Giles, John Griffiths, Bill Gwynne, Keith Hickman, Jim Holt, Billy Jackson, Mike Jackson, Alan King, Arthur, Alan and Martin Lampkin, Andy Lee, Ken Lywood, Freddie Mayes, Bob Norman, Charlie Ralph, Derek Rickman, Andy Roberton, Ken Sedgley, Terry Silvester, Dave Treleaven, Bryan Wade, Jim Webb. My sincerest apologies if I have missed anybody out.

Special thanks are due to the Grandstand Trophy winners, Dave Bickers, Jeff Smith, Chris Horsfield, John Banks, Alan Clough, Bryan Goss and Dave Nicoll, and also Torsten Hallman and Murray Walker for their contributions to the book.

Of course, this publication would not have been possible without the outstanding contribution of the photographers, who braved the elements, worked in atrocious conditions and had to keep to exacting deadlines to supply a photographic record for the motorcycle press of the day. They are identified on the photo captions as follows:

CB	Cecil Bailey	RD	Ray Daniel
MC	Malcolm Carling	GF	Gordon Francis
BC	Bill Cole	BH	Brian Holder
PD	Pat Dalton	IB	Ian Berry (Author)

Thanks also to Bob Light (custodian of Bill Cole's photographs), Jill and Chris Francis for their help in furnishing Gordon's photographs and to Nick Haskell for his tireless work in supplying the photographs by Cecil Bailey and Malcolm Carling.

Also, on the production side, I am indebted to João Matos and Vasco Corrando for their help on the cover artwork.

Finally, I would like to thank Rollo Turner of Panther Publishing, for his unwavering support as always.

About the Photographers

Malcolm Carling

Malcolm Carling was behind his camera for the inaugural round of the BBC Grandstand series at Hawkstone Park in October 1963, and over the next six and a half years, he covered more than 30 BBC TV events for Motor Cycle News. Often this entailed a short drive from his home in Audenshaw, Manchester, to venues such as Cuerden Park, or Hatherton Hall, both less than 50 miles away. But on occasion he would be required to make a round trip in excess of 450 miles, to far-flung destinations such as Tweseldown, Hants, or Somerleyton Hall near Lowestoft.

Carling's first love was cycling. 'When I was a lad, living in Ripon, I was a cyclist and a keen photographer. I'd go out to the races run by the British League of Racing Cyclists and take photos. Then I moved to Manchester and I remember going to watch a road race meeting at Aintree and how I liked the speed! Not long after that I started Event magazine (1960) with Harry Stansfield, who had a shop selling cameras and photographic equipment.' Stansfield wrote the text and between them they shared photographic duties. 'I'd take them out to meetings and sell them between races. However, it took us a whole season just to sell the first issue.'

Malcolm had ridden bikes in his youth, but never in competition. 'I used to have a 197 James and then a Norman TS with a 250 Anzani twin engine. In the early days doing the TV scrambles, I used a Mini Countryman, which wasn't very comfortable for long runs. After that I got a 1275 Mini Cooper, which went well and I'd often beat some of the lads to the meetings. But it wasn't so good for getting across a muddy motocross paddock! I'd set off to a meeting in the early hours of the morning and spend the day, or sometimes the weekend, taking photos, often in really terrible conditions. When the meeting was over, I'd race home, develop the film then get the negatives, or sometimes prints, and send them off by Red Star to MCN at Kettering on the midnight train.'

In spite of working in such difficult conditions and having to follow such a rigorous schedule, Carling regularly produced photos of the highest quality, as those featured on the pages of this book demonstrate. *(Photo Brian Holder, Brill, March 1966)*

Cecil Bailey (1918-2008)

As a school leaver, Cecil Bailey was employed at the Supermarine works in Southampton and was a keen motorcyclist, competing in trials, grass track and scrambles before the outbreak of the Second World War, when he served as a despatch rider.

After the war he returned to motorcycle sport winning a factory ride with BSA and competing in grass track and scrambles. In 1947 he was selected to represent Britain in the very first Motocross des Nations in Holland. The same year he turned his attention to the growing sport of speedway, racing for Southampton and Plymouth through till 1951, when he retired.

Bailey then turned to photography, with equal success. From 1958, he was a staff photographer for Motorcycle News and, when scrambling hit the TV screens, Bailey was one of the first to cover events, especially in the South and South Western centres. He covered the BBC meetings from January 1963, at a very wintry Hankom Bottom, and when the Grandstand series came to an end in March 1970, Bailey was behind the lens at Dodington Park. *(Date and photographer unknown)*

Gordon Francis (1935-2008)

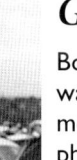

Born in Sturminster Newton, Dorset, in 1935, from an early age Gordon Francis was interested in all things mechanical and as a result, was drawn to the local motorcycle club scrambles at nearby Bulbarrow Hill. His first love, however, was photography and he was able to hone his skills at those local scrambles when marshalling and generally lending a hand.

National Service soon beckoned and he joined the photographic section of the RAF, where he spent his first month near Oxford, followed by a year stationed at Laarbruch in Germany, which gave him the opportunity to visit the (old) Nurburgring and Holland for the Dutch TT at Assen.

In 1955 when Cyril Quantrill set up Motorcycle News, Francis was recruited to cover the South and South West Centres as a freelancer. Until the mid-1960s, he worked for most of the weekly and monthly publications, covering all disciplines of motorcycle sport, and developed a reputation for producing quality results come rain or shine. He frequently travelled to Europe, often accompanying the riders to GPs or team events and these trips resulted in some of his work featuring in foreign publications such as the Swedish magazine MC-Nytt.

In 1966, he gave up photography when he started a new career in the fuel and lubricants industry. He also tried his hand at car motorsport and was particularly successful in production car trials at local and national level. 30 years later, following his retirement from business, he returned to his first love, this time embracing the digital age and was regularly seen photographing popular classic bike events, renewing old friendships and producing the same top quality photos. This return to the scene ultimately culminated in the publication of two limited edition books showcasing Gordon's archive of the 'Golden Era', *Bikes - Camera - Action* and *More Bikes - Camera - Action*. *(Photo Cecil Bailey, at Hants GN)*

Brian Holder

In his youth, Brian Holder was a keen trials rider, competing at clubman level and riding a factory James in the 1961 Scottish Six Day Trial. However, in the early 1960s he started taking pictures of trials, scrambles and road racing, and when his pictures started appearing in *Motorcycle Sport* and *Motor Cyclist Illustrated*, it was clear that he was a better photographer than trials rider, so he hung up his boots in 1964 to concentrate on motorcycle photography.

It was around this time that he began to cover the BBC meetings, the first of these coming at Tweseldown, in December 1964. From 1966 onwards, by then working as a freelancer for Motor Cycle News, Holder became increasingly active on the Grandstand Moto-Cross series, covering events right through to its conclusion in 1970.

At weekends, the London-based photographer found himself covering every sort of motorcycle event in the East and South Eastern centres, including many international road racing, motocross, speedway, trials and sprint events for *MCN* and *Motorcycle Sport* untill the late 1990s.

He is still involved in photography, and is currently converting many of his motorcycle files into digital format to meet demands from publishers, including many previously unpublished pictures especially for this book. *(Photo Malcolm Carling, Brill. March, 1966)*

Cecil Bailey was on hand at Asham Woods in March 1966, to capture the action as Don Rickman on the Triumph Métisse, left, slips past Rob Jordan on the Triumph Wasp. Trailing them are Bryan Goss, Jeff Smith and Vic Eastwood

Contents

Winners Then - Winners Now	viii
Foreword by Dave Bickers	x
Foreword by Murray Walker	xi
The Best Of Times...	1
Introduction	4
ABC Television Picks Up The Baton	9
Enter The BBC	18
Into The Grandstand Trophy Series	33
1963-64 The Winter Of Living Dangerously	37
Royal Enfield Project Bike	44
Anyone for a Pacemaker	60
1964-65 The Times They Are A-changin'	82
Chris Horsfield's 'Special' Matchless	132
1965-66 Normal Service Is Resumed	134
Jerry Scott	168
1966-67 The Dave Bickers Spectacular	172
1967-68 The Year Of Foot-And-Mouth	208
Grandstand Trophy Series On Pause	215
Jeff Smith's Lightweight Special	236
1968-69 Going Into Orbit	238
1969-70 The End Of An Era	264
The BBC Pulls The Plug	283
International Races	294
Sidecar Motocross - Into The Lions Den	299
All Good Things...	301
Grandstand Trophy Winners Table	304
Grandstand Trophy Race Winners Table	304
Index	305

Winners Then

Dave Bickers (MC)

Jeff Smith (BH)

Chris Horsfield (MC)

Alan Clough (MC)

John Banks (BH)

Bryan Goss (CB)

Dave Nicoll (BH)

Winners Now

Dave Bickers (IB)

Jeff Smith (Photo Christine Smith)

Chris Horsfield (IB)

Alan Clough (IB)

John Banks (IB)

Bryan Goss (IB)

Dave Nicoll (IB)

Foreword
by
Dave Bickers

What a great book. It brings back so many memories – some of which are probably best forgotten! Nevertheless, although we were often very cold and wet, with the added problem of snow, we did have some great times. Weather never cancelled the races; we just got on with the job. The TV brought 'scrambling' into the front room, bringing with it recognition and very often a few favours; even to the present day.

On the start line, it was always a good plan to be near Badger (Bryan Goss), who was always one of the first away. The programmes were live on air and the race would not be restarted for any reason. There was a lot of hard and fierce competition on the track, but as soon as it was over it was all forgotten over cups of tea and a few laughs and excuses.

We always stayed in hotels. No big camper vans then, just a trailer, an old van or maybe a Morris 1000 pick-up. We had tea and beans on toast at transport cafes and often got back home in the early hours with eyes still full of mud; making driving difficult. (No motorways then) We always had to keep an eye out for the police as trailers were restricted to 30mph in those days.

Many of the friendships made in those years are still ongoing and we still maintain contact through old vehicles, tractors and of course, old bikes. Most of us seem to be naturally drawn towards wheels and engines and a bit of competition, even in our old age.

Ian has got it dead right. He has very much re-created the times and memories of when we old 'scramblers' were young and living in a different world to the world of today. It's well worth the read and I personally am proud to have played my part.

Dave Bickers
May 2013

The style is unmistakable; head set characteristically to one side, jaw set in determined fashion, every sinew in his body tensed as he leans his bike into a corner. Cecil Bailey captures Dave Bickers, racing his 250 Husqvarna, on the way to the first of his five Grandstand trophies, at Tweseldown, Hampshire, on January 4th, 1964.

Foreword by Murray Walker

I love this book because Ian Berry has done a great job of recording an aspect of motor cycle sport - 'Scrambling' as it used to be called and 'Motocross' as it is now - that gripped the nation with over ten years of dramatic television.

For me every page and every picture remind me of places I went to, racing I saw and things I did. Happy memories of truly spectacular events and the outstanding riders, organisers, enthusiasts and TV people who made it all happen.

In the early post war days of scrambling I used to go to meetings such as the Hants Grand National and marvel at the exploits of people like Brian Stonebridge, Geoff Ward, Bill Nicholson, John Draper and Les Archer on his unique Manx Norton-powered bike. They were summer events and when the conditions were dry, as they usually seemed to be, the spectacle was enhanced by great plumes of dust as the knobbly tyres clawed the ground. But when the winter TV scrambles took off those dust clouds were replaced by driving rain, glutinous mud, and even thick snow which offended the Sport`s enthusiasts but made it for the millions at home gazing spellbound at their TV sets. Something they`d never heard of became a weekly fix.

Until the advent of scrambling on the box I`d been a radio commentator, mainly on motor cycle road racing, but my life was transformed when ABC Television, which then covered the Midlands and the North of England, invited me to handle the commentary for a series of scrambles they were to transmit. That led to literally years of weekend events, mainly in Lancashire and Yorkshire, with multiple Manx Grand Prix winner and arch enthusiast Denis Parkinson as my co-commentator,

Looking very dapper in his Gannex raincoat and gloves, the voice of the BBC Grandstand Moto-Cross series, Murray Walker, introduces viewers to Chris Horsfield at Caerleon, South Wales, in November 1964 (MC)

excitedly talking about the dramatic racing we were watching. Such was their impact that, as Ian Berry recounts, the BBC decided they wanted scrambling and set about getting it, which they did, although not without a vast amount of ill-feeling, friction and political uproar.

It was worth it though for the BBC did a superb job, with national coverage of a major series, with all the stars and works support from BSA, Matchless and Greeves. The 'Grandstand Trophy' programmes became a major talking point in the pubs and the top riders - Jeff Smith, Arthur Lampkin, Dave Bickers, Chris Horsefield and Vic Eastwood - became sporting stars of the box. I`m very proud to have been a part of it all because it was great entertainment that promoted a great sport which took me all over the country and which kick-started my TV career.

Sadly, scrambling was over exposed and gave way to Rallycross and, even more sadly, Britain lost its dominance in the sport it had created but I shall always remember the years of the 'Grandstand Trophy' with great affection and warmth. If you are old enough to have seen the programmes I am sure you`ll remember them that way too but if you aren`t then read on and see what you missed!

Murray Walker
April 2013

The Best of Times...

The conjurer's trick – pulling the names of Bickers, Lampkin and Smith from thin air! The 'Big Three' at Brill, March 1964 (MC)

'It was the best of times, it was the worst of times...'

I borrow the opening words from Charles Dickens' *A Tale of Two Cities* as for me they so aptly describe the televised scrambles that the BBC broadcast during the 1960s.

The best of times, because scrambles fans nationwide could see the stars of their favourite sport in action on Saturday afternoons from the comfort of their own homes. Furthermore, there is little doubt that the exploits of the merry band of riders who turned out in all weathers helped raise the profile of the sport.

The worst of times, because it showed the sport in the most unflattering light, as scrambling was essentially a sport that took place during the spring, summer and autumn, where dust was more of a problem than the axle deep mud that riders so often had to contend with in the winter months. Having said that, for many of the uninitiated who tuned in to watch, the thrills and spills afforded them plenty of entertainment.

The Grandstand Trophy series also provided a showcase for the British motorcycle industry and major manufacturers such as BSA and AMC were quick to realise that results on TV on a Saturday afternoon would be reflected in sales in the showrooms on Monday morning. At the same time smaller companies such as Greeves and Dot, who

The best of times ... Chris Horsfield drifting his Matchless special in the November sun at Nantwich, 1964 (MC)

The worst of times ... but this Cotton rider refuses to throw the towel in just yet. Caerleon, New Year's Day, 1966 (MC)

predominantly manufactured lightweight two-stroke competition machines, seized the opportunity to promote their wares on the small screen, thereby increasing sales to the clubmen who saw themselves as a budding Dave Bickers or Alan Clough.

For the young up-and-coming riders of the day the televised meetings also provided an opportunity for them to demonstrate their worth and to establish themselves as the stars of tomorrow. The more successful of these would often find that a good run of results on TV could provide them with some leverage when negotiating their contracts for the coming season.

The BBC were also on to a winner, as they soon discovered that motocross riders would perform, when all around them other sports were being postponed due to extreme winter conditions. The racing also served to fill gaps between other, 'higher profile' sports, most notably horse racing, though some riders were genuinely aggrieved at having to frequently play second fiddle.

For many, the televised meetings also served as an introduction to the joys of off road motorcycling. I, for one, feel privileged to be part of a generation that was reared on the BBC Grandstand Trophy series. When friends and acquaintances learn that I write about motocross they often ask, 'Is that what they used to call scrambling?' and when I answer, 'Yes' they often recall tuning in to *Grandstand* in their youth and can conjure the names of 'Bickers', 'Smith' and 'Lampkin' from thin air.

On a personal note, the riders I saw regularly competing on TV were my first sporting heroes and when my first bicycle came along a few years later, a BSA no less, it felt as if I'd joined the ranks of Smith and Lampkin! Once the racing had ended, I'd be sprinting out the back door and jumping on my bike, pedalling for all I was worth, up and down our street, around our garden and in and out of the nearby building site, desperately trying to re-enact the racing I'd witnessed on the box and I'd wager that all across the nation young lads and lassies of a certain age could be found doing the very same thing.

Many of those kids, who'd be 50-somethings today, have probably never been to a motocross meeting in their lives, but by the same token there are also those who used the *Grandstand* experience as a springboard to becoming life-long followers of the sport. What we all have in common, is the memory, albeit rather grey, or should that be 'black and white', of some thirty of the nation's top riders lining up under starter's orders on our television sets and flying into action as the words of the inimitable Murray Walker reverberated off our living room walls and brightened many a gloomy winter's Saturday afternoon.

My wish in writing this book is that I will help bring those blurry images back into focus, aided and abetted by the wonderful photographs that grace these pages, and by the stars of the show, the riders themselves, who have provided so many wonderful insights as to how things really were back in the day.

The Grandstand Trophy Moto-cross series has passed, but long may it be remembered!

Introduction

Brian Stonebridge racing the 500 Matchless to victory in the inaugural British Motocross GP, at Nympsfield, Gloucestershire, September 1952 (BC)

Oxford's John Avery, winner of the 1952 ACU Star, seen here racing his 500 BSA Gold Star to a win at the Experts GN at Rollswood Farm the same year (BC)

Long before the advent of television, motorcycle scrambles had been a popular form of entertainment, taking place across the length and breadth of Britain, especially in the summer months. I use the term 'scramble' as opposed to 'motocross' as this was the name that the pioneering events were tagged with.

According to motorcycling folklore, the name 'scramble' first appeared when members of the Camberley and District MCC were searching for a name for the first recognised event to carry that title, the Southern Scott Scramble, which took place on Camberley Heath on 29th March, 1924. Much debate ensued when the club sat down to attempt to draft the regulations. Legend has it that one club member noted, 'It isn't a trial and it isn't really a race. What shall we call it?' to which a second member remarked, 'Whatever we call it, it's sure to be a right old scramble!' That obviously struck a chord with the club members and 'Scramble' it was.

The Auto Cycle Union (ACU) had been founded as early as 1903, with the aim of organising motorcycle sport through clubs. Off-road motorcycling was popular between the world wars and by 1923, membership was growing so rapidly that the decision was made to form 14 individual 'centres'. Off-roading really blossomed in the post war years when the big motorcycle manufacturers realised that success in competition would result in sales in the showrooms and by 1953, as the ACU celebrated 50 years of activity, it boasted 54,000 members in 750 clubs nationwide.

Early Developments

By the 1950s scrambling had become a very popular spectator sport, with the top meetings of the day, such as the 'Grand National' events - the Lancashire, Hampshire and the recently added Experts at Rollswood Farm, Warwickshire - readily attracted crowds in excess of 10,000 spectators, whilst smaller centre events could expect 3-5,000 paying customers through the gates.

As a result of such popularity, in 1951, the ACU ran its first 'Scrambles Drivers' Star' - a national championship based on a series of twelve scoring events - with factory AJS rider Geoff Ward, from Maidenhead, Berkshire, lifting the title, an achievement he would go on to repeat in 1953 and 54.

A year later the Stroud Valley Motor Club staged Britain's first motocross* Grand Prix at Nympsfield, Gloucestershire, the famous Cotswold Scramble having been a regular fixture on the scrambles calendar since 1934. On Sunday 13th September, 1952, home rider Brian Stonebridge, racing his factory Matchless, emerged victorious ahead of the BSA's of Phil Nex and Derek Rickman.

Roll Cameras

It was in such a well-structured and organised climate that the very first televised meeting took place. Although many remember ITV's efforts in the late 1950s in the Midlands and the North as being the pioneering televised scrambles events, when in fact, it was the BBC. They set the wheels in motion and the cameras rolling, when they televised a meeting from Church Woods, Beenham, Berkshire, on 4th December, 1954, under the guiding hand of top ACU official, Harold Taylor.

---

* The term 'motocross' was widely used on the continent at that time and would, in time, replace 'scramble' and its derivatives in the sport's vernacular.

The moment Bob Manns (foreground) gifted victory to Les Archer in the very first BBC scramble, Church Woods, Beenham, December 1954

(Photo here and opposite from Motorcycling Dec 9, 1954, courtesy of Mortons Media Archives)

Although racing began mid-afternoon, the many tons of equipment that the BBC brought with them had arrived several hours earlier and a lengthy practice session preceded racing. As the *Motor Cycle* reporter of the day commented: 'Many more laps were ridden before 2:45 than after, chiefly to enable the cameras to swing in all directions and thus determine whether any alterations in siting were necessary.' The BBC viewers who tuned in to watch the spectacle, were then treated to 45 minutes of action-packed racing, comprising two solo heats and a sidecar race, topped off with the solo final.

On that winter's day at Beenham, the silky voice of the BBC's own motoring correspondent, Raymond Baxter, supplied the commentary. As a keen aviator, who had flown Spitfires during the Second World War, and an expert rally driver, Baxter would, I am sure, have had a good feel for the sport. It is also testament to his versatility that the same man who had provided commentary for the funeral of King George VI, with all its pomp and ceremony, should do likewise for a motorcycle meeting in the depths of rural England in midwinter.

Out on the track, it was Les Archer on his 'Cammy' Norton who did the talking, finishing second in his heat and winning the final, though the unluckiest rider on the day was unquestionably Bob Manns on his factory AJS. In the final Manns led Archer all the way, but was denied victory on the last lap when he became well and truly bogged down in the mud. That left Archer to ride on to a comfortable victory ahead of John Draper, on the factory BSA Gold Star, and John Giles, on his factory Triumph.

Unlike the vast majority of the BBC Grandstand scrambles that followed, the South Reading MCC promotion also included a sidecar race, with 6 outfits taking to the line. A great battle ensued between two of the top charioteers of the day, with Jack Stocker, on a Royal Enfield, eventually getting the better of Bill Turner, on an Ariel, the two outfits never being separated by more than about 10 yards, with Bill's brother, Cyril, third on a second Ariel outfit.

Mixed Reception

The *Motor Cycle* report also carried a commentary from Leonard Marsland Gander, who they billed as 'the World's First newspaper TV Critic'. As a war correspondent for the Daily Telegraph, he'd just about seen it all. However, as a former motorcyclist himself, Marsland

Famous sidecar exponents Jack Stocker and Bill Turner locked in combat as they pass the BBC camera gantry

Gander was quick to appreciate the skills of the riders, though he was less complimentary about the appeal of the sport. 'One point about scrambling that could be admired and appreciated without any expert knowledge was the astonishing art of the riders in maintaining racing speed and equilibrium. The pity is that it is not more picturesque as a spectacle for the uninitiated.' He went on to conclude: 'But with or without a beauty chorus and fancy trimmings, let us, in fairness, have it on TV again under drier conditions, BBC.'

Previously he had raised some very pertinent points. 'Obviously the sport has exciting possibilities, but viewers will need to know more about it before they take it to their hearts. I imagine the chief trouble for the majority was that they had never heard of the contestants. There was no Chataway, no Stanley Matthews, no Hutton, no Bannister. Moreover, riding numbers were soon mud-covered, riders were all disguised in almost identical kit, and a dozen competitors is a lot for the small TV screen to show, especially on a grey day.' For those younger readers, who won't recall these names, Christopher Chataway and Roger Bannister were top athletes of the day, Stanley Matthews an England footballer and Len Hutton a cricketing hero.

By the time the Grandstand Trophy series began, however, the BBC had addressed all the problems raised by Marsland Gander, not least of all enlisting the talent of commentator, Murray Walker. Walker, the son of former road race ace and fellow commentator, Graham, had cut his teeth providing radio commentary for the BBC, in company with his father, on the TT and Manx GP meetings, before providing most of the commentary for the ABC Television meetings.

Walker was the consummate professional. He worked very hard to be as good as he was, putting in hours chatting to riders, organisers, ACU officials and the captains of the British motorcycle industry, in order to provide viewers with a truly informed commentary. As a result, *Grandstand* viewers were always highly informed as to who the riders were and what machines they were riding.

In terms of rider recognition, in addition to carrying numbers on their machines, riders were generally required to wear a numbered bib, to further aid identification. And as for a dozen competitors racing at once, well in comparison with speedway that was a lot, but come the Grandstand Trophy, the cameramen were really kept on their toes having to contend with fields of up to 30 riders!

The Evolution Of TV Scrambles

The BBC had taken the first step in televising scrambles, though in the immediate years to follow they would focus their attention on the annual Television Team Trial, an event introduced in 1953, with three solos and a sidecar representing teams from the North, South, Midlands and West. At that time, despite the scrambling boom, trials events were still more popular with clubmen and they were also the main competition focus for the motorcycle industry.

In the late 1950s and early 1960s, Associated British Corporation (ABC) Television, which supplied weekend programmes for the North and the Midlands, began broadcasting scrambles within those regions. These events, whilst attracting some of the top riders of the day such as Les Archer, Brian Stonebridge, Jeff Smith and Arthur Lampkin, often lacked strength in depth in terms of the entry and would only be seen by viewers in the North and Midlands. They were also primarily broadcast during the winter months, not traditionally associated with scrambling but more so with trials events, and this discouraged some riders from participating.

Other independent stations were soon transmitting scrambles, most notably Southern TV, but it was only when the BBC decided to broadcast racing on its *Grandstand* programme that viewers nationwide could watch up to 30 of the nation's very best riders go head-to-head. Not only were the images beamed out to homes throughout Britain, but they were also transmitted from venues as far flown as Caerleon in South Wales, Winchester in the South of England, Lyng in East Anglia and even north of the border in Kirkcaldy, Scotland, giving the Grandstand Trophy Moto-cross series a truly national feel.

The TV Effect

The advent of the Grandstand series benefitted riders and manufacturers alike. The races helped the riders stay fit during the 'off-season' when they would traditionally have been resting, or turning to the more leisurely pursuit of trials riding. For manufacturers it presented the opportunity to develop their bikes for the coming ACU Star contest and the world championships, whilst (hopefully) serving as a good advertisement for the ruggedness and reliability of their machinery.

There is no question that it also raised the nation's awareness of the sport and led to its stars becoming household names, putting the likes of Dave Bickers and Jeff Smith up there with Formula One's Jim Clark and John Surtees and rally star Paddy Hopkirk. However, by the mid-1960s when the TV events were seemingly at the height of their popularity, with ITV returning in tandem with the BBC with its World of Sport series, some would argue TV coverage would prove to be the death of the sport as spectators no longer ventured out to meetings in such numbers, content to watch the meetings on the box from the comfort of their own homes.

Arthur Lampkin, the tough, pragmatic Yorkshireman who through his exploits in the ABC Television meetings earned himself the title 'Mr. Television', summed it up nicely when he drew a parallel with football:

> *Who would pay to go along to Elland Road to watch Leeds United, when they could watch it on TV on Saturday night for free?*

The topic of how much good the TV events did or did not do for the sport would make for a very interesting debate, but for now let's just say that they certainly put motocross on the sports map and entertained millions of viewers for a few short years.

ABC Television Picks Up The Baton

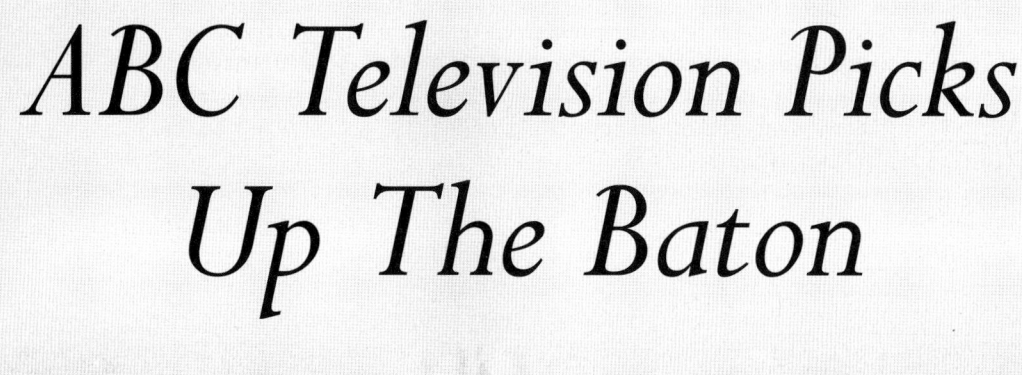

Man of the meeting, Don Rickman, receives his trophy from Alderman Edgar Wallace at the Southern TV scramble at Weymouth, New Year's Day 1961 (GF)

The early 1950s was a very exciting period in broadcasting circles, when the newly elected Conservative government moved to set up a commercial television channel, though this was greeted with much scepticism at the time. However, by 1954 they had managed to push through the Television Act, which hastened the arrival of Britain's first commercial TV network, ITV (Independent Television), operating under the watchful eye of the Independent Television Authority.

The first programmes on the new network were broadcast in September 1955, initially in the London area, which was served by Rediffusion. ABC (Associated British Corporation) Television was established to serve the ITV in the North and Midlands, furnishing viewers with innovative weekend programming. Broadcasting started in February 1956 and after a successful run where it pioneered several ground breaking programmes, such as *Armchair Theatre, Oh Boy!* (one of the earliest Pop music shows), *The Avengers* and *World of Sport*, originally presented by Eamonn Andrews, it merged with London Television in July 1968.

ABC was broadcasting television scrambles from as early as 1957, with the sport competing for air time with horse racing, rugby, wrestling and even motorcycle racing. On Saturday, April 13th, 1957, the channel allotted a very generous two and a half hours to scrambling from Bentley Springs, near Wakefield, Yorkshire, the programme being presented by David Southwood, who would go on to become Chief of Outside Broadcasts for the channel.

A Man With A Mission

The driving force behind the early ABC transmissions was former Manx GP and Isle of Man TT winner, Denis Parkinson, who was a founder member of the Wakefield and District Motor Sports Club. In that first televised meeting, Parkinson put the aforementioned air-time to very good use - running off no less than 14 races, including sidecars, with top honours going to local man Frank Bentham (AJS) in company with Jeff Smith (BSA), Brian Stonebridge, on his 197 Greeves, and Eric Atkinson (BSA) in the sidecars. Other winners on the day included top all-rounders Terry Cheshire (BSA) and Jim Sheehan (Ariel).

For this event, and several others run by the Wakefield Club, it was local sports goods manufacturer, Slazenger, better known for their association with lawn tennis than off road motorcycling, who sponsored the main event - the 'Slazenger Trophy'. This was won by Smith from Stonebridge and Ron Langston (350 Ariel) and proceeds from the meeting went to the Sailors, Soldiers and Airmen Families' Association and the ACU Benevolent Fund.

Denis Parkinson, the man who brought us scrambling on TV and 'Undulating straights' (MC)

Another event was run on the same circuit in the autumn that year and a glance through the list of winners reveals that many of the placed riders belonged to a 'pre-Grandstand Trophy' generation, with names like Les Archer, Eric Cheney, Geoff Ward and the Taft brothers, Peter and Paul, to the fore. Two leaders of the new vanguard, Jeff Smith and Arthur Lampkin, were notable absentees as they were away doing military service at the time.

Making A Weekend Of It

A subsequent meeting at Bentley Springs also broke new ground, as it was a two-day event. Staged in mid-March 1958, the organising Wakefield Club had to work overtime to keep it running, as there were four inches of snow on the ground at the time. The TV cameras and crew were only there on the Saturday, but in spite of the inclement weather conditions, a massive turnout of some 10,000 spectators attended on the Sunday to watch some very entertaining racing.

Murray Walker, who would go on to provide the commentary for the Grandstand series was the principal commentator for the ABC events, aided by Parkinson. This is how a typical weekend would pan out for him:

> *I'd leave the office in St. James' Square on a Friday afternoon and get on the tube to Cockfosters, which was the end of the Piccadilly line, where my wife would meet me in the car, our Austin A40, with our dog and then we'd drive to Yorkshire. Of course, there were no motorways at that time and it was a long journey and mostly after dark. Then we'd be up with the lark on Saturday morning to cover the racing from Bentley Springs or wherever. On the Saturday the racing went into the national network, with riders such as Bill Barugh on the Dot and Brian Stonebridge on his Greeves making the news, then on*

Murray Walker in the commentary box with his wife, Elizabeth, keeping tabs on the riders (MC)

Sunday at the same venue with the same riders, they'd compete again and that would go out on the regional network.

When I say national network, it was by degree. I'd often be in full flow when my producer would come on and say, 'Tyne Tees have left us, Murray, please welcome Westward Television.' so all the way through I was saying goodbye to this and hello to that. But they were enormously successful, partly because it was different, partly because it was noisy, muddy and exciting and partly because there often wasn't much else on.

Despite the snow, riders were treated to two gloriously sunny days and of the televised races, Stonebridge won the 250cc and Unlimited finals and was only denied a hat-trick in the 1000cc by fast-gating Peter Taft. Typifying the hospitality of that era, the organising club provided riders with supper on the Saturday evening, followed by a film show and dance.

Reading this you might think that the Wakefield Club had a monopoly on ABC's televised scrambles. Not so, in fact there were a whole host of venues used throughout the North and the Midlands. Amongst the most popular were: Ringinglow, near Sheffield, Hutton Conyers, near Ripon, High Hoyland, near Barnsley, Farnsfield in Nottinghamshire, Bevercotes near Retford, Nottinghamshire, Bredbury near Stockport, Clifton near Ashbourne, Tunstall in Staffordshire, Hatherton Hall near Nantwich and Larkstoke in Warwickshire, though many others were used over the years.

Below is the programme schedule for ATV (London) for Sunday, November 2nd, 1958, with a 55 minute spot scheduled for scrambling from Ringinglow, courtesy of ABC Television:

11.15	*Church St Joseph & St Francis Xavier* Richmond York - 12.15
1.30	*Motor Cycle Scramble* from Mayfields Course, Ringinglow, York (ABC)
2.25	*Free Speech* with Lord Boothby, WJ Brown, Michael Foot, Alan Taylor
2.55	*Music Shop* host Teddy Johnson with Joan Regan, Billie Anthony
3.25	*No Parking*, film starring Gordon Harker
4.40	*Slater's Bazaar*, ad mag with John Slater, Bert Weedon, Mavis Sage, Tony Hilton, Ray Cooney
4.55	*Caroll Levis Junior Discoveries*
5.25	*The Adventures of Robin Hood,* The Devil You Don't Know
5.55	*It Can Happen Tomorrow,* scientist Ritchie Calder with the latest scientific news (ATV)
6.00	*News*
6.15	*The Sunday Break* with Rev David Sheppard
7.00	*About Religion* - School Religion
7.25	*News*
7.30	*Wyatt Earp*, Ballad and Truth
8.00	*Sunday Night at the London Palladium*, Dolores Gray
9.00	*Dotto*, quiz with Robert Gladwell
9.30	*News*
9.35	*The Invisible Man*, Shadow on the Screen
10.05	*Armchair Theatre*, The Witching Hour starring Dennis Price, Thora Hird
11.10	*After Hours*, Shirley Bassey, Bernard Braden, Stirling Moss
	Epilogue, Rev Robert Duce, Minster of Pett's Wood Congregational Church & Close down.

Mr Television

Arthur Lampkin, who would become a double-British champion and top GP runner, cut his teeth on meetings such as the one above, where on his factory BSA Gold Star he was the star of the meeting. A report in *The Motor Cycle* (6th November 1958) noted 'Arthur Lampkin proved invincible at the Sheffield and Hallamshire Club's Television Scramble on Saturday' despite the fact that 'overnight rain had turned the 1,400 yard course into a gigantic slide and conditions were described as the worst ever.' Lampkin always performed to his best in front of the cameras and it was results such as this that earned him the unofficial title of 'Mr Television'.

'Mr. Televison'. Arthur Lampkin pictured at an ABC TV meeting at Rollswood Farm (MC)

Wherever Arthur went in those early days, his younger brothers Alan, or as he's known to the family 'Sid', and Martin, would tag along. Alan, who would also feature prominently in the BBC meetings remembers, "I used to go along to all those ABC meetings, later on with Martin in tow." Martin, who rode both trials and scrambles in his youth before going on to become world trials champion in 1975, recalls that at the time of the ABC meetings the Lampkin family didn't have a TV of its own:

> My dad wouldn't have a TV in the house. We had all the board games and cards but even though Arthur was on the telly, he wouldn't let us have one. We used to go to the next-door but one neighbour and huddle round the TV. Those were the best days. Setting off in a car with Arthur and Smithy to go to a meeting when you were only a kid was something special.

The turn of the 60s saw Lampkin challenged by the likes of Dot factory riders John Griffiths and Alan Clough and occasionally in the bigger meetings by Dave Bickers, Jeff Smith, John Burton, John Harris and Vic Eastwood. But he also had to contend with local riders such as Norman Crooks, the Tate brothers (Maurice and Ron), Gordon Blakeway, Dickie Preston, Ron Fairburn and Terry Silvester.

Alan Clough, Jeff Smith, Bernie Andrews and John Burton on the startline at Clifton, Derbyshire, October 1962 (MC)

Televised Scrambling Sweeps The Nation

Other ITV regional stations soon followed the lead of ABC, most notably Southern Television, who only began broadcasting in August 1958 and were drawing up plans for their first televised scramble just a few weeks later to be run on Lord Montague's estate at Beaulieu.

Just as the ABC network had Denis Parkinson to act as a liaison man between them and the ACU, so Southern TV had Neville Goss, an ACU official and well-respected figure in the Southern Centre. Goss helped put Southern TV on the scrambles map, organising events at venues such as Beaulieu, East Chickerell, near Weymouth, Portsdown Hill, Hants and Hankom Bottom, Winchester.

Southern TV invited Goss and the Southampton and District Motorcycle Club Club to organise that inaugural meeting at Beaulieu Old Park, in October 1958, as an 'experiment', and said that if they were happy with the outcome of the event they would run a series of televised scrambles the following season. It would seem that those in charge back in the studios liked what they saw, as not only did Goss get his series of events, but on that first Saturday afternoon, they granted an extra 10 minutes to cover a second sidecar race!

Not surprisingly, that first Beaulieu event threw up some new names for TV viewers, though as the ITV network was always regional, Southern and South Western scrambles fans would certainly have recognised the names of the winners. Bryan Sharp took the Lightweight and Lightweight Star races on his Francis Barnett, Derek Rickman the Unlimited and Solo Star races, and brother Don (both BSA mounted) the Expert's race, whilst sidecar stalwarts Frank Wilkins (Ariel) and Frank Darrieulat (BSA) won a race apiece.

On New Year's Day 1961, the Weymouth and South Dorset Motor Cycle Club in conjunction with Southern TV ran their first televised meeting at East Chickerell. Despite the inclement weather there was a good turnout of riders, with Don Rickman, riding his Triumph Métisse, winning the day's three big finals, though Geoff King (TriBSA), John

'Twist' Visits the Great Cornard Television Scramble

The cartoonist 'Twist' was on hand at the Sudbury Motorcycle Club's meeting in September 1962 to record the events of the day.

Clayton (AJS) and Triss Sharp (Greeves) all made sure that he had to fight for his trophies. Sidecars also featured and it was Ken Robertson riding an AJS powered outfit, who had the edge on Rufus Rose who was under Triumph steam.

Anglia TV were also bitten by the bug, broadcasting their first meeting from Tye Farm Gt Cornard, which was organised by the Sudbury Motorcycle Club, in September 1962. The Jack Hubbard Television Trophy event, saw Dave Bickers (Greeves) take a comfortable win after local ace Jim Aim had dropped his 500 Orcadian whilst leading on the first lap. Race sponsor and top local expert, Hubbard, finished second, as John Banks won a great three-way tussle with fellow Dot rider Tim Robinson and John Pease (Greeves).

The local Suffolk Free Press newspaper reported at the time that:

Although the main objective of the meeting is to cater for the television cameras, the public will be admitted. However, there will be no special facilities for them such as programmes and a public address system. The car park will be open at a reduced rate and club president, Mr Donald Steed, tells me that the public will at all times be under the direction of Anglia TV.

Makes you wonder what sort of 'direction' the general public might have been given! The races were recorded and transmitted on Anglia TV's About Anglia programme on Tuesday 18th September, and the Sudbury Club would go on to stage a meeting for the BBC the following month (see p22)

Over the coming years Anglia TV broadcast several meetings from Tye Farm and other venues in the region.

It's A Hard Life, But ...

The televised races always had their share of drama and heart-breaking stories, though sometimes they also had a happy ending. In February 1962, Cotton runner Jim Timms raced at Beaulieu Old Park on Saturday 10th, apparently without much success. However, he then loaded up his bikes on his trailer and headed off for the following day's ABC TV meeting at Accrington, some 270 miles away in Lancashire. Then his luck really deserted him, as a MCN reporter of the day informs us:

Shortly after leaving the Southampton TV event a sports car ran into the back of his trailer, wrecking it completely. Timms' N°1 machine was twisted and with the trailer a write-off, the two bikes were fitted into his car boot and taken to Gloucester, where a Land Rover was obtained for the rest of the journey north.

Despite getting no sleep and having to ride a third-string Cotton, Timms still managed to challenge the leading riders and his sterling efforts were rewarded with 6th place in the 'Event of the Day' and 4th place in the Allcomers Unlimited.

Timms' effort was typical of many at the time, with riders often travelling hundreds of miles in the worst imaginable conditions to compete in events. More often than not, however, they were happy to do this and enjoyed the company and camaraderie of their friends and fellow competitors.

So, by the early 1960s, Britain's TV viewers had the possibility of regularly watching live scrambling thanks to the efforts of the Independent Television Network and individuals such as Denis Parkinson and Neville Goss. However, at the same time, a young TV producer working for the BBC in Bristol was hatching a plan that would see the BBC enter the arena and take coverage of the sport on television to a new level, with meetings being broadcast nationwide.

17

Even the big freeze-up of 1963 couldn't stop the TV scrambles going ahead and scenes such as this, taken at Tunstall in January 1963, were common (MC)

Enter The BBC

Murray Walker interviewing in the snow (GF)

Following the initial televised meeting at Beenham Park, the BBC had flirted with coverage of both scrambles and trials events. However, it wasn't until the early 1960s that things really gained momentum, when Brian Johnson, a young producer working for BBC Bristol, came on the scene.

> *I had been watching the ITV scrambles and as a motorcyclist myself, thought that we (the BBC) could do better. I put the idea to Bryan Cowgill, the producer of the very popular Grandstand programme, and suggested we change the name of the sport to the continental one of 'Moto-Cross', as ITV had billed their events as 'scrambles'.*

Much to his surprise, Johnson's suggestion was accepted by Cowgill. A meeting with the ACU's Harold Taylor (best remembered as the manager of the *Motocross and Trophee des Nations* teams) was arranged, where the ground rules for a short series were agreed. I wrote to the then leading factories such as BSA, AMC and Greeves, all of whom agreed to field a works team. Murray Walker was then tempted away from ITV as the commentator and the first programme was on the air in October 1962 at Naish Hill in Wiltshire.

Walker recalls how Cowgill applied a little 'leverage' to help him decide where his loyalties lay!

> *At that time ITV were knocking seven bells out of the BBC on viewing numbers and Bryan Cowgill, a tough uncompromising Lancastrian, called me in one day and said, 'We like this scrambling Murray and we're going to do it and you're going to do the commentary.' And he continued, 'I'm well aware that ITV have been doing it and that you've been doing the commentary for them and should you sign this contract you will in no way be inhibited from doing it for ITV and should you do so, we will continue to use you for as long as it takes us to find a replacement!' It wasn't until he had said the last word that I realised my days commenting on ITV scrambling were over!*

Peter Dimmock, who was the Head of Outside Broadcasting at the time, chaired the early meetings between the BBC and the ACU, with Taylor, who had been the driving force behind the first ever televised scramble at Beenham, in 1954, representing the ACU, and Johnson also present. In one of the meetings, the West Wilts Motor Club, who used a piece of land at Naish Hill near Chippenham, was suggested as a possible organiser for a pilot televised event.

In fact, both the club and venue were already known to the BBC, as the 1962 Television Team Trial had been broadcast from there in May, with the Midland team of Sammy Miller (Ariel), Scott Ellis (Triumph), Bryan Povey (James) and Peter Wraith (Ariel sidecar) winning the event.

At that time, the West Wilts Club was fortunate enough to have a dynamic, young organiser, Ken Lywood, amongst its member and he would be responsible for putting together the inaugural Grandstand Trophy event at Naish Hill. Harold Taylor would become a guiding light for both Lywood, and the West Wilts Club, which would go on to enjoy a happy association with the BBC and the ACU.

Over the coming years, events would be filmed at both Naish Hill and Farleigh Castle, the latter going on to host a string of 500cc British Motocross GPs from 1966 through till the end of the 80s. As Lywood recalls, 'Once the ACU took an interest, with Harold Taylor getting involved with the first TV event at Naish Hill, it just gelled from there, as simple as that.'

The 'pilot' programme was aired on BBC Television's *Grandstand*, a show that ran throughout Saturday afternoon and was dedicated entirely to sport, covering, amongst other things, athletics, football, rugby league, cricket and motor racing and closing with *Final Score*, which brought the viewer up to date with all the Football League results.

The BBC had launched its seminal sports programme on 11th October, 1958. Originally the programme was conceived by Paul Fox, the brainchild behind the *Sports Personality of the Year*, and Cowgill, who was a sports producer at the time. The programme was designed to showcase BBC's live Outside Broadcast links in one programme, though it had its roots in *Sportsview*, a mid-week sports show, and *Sports Special*, which ran on Saturday evenings from 1955 until 1964, when it was replaced by Match of the Day.

The original presenter was Peter Dimmock, who had previously presented *Sportsview*, but after just three programmes, Dimmock was replaced by David Coleman, a fresh-faced, former athlete with a vast sporting knowledge, and it would be Coleman at the helm when the BBC launched the Grandstand Trophy series in October 1963.

Avon Calling!

The land that had been used for the televised trial was on the site of the Avon Tyre Company's dump and it was through connections with the tyre manufacturer - club Chairman Jim Dykes being the Competitions Manager there - that the West Wilts Club secured the use of the land. A few months later, the club was approached by the ACU and the BBC and were asked to start making plans for a televised scramble to be run there in the coming autumn.

Naish Hill was a good choice as Ken Lywood explains:

Naish Hill was simply very well suited to the requirements of the BBC for televised meetings. It was a short circuit that was perfect for the 10 to 15 minute races and it offered some good vantage points for the cameramen. It also had a very good approach road, which helped getting the heavy equipment in and out, and the track itself had a very hard base, compacted when a Super Fortress crashed there at the end of the war, which made it a good track to use all year round.

Fast starter Bryan Goss in full flow on his factory Greeves in the Grandstand Trophy at Naish Hill, October 1962 (GF)

Murray Walker with Grandstand Trophy winner Dave Bickers and Mike Hailwood, who is about to hand over the splendid trophy (GF)

So it was, that on 20th October, 1962, the club, in conjunction with the BBC, whose Brian Johnson would produce the programme, ran a scramble for the Grandstand Trophy. Many of the leading riders of the day were present, including Dave Bickers and his Greeves teammates, Joe Johnson and Bryan Goss, and AMC's big guns, Chris Horsfield, Vic Eastwood and Dave Nicoll.

On their arrival on Saturday morning riders found the track shrouded in mist, but by the time the TV cameras were called into action it had cleared away. Ralph Venables, who was there to report on the day's racing for *MCN* accompanied by his good friend and ace photographer, Gordon Francis, was quick to note an irregularity in scrambling etiquette!

Proceedings began with a couple of 250cc heats - and promptly at one o'clock Bryan Goss started the first of these two races (to the surprise of the official starter!) and led for one lap.

Bickers was in imperious form, however, taking the First Unlimited final, the Lightweight final and the main event, and receiving his trophy from none other than the newly crowned world 500cc road race champion, Mike Hailwood, who ran on Avon tyres and was invited along by chairman Dykes. Murray Walker still remembers his first day on the microphone for a BBC motocross very clearly:

Brian Johnson was the producer on the spot with a man called Alec Weeks sitting in the gallery in London. Dave Bickers stalled his engine at the start and was last away by a long, long way. Remember, this was the first one and it was always going to be a bit sensitive. Is it going to be successful? Do we want to continue doing it if it is? But Dave rode an absolute blinder and stormed his way through the field and as the last lap began he was closing in on the leader when Weeks, from London, screams down the line, 'This is bloody marvellous, tell them to do another two laps!'

The meeting was a huge success and by this time talks were underway between the ACU and the BBC to stage a series of televised races to be broadcast on the *Grandstand* programme. Harold Taylor had great confidence in Lywood, the man who would ultimately replace him as *Motocross des Nations* team manager in 1971, and invited him along to the meetings with the BBC as his assistant. As a result, the West Wilts Club was always well informed as to any developments in this area.

Opportunity Knocks

The Naish Hill meeting was just one of a series of 'try-outs' over the winter of 1962-63 and for Brian Johnson especially it was a time of excitement, tinged with a certain amount of trepidation. Johnson had been posted to the BBC's West Region in 1961 as a TV production assistant, but was not happy there as he felt he had to play second fiddle to another 'homegrown' PA.

I realised that I would not be allowed to produce any worthwhile programmes in Bristol unless I had devised them. All I was doing there was directing a weekly regional studio-based programme, entitled 'View'.

However, the success of the motocross experiment ruffled a few feathers at BBC Bristol. Johnson remembers:

The result was more trouble with the suits at Whiteladies Road (the home of BBC West Region). As the programme had been a hit they felt that their man would direct the next programme. Cowgill flatly refused to agree: saying in a classic BBC memo of their man: 'Anyone who can fuck-up ping pong is no use to me.' It would appear the local producer had 'previous'.

As it turned out, Johnson would not produce the next broadcast, though he would soon return to that position and make it his own.

Anyone For Cricket ...

A fortnight after the Naish Hill event, 18 year-old Barry Chaplin, an aspiring Sudbury MCC member, was responsible for organising an Inter-Regional Team event at the club's track at Tye Farm, Gt Cornard. The go-ahead club had only been in existence since 1958, but four years on it was forging a reputation for itself as a promoter of excellent off-road meetings, with Chaplin being ably assisted by his brothers, Tony (AKA Chas) and Roger, the youngest, who was just 16 at the time. Here, Roger Chaplin takes up the story:

Peter Wigg of the Ipswich Club, who was also a leading ACU official, had been asked by the BBC to run a meeting to be filmed in the Eastern Centre. This was during the first season that the BBC transmitted scrambles on Grandstand in 1962 and would be only the second to be screened. The Ipswich Club could not run it at Shrubland Park, nor could the Halstead Club at Wakes Colne, so Wigg approached the Sudbury Club and asked us to run it. Some of the committee members including my brother Barry (who was just 18 years-old at the time), attended a meeting at Wigg's home to discuss the event. Barry pointed out that we were only in our second year of promoting scrambles and it was all quite new to us, but Peter Wigg made it clear that he wanted the Eastern Centre to run this meeting and promised to help us get riders for the event. Thus the planning began.

A taste of things to come! Andy Lee ploughing through the mud at Tye Farm, Gt. Cornard in the BBC Grandstand Team Trophy event, November 1962 (MR)

The club had already run a demo scramble for Anglia Television at their track at Tye Farm, Great Cornard, in September 1962, when Bob Welling and John McGregor did the presentation and interviews. BBC producer Philip Lewis, better known for his cricket coverage, came to view the track in late October and a party of club members gave him a guided tour of the course. Barry suggested various vantage points for the cameramen to film from and eventually five cameras were used on the day; two from the spinney and the other three on the track's hillsides.

Lewis thought the riders would stop and do a few tricks then continue (I fancy he'd seen the odd trial or two) and he had no idea what a scramble was. The whole party then retired to the farmhouse of the landowner and Club President, Donald Steed, where the men from the BBC were shown cine footage from the club's previous scrambles and they then understood the concept.

The hilly Tye Farm circuit proved ideal not only for filming, but also for transmitting the pictures across the valley where it was relayed to the studios in London. On the day, Saturday 3rd November, 1962, it rained all day. Barry (whose organisational skills won him second place in the 1962 Pinhard Prize - beaten only by ace off roader, Malcolm Davis) was interviewed by Murray Walker before the racing got underway.

He was Secretary of the Meeting and Clerk of the Course, but in addition to this he sat alongside Murray in the commentary box and helped him identify the riders. I was assistant to starter Albert Carter, and I helped the lap scorers by shouting out the riders' numbers many of which were covered in mud, but I knew the riders riding styles and had memorised their numbers.

Out on the track, the riders were struggling to get round and the racing was far from scrambling at its best, but it certainly kept the crowd and the viewers at home entertained. In the Grandstand Team Trophy race, much to the delight of the partisan crowd, a quartet representing the East led by Dave Bickers and Freddie Mayes, who finished first and second, and ably supported by Jim Aim and Tim Robinson, finished first overall. The other televised race was an Open Invitation and looked like being a Vic Eastwood benefit. Riding his big Matchless with great aplomb, he led for eight of the nine laps, but was forced to stop to clear the mud from his eyes on the last lap, allowing Geoff King (Triumph) and Bickers to storm through.

... Or Ice-Skating, Perhaps?

Of course, the winter of 1962-63 saw the big freeze up, when a blanket of snow fell across southern England on Boxing Day and spread both west and north in January. However, for our intrepid riders, it simply gave them another chance to demonstrate their amazing skills and a chance to show armchair sports lovers that they would go out racing no matter what the conditions!

In mid-January, the Southampton and District MCC, led by Neville Goss, organised a BBC televised meeting, at Beaulieu Old Park, in the snowbound New Forest. Goss had done a marvellous job in promoting this event and had managed to enlist the services of Sweden's world champions, Torsten Hallman (250) and Rolf Tibblin (500), to bolster an already impressive gallery of riders, which included factory runners Dave Bickers, Bryan Goss and Bill Gwynne, all on Greeves, John Burton on his BSA Gold Star, Chris Horsfield on the Matchless and local favourites and top 'privateers', Don and Derek Rickman, racing just 15 miles from their New Milton home.

Following the Team Event at Gt Cornard, Brian Johnson had returned to the role of producer and he remembers this as the event that really sold the BBC on motocross.

The very cold weather - the BBC riggers found a hare frozen in a walking position - had caused all the other events such as horse racing to be cancelled. But the racing from Beaulieu practically filled Grandstand that Saturday.

This event was a real spectacle, with riders racing in sub-zero temperatures on a bone-hard, frozen track. Naturally, there were a lot of fallers, but it was the Swedes, who were used to training in similar conditions, who adapted best and took a clean sweep in the major races.

Torsten Hallman sheds some light on the event with this account of things:

After being crowned World Champions during 1962, Rolf Tibblin and myself got lots of invitations from race promoters all over Europe. One of these came from the Southampton and District Motor Cycle Club to race at Beaulieu, where they were hosting a BBC TV Motocross during the early part of January 1963. We accepted without hesitation and we were eager to get experience from a race, specially prepared for TV. This was also the perfect occasion for us to escape the snow in Sweden and get an early start to the season. But when we accepted we had no idea what to expect coming to England at the beginning of January!

Murray Walker helps Grandstand viewers become acquainted with Rolf Tibblin and Torsten Hallman, whilst Dave Bickers looks on. Beaulieu Old Park, January 1963 (GF)

We met at the Husqvarna factory, loaded our bikes on the trailer of Rolf´s Mercedes and drove to Gothenburg where we embarked on the ferry boat to Ipswich (Felixstowe). We wanted to get to England in good time so we could do some riding for training purposes and get our bikes dialled in. We were headed for St Albans to meet a friend of mine, Chris Lavery, a journalist who had been travelling with me to several races throughout Europe. With his contacts he should be able to find some training ground for us.

But what a surprise when we got to England! A heavy snow storm with really cold weather was on the way and it took the whole country by surprise. For us Swedes this was nothing to worry about. But in England at that time, two inches' of snow was a disaster! We could not believe that the equipment for the removal of snow on roads was so outdated and completely worthless. Traffic was standing still, roads were blocked, and there was complete chaos! Our plans to do some riding on a nice, grassy English motocross track were dramatically changed. Instead we ended up spending our day at my friend's house, and what an experience! Because of the cold weather the water pipes and the heating system were frozen, so no water and no heating in the house - in those days the pipes for heating houses were fitted on the outside. We couldn't believe that a little snow and cold weather could cause so many problems.

The best and warmest place was in the car, so we headed for Beaulieu knowing that we might have to wait many, many hours in the slow traffic because of the snowy weather conditions. We found a hotel in the town close to the race track, our requirements were simple - the rooms should be heated. Unfortunately the 'heating' was like an electric wire on the wall. One had to put a shilling in a slot every hour to get some 'heating' in the room! I still remember how I pushed Rolf to wake him up during the night when it was his turn to drop a shilling in the machine! We have never, ever, in our lifetime been so cold, frozen and homesick!

Finally: Race Day arrived. As stated before - the warmest place was in the car so we took off early in the morning and headed for the race track. On arrival many of the cars in front of us had big trouble getting into the paddock area. However, we were used to driving in snowy conditions so we had no problem at all manoeuvring our Mercedes with trailer and two bikes to our designated area.

Anyway, we unloaded the bikes, met with several of our friends and competitors and started to prepare our bikes. First on our agenda – to cut our tyres to be prepared for the snowy and icy conditions! We were used to riding and training in the snow, so we knew how to set up our bikes. By getting better tyre grip, adjusting the pressure, preparing cables and the air filter to avoid the throttle sticking, we felt confident with the preparation of our bikes. Now we were ready to race!

However, we also knew from earlier experience that racing against English riders on home soil was a completely different experience than racing against them on the continent. At home they were always a different class!

The 250cc race was the first on the schedule. I expected it to be a tough race, especially against David Bickers, my main competitor. He was also a good friend of mine and in my opinion one of the best riders ever, as he had fantastic balance and throttle control.

Right after the start I lost track of him and the rest of the riders. I was alone and it was like having a training session as I was way ahead of everyone! Next was the 500cc race and now it was Rolf's turn to show. The same thing happened to him - no opposition, he won easily.

After these two races, Bickers came up to me, his face like a question mark and he said, 'How can you get such grip when it's so slippery and icy? I can't compete'. I said, 'David - I'll show you our tyres - that's the secret! We cut our knobs with a saw in tiny small pieces. So instead of getting grip from one edge, we get it from 7 - 8 edges. Go ahead, please use my saw and do the same!'

The next race was a mixed 250 - 500cc race. The same thing happened again with the competition, nobody could follow us, except Bickers, now on the new 'secret tyres'! However, after a while Rolf and I were by ourselves in the lead again, trying to find out how to outsmart each other on the icy surface. Rolf was not very happy when I crossed the finish line ahead of him - he did not expect that I could beat him. And as a matter of fact - I was surprised myself! The last race was what was called the Grandstand Final. Once again it was the same battle between Rolf and me, but this time Rolf was the winner with me on his rear tyre.

That evening, two happy Swedes left Beaulieu with most of the prize money and the glory of dominating the racing. Luckily we had a tremendous advantage in the snowy and icy weather conditions. I'm afraid, it would have been another story in dry or muddy conditions!

Dave Bickers took the challenge to the invincible Swedes. Here he leads Torsten Hallman and Bryan Goss (GF)

Once again, Murray Walker remembers it as if it were yesterday. 'I remember that Beaulieu event very well, the Swedes made us look like a bunch of fumbling amateurs. I remember Rolf Tibblin and Torsten Hallman riding round together - light years ahead - and to rub salt into the wounds, as they approached the finish they joined hands and crossed the finishing line together.'

BSA Show Of Strength

Two weeks later the racing came from Hankom Bottom, near Winchester, just over 20 miles north of Beaulieu. The weather had failed to improve, but at least this time the home riders didn't have to contend with the threat of humiliation at the hands of the Viking invaders. On this occasion, the master class was meted out by Streetly's finest skating exponent, Jeff Smith, as the threat from Bickers evaporated when his Greeves was arrested by a waterlogged electrical system.

Bickers led Smith, who for this meeting abandoned his new lightweight 420 BSA in favour of a Gold Star, for the first six laps of the Grandstand Trophy before running out of grip on the big hill and then retiring when the Greeves spluttered to a stop. But from there on, it was pretty much processional for Smith, who lead home teammates John Harris and John Burton.

In the Allcomers race, Vic Eastwood managed to get the Matchless out front briefly on the second lap, but Smith soon recaptured the lead and when Eastwood tumbled, Harris and Burton guaranteed a BSA-BBC whitewash. Burton eventually got the better of Smith in the Invitation race, after deposing early leader Harris, who held on for third ahead of Eastwood for yet another BSA 1-2-3!

Action, Drama And Suspense

In mid-February 1963, the West Wilts Club ran, what would be the first of three televised meetings they would organise that year. Once again, the venue was Naish Hill and, like the Beaulieu and Hankom Bottom events, this event was run on a snowbound track.

Despite the absence of Smith and Burton, the riders put on a great show for the TV pundits, though Dave Bickers was once again to be denied. A poor start in the 250 race saw Bickers back in eighth place, whilst Vic Eastwood on the James was away from the rest of the field at the front. Never one to shirk a challenge, Bickers pushed on throughout the race and as they entered the penultimate lap Eastwood's 250 yard lead had been reduced to nothing. Starting the last lap it was advantage Bickers, but Eastwood matched his determination and energy and blasted back into the lead, which he held to the flag.

The Open Championship lived up to the excitement of the lightweight duel. Local man Brian Curtis initially led, but was soon passed by John Harris, and the flying Greeves pair of Joe Johnson and Bickers. These three riders were locked in combat, but something had to give and Johnson was the first to lose contact. However, the front two kept the viewers guessing as to who would take the win, with Bickers gamely hanging on to Harris' back wheel, before making another bold, last lap passing manoeuvre, but Harris withstood the challenge to claim his first BBC victory.

Worthy of mention were leading scrambles exponents from the north of England, Jack Matthews, John Griffiths and Alan Clough, who'd all made the long arduous journey down from Cheshire, only to arrive after the meeting had started. However, they soon got stuck in, and although Clough had little to show for his efforts, Matthews scored a couple of fifth place finishes and Griffiths took fourth place in the Open Championship.

Jim Timms (13) leads Dave Nicoll (11), Ken Messenger (55), John Banks (22), Joe Johnson (6) and Bryan Goss (46) in a 250 race at Naish Hill, February 1962 (GF)

Setting The Tone

On 9th March, 1963, the BBC televised a meeting held at Lower Hill Farm, Prestbury, Gloucestershire, which coincidentally was home to former European Motocross champion, John Draper. By this time the big thaw had already begun, leaving the track very soggy underfoot and when the rain set in it provided the BBC technicians with the kind of conditions that would come to typify the racing presented on the *Grandstand* programme over the years. Competitors had to force their way forward through a glutinous mudbath, whilst the cameramen tried to follow the leaders and commentator Murray Walker, aided by Cheltenham Home Guard MC and LCC (Motor Cycle and Light Car Club) members, did his best to identify the riders. Walker recalls:

> *Very often the riders were so muddy that they were literally unrecognisable and I would get very worried about it. But subsequently I thought, 'Well if I don't know who they are the viewers certainly don't know who they are!'*

Due to the conditions, the race programme was changed with three televised Invitation races being run, which provided three different winners. 18 year-old AMC runner Dave Nicoll, who was always an ace in the mud, stormed the first race and although he was briefly passed by teammate Vic Eastwood, who then immediately landed on his ear, he raced on to a comfortable win, his first on television, ahead of Bryan Goss and Eastwood, who had made a speedy recovery. Even the great Jeff Smith was having trouble, despite his knowledge of the track (he married Draper's sister, Irene). He could only finish sixth to the flying Nicoll, a lap adrift. Nicoll, who currently acts as the FIM's Clerk of the Course for Motocross GPs, recalls, 'Looking back I came up on the scene very quickly. At 19, I got several hours of prime time live exposure.'

It was Nicoll who also set the pace in the second race, though he got a little over-confident and spun the big Matchless at the bottom of the hill, allowing his other teammate,

Jeff Smith keeping his hand in on the 500 Gold Star, Winchester, January 1963 (CB)

Chris Horsfield, to take up the running, hotly pursued by Greeves runners Alan Clough and Goss, who would run out the race winner.

The third race, which provided the day's best racing, eventually saw Smith rediscover his winning ways, but only after ousting Nicoll from the lead and then holding off a grimly determined Horsfield, who also wanted to get in on the winning act. Smith, who had elected to ride his full-500 Gold Star, rather than the lighter 420, raced for the line side-by-side with Horsfield, getting the verdict by half a wheel, whilst Nicoll edged out Goss for 3rd place.

Dry Run

On 30th March, 1963, the BBC televised three races from Hawkstone Park, home to the 500 British GP since 1954 and the track that would play host to the first Grandstand Trophy round some seven months later. The televised races were run on the Saturday afternoon, whilst the following day there was also a full programme of races, including the opening round of the 500 ACU Star contest.

Leading BSA rider Jeff Smith knew Hawkstone Park like the back of his hand, having won countless races at the Shropshire track, including three 500 GPs by that juncture, and he turned in another peerless performance over the weekend, winning six of the seven finals, including the ACU Star race. His first victory came in the televised seven-lap Up to 650cc race, when, mounted on his 350, he stormed through from fifth on the first lap to lead in a BSA 1-2-3 ahead of teammates John Burton and John Harris on their 500 Gold Stars.

He added his second in the 250 to 500cc when for the second race in succession Burton got the start. The Leicestershire rider must have fancied his chances this time, as it was just a four-lapper, but Smith again showed his pedigree by overhauling his teammate on the last lap, with Chris Horsfield on his factory Matchless third.

The performance of 18 year-old Dave Nicoll was a bright spot on a murky day at Draper's Farm, March 1963 (GF)

The only man to beat Smith all weekend was 22 year-old Bryan Goss, who was rarely at his best in the deep sand of Hawkstone Park. Goss gated fastest, but Horsfield shot past the factory Cotton runner as they rocketed up the hill on the second lap. However, the James rider's lead was short lived as he crashed in dramatic style just a few yards further on. This left Goss well clear of the pack, as Smith, who had started ninth, worked his way through the field to eventually pip Greeves' Joe Johnson for second place.

The Grandstand Trophy Moto-Cross Series

Following the success of the televised meetings shown on *Grandstand*, and a prolonged battle with ITV over the rights to televise the sport, the BBC, with the ACU's blessing, took the decision to televise a winter motocross series, as Brian Johnson explains:

> *Bryan Cowgill and Peter Dimmock realised that in motocross they had an unstoppable sport for the winter months and what had been a series of one-off meetings, was for the winter of 1963/64, to become the Grandstand Trophy series'.*

Johnson started work at the BBC in Shepherd's Bush in August 1963 and the same month was given responsibility to liaise with the ACU in a series of meetings to establish rules, fees, locations and roles for the coming series. This accomplished, the first Grandstand Trophy Moto-cross series round was scheduled for 12th October, 1963 at Hawkstone Park.

Technology has arrived! Smith with mobile camera at Caerleon in December 1963 (MC)

How The Grandstand Trophy Series Worked

In the opening 1963-64 series there were 12 rounds, with one 250 and one 500 race counting towards the respective Grandstand trophies staged at each round. Points were awarded to the first six riders to finish in each of these races. These were awarded as follows:

1st place	8 points
2nd place	6 points
3rd place	5 points
4th place	4 points
5th place	3 points
6th place	2 points

At the end of the series the rider with the most points accumulated in each category would win the coveted Grandstand Trophy.

Supporting Races

In addition, the organising clubs would generally run a third televised race, though in some instances only the 250 and 500 Trophy races would be broadcast. However, on a few occasions there would also be a fourth televised race.

These non-Grandstand Trophy races were generally 'Invitation' races, where the organising club would pre-select a field of riders to compete. However, they could also take the form of 'Unlimited' or 'Allcomers' races where all riders would have to compete in heats to qualify for the final, which would then be televised.

Though the terminology may have changed from round to round, the idea behind these 'supporting' races was generally the same: riders of 250 and larger capacity machines could race together. They also tended to produce some of the most competitive and exciting racing ever seen on television, especially on the tighter, twisting courses that favoured light weight and manoeuvrability over sheer horsepower.

Changes to the format

Sidecars
Sidecar racing was briefly included in the programming for *Grandstand*, the first event being televised in January 1965. However, these races were, by and large, unsuccessful and although it was discussed at meetings between the BBC and the ACU, there was never really a possibility of a Grandstand Trophy for sidecars. The last sidecar race to be included during the time of the Grandstand Trophy series was screened in March 1966.

Reduction in the number of rounds
The 1965-66 series saw a reduction in the number of rounds, from 12 to just 8.

Capacity increase to 750cc
From 1966-67 onwards, the larger capacity class was opened out to 750cc. The thinking at the time was that the 'big' (350 plus cc) two-strokes would come to dominate the larger capacity competitions and that the four-stroke machines would benefit from using larger engines. With hindsight we know that the thinking was right on the first count, but

wrong in assuming that larger capacity engines would make four-stroke machines more competitive. However, the BSA factory, which had decided the future of the four-stroke motocross machine lay in reduced weight, managed to produce competitive motorcycles right through till the end of the Grandstand series in 1970.

Impact of foot-and-mouth
There were some anomalies in the 1967-68 series due to an outbreak of foot-and-mouth disease, which severely restricted competition motorcycling and led to wholesale cancellations. As a result, when the series reconvened at Bury St Edmunds in January 1968, a meeting that was hastily arranged once the ban had been lifted, there was no 250 race, only a race which counted towards the 750 Grandstand Trophy. In addition, the series was reduced to just 5 rounds and to compensate for the missing 250 race, two 250 races were staged at the final round at Caerleon in March 1968, with both races counting towards the Grandstand Trophy.

Conditions were often less than ideal! Underneath the mud is Bryan Goss (BH)

Into The Grandstand Trophy Series

The stylish John Griffiths, arguably at his best during his Dot days, in an ABC TV meeting in 1963 (MC)

At the same time that the BBC was in negotiation with the ACU over the forthcoming Grandstand series, Britain's leading motocross riders were contesting the GPs, though with greatly contrasting levels of success. Mid-June 1963, found twice European 250 motocross champion Dave Bickers racing at the Finnish GP, an event that was to prove pivotal in Bickers' career. Meanwhile, BSA's Jeff Smith and Arthur Lampkin, who after several years of chasing the 250 crown had moved over to the 500 class, had just returned from Russia and were racing in their home GP at Hawkstone Park.

A week earlier Swede, Torsten Hallman, had clinched his second 250 world title on his Swedish Husqvarna machine at his home GP at Vannas, much to the delight of the partisan crowd. For Bickers, however, it was a very different story. He had suffered a torrid time in the world championship, despite winning the curtain raiser in Spain, and was far from pleased with the Greeves' performance. In Sweden the bike broke down in both legs, but it was the Finnish GP the following week that proved to be the straw that broke the camel's back.

> I'd been breaking down in the GPs on the Greeves and I was so fed up that on the way back from Finland I called in at the Husqvarna factory and bought a bike off them. I took it apart, put it in the back of the car and brought it back home. I fitted some Greeves forks and even wanted to paint it blue and call it a Greeves, but Mr Greeves didn't like that idea!

Dave Bickers flying his recently acquired Husqvarna, fitted with Greeves forks and petrol tank, on his way to victory in the 250 Experts Grand National, Larkstoke, Warwickshire, August 1963 (MC)

In July 1964 Jeff Smith notched up his fourth victory in the 500 British GP at Hawkstone Park (CB)

It didn't take Bickers any time to adapt to his new mount and at Shrubland Park on August Bank Holiday Monday, he took the bike (entered in the programme as a '250 Special'), to a winning debut in the ACU Star race, beating Arthur Lampkin by some 150 yards! A fortnight later, the combination also proved too strong for the likes of Greeves runners Alan Clough and rising star Malcolm Davis, as he won both legs of the 250 Experts GN at Larkstoke, Warwickshire.

As the summer drew to a close, he added wins at the Brian Stonebridge Memorial, at Hawkstone Park, and at the Thirsk GN meeting, where he clinched his third 250 ACU Star (British championship), winning the Star race and taking the first leg of the GN event from Jeff Smith and Don Rickman. But Bickers really caught the eye on the Husqvarna in the Grandstand Trophy that brought scrambling into our living rooms and made household names of its stars.

In the meantime, at Hawkstone Park, Smith had won his fourth 500 British GP, on a memorable day for British motocross, with the podium comprising three British riders on British machines, with Lampkin as runner-up and Derek Rickman third on his Matchless Métisse. Smith would go on to finish third in the world championship, behind the Swedes, Rolf Tibblin and Sten Lundin in his first full season of GPs on the 420 BSA.

By the end of the summer though, Smith had secured his sixth 500 ACU Star, despite missing the final round at Elsworth in September, ironically whilst on duty with the British team at the *Trophee des Nations* in Belgium.

There is no question that at this time, Dave Bickers and Jeff Smith were the best of British motocross riders, but a new crop of very talented riders was emerging to prevent them from resting on their laurels.

In the 250 class, Bickers was continuously having to look over his shoulder in order to fend off the likes of Dot factory man John Griffiths, whose career would sadly be cut short due to injury, and his Greeves teammates, Alan Clough, who had recently switched from Dot, and Bryan Goss.

Also waiting in the lightweight wings, eager to flex their muscles, were young riders such as John Banks and John Done, on their factory Dots, Freddie Mayes, who was racing a factory Cotton, and Malcolm Davis, who was beginning to make a name for himself on a works Greeves.

In the 500 category, Jeff Smith, and especially BSA had been dominant since the outset of the 60s, primarily through Smith and Lampkin, but also with stalwart performers, John Burton and John Harris. But in the 1963 ACU Star contest, AMC's new prospect, Vic Eastwood had pushed Smith all the way, and in Eastwood, AMC had a rider who could perform for them at the same level that Geoff Ward and Dave Curtis had previously done. The AMC group could also call on the talents of Chris Horsfield and the teenager with a bright future ahead of him, Dave Nicoll, and in the Grandstand Trophy series they would challenge, in both the 250 and 500 classes, on James and Matchless respectively.

The Rickman brothers, Derek and Don, who were well-established riders of the highest quality and capable of beating any rider in the world on their day, posed a potential threat in both classes, with Don a double threat on the 250 Bultaco Métisse and a Matchless or Triumph-engined Métisse in the 500 class, whilst Derek always preferred to race the larger capacity machine. However, as we will see, product development and running a full time business required a lot of time and energy and, sadly for TV viewers, the brothers would only make a few fleeting appearances on the TV screens.

Murray Walker remembers his transition from the ABC TV meetings to the BBC and the impact that the Grandstand series had on TV viewers very well.

The BBC started to televise scramble meetings in 1963 and the ACU had big plans for this. They wanted to make it an all-singing, all-dancing national sport, and a massive battle ensued between the BBC and ITV for screening rights which the BBC won.

The ACU had Harold Taylor, a nice guy, but very irascible, who dragooned everybody into shape and did a very good job. As a result, the BBC Grandstand Trophy series became enormously popular, firstly by virtue of the sort of sport it is - exciting, fast-moving, noisy and dramatic - and secondly, because it was the BBC and it went out nationwide and was no longer confined to Yorkshire and Lancashire as it had primarily been with ABC Television.

Top, Alan Clough was a constant thorn in the side of Dave Bickers. In 1963 he made the move to Greeves after a string of impressive rides for Dot (MC)

Middle, racing his factory Matchless, Vic Eastwood led the challenge to BSAs supremacy. Here he is pictured in the BBC meeting at Naish Hill, October 1963 (GF)

Bottom, Dave Nicoll, the youngest member of the AMC team, got a taste for TV success at Larkstoke, in March 1963, winning two finals on the Saturday (MC)

1963-64
The Winter Of Living Dangerously

Dave Bickers, Hankom Bottom, 30th November, 1963 (GF)

On the same weekend that reputedly saw the birth of 'Beatlemania', when the mop-topped Liverpudlians played live on ATV's *Sunday Night at the London Palladium*, hosted by Bruce Forsythe, the very first Grandstand Trophy Series took to the airwaves at what had become the ancestral home of British motocross, Hawkstone Park, Shropshire, on Saturday 12th October, 1963.

Of course, scrambling was not unfamiliar to TV viewers following the pioneering efforts of the ITV network, but the BBC, having fought off a spirited challenge from ITV for broadcasting rights, were launching an ambitious 12-round series that would run from mid-October through to early March, with riders scoring points and competing for the Grandstand Trophies for 250 and 500cc classes, to be awarded to the rider in each category who had accumulated the most points at the series' close.

One of the three or four cameramen who would have covered the racing at Hawkstone Park (MC)

Round 1

Hawkstone Park, Shropshire, October 12, 1963

The racing at Hawkstone Park cannot have failed to catch the attention of those who tuned in to their favourite TV Sports programme, and those with little or no knowledge of the sport were soon educated as to just who the stars of the day were. Britain's leading scrambles riders, Dave Bickers and Jeff Smith, who was two days shy of his 29th birthday, recorded emphatic wins in the 250 and 500 Trophy races and each then added a second win in their respective classes, though armchair viewers would have to wait a while before they would see these two giants of off-road racing go head-to-head in an invitation race.

The programme for the opening round of the Grandstand Trophy series at Hawkston Park with none other than 'Mr. Televison', Arthur Lampkin, gracing the cover

Dave Bickers looking supremely focused as he races to victory in the 250 Trophy race (MC)

250 Trophy Race

In the 250 Trophy race, Bickers got the start and soon established a comfortable lead over the chasing pack, led by John Griffiths, Dot's top factory runner from Crewe, Chris Horsfield from the Midlands on his factory James and North-West kingpin Alan Clough, who was in his first season on a factory Greeves, having previously ridden for Dot.

With the race under control, Bickers eased back a little maintaining the gap to Griffiths, who finished 2nd, whilst Horsfield had to remain attentive to the flag, as Clough, Hawkstone debutant, John Banks, and fellow Dot rider, Ernie Greer, almost closed him down. Curiously enough, Horsfield, Clough and Banks would all go on to become holders of the coveted Grandstand Trophies, a few years down the line.

With the 250 Trophy race finishing at 2:40, racing did not return to the airwaves again until 4.25, at which time, inexplicably, the 250 Invitation was run rather than the 500 Trophy race with Dave Bickers taking his second win of the day, again from Griffiths with Banks improving to a brilliant 3rd place.

500 Trophy Race

The result of all this was that the 500 Trophy race was run in fading light, giving the BBC technicians and the ACU officials some food for thought, though as former BBC producer Brian Johnson has assured me, such conditions were more problematic to the riders and officials than to the BBC cameramen.

However, Smith had no problems, expertly piloting his way through the gathering darkness to his second win of the day on the 420 BSA. From the start it was BSA

Big John Burton, was on fine form for the TV cameras, finishing as runner-up to Jeff Smith in the 500 Trophy race on his trusty Gold Star BSA (MC)

With shadows lengthening and daylight fading Jeff Smith rides on to victory in the 500 Trophy race (MC)

teammate John Burton, who favoured his trusty 500 Gold Star, who took the lead and fended off Smith till mid-race distance. Whilst Smith was comfortable at the front, Burton, affectionately known as 'Burly' on account of his robust physique, came under increasing pressure from top AMC runner Vic Eastwood, who in turn had to quell the advances of fellow Matchless rider Bill Gwynne for third spot.

At the flag Smith lead in Burton, Eastwood and Gwynne, with Jerry Scott on a Gold Star BSA getting the better of young Dave Nicoll on the factory Matchless.

The Press

The man MCN (Motor Cycle News) despatched to Hawkstone Park was their 21 year-old fledgling reporter, Chris Carter. Chris had only joined the paper the previous year, but he was already their leading motocross expert as a result of the big reshuffle on the paper when Brian McLaughlin was appointed Editor-in-chief. When Carter took the job he had been totally oblivious to the fact that within a few months he would be travelling all over the country covering a motocross series promoted by the BBC.

Motorcycle News reporter Chris Carter (left) in conversation with Harold Taylor (centre) in the paddock at Hawkstone Park (MC)

> No, the best I could have hoped for at that time was to cover an ACU Star round. But when the BBC television meetings came along it was a really big deal.

Carter went on to cover eleven of the twelve rounds of the opening series, having to cede to Ralph Venables at Tweseldown in January, and in total he reported on twenty-three of the fifty-seven meetings staged over the seven series that the BBC televised.

Grandstand Trophy Results

250 Trophy
1 D Bickers (Husqvarna)
2 J Griffiths (Dot)
3 C Horsfield (James)
4 A Clough (Greeves)
5 J Banks (Dot)
6 E Greer (Dot)

500 Trophy
1 J Smith (420 BSA)
2 J Burton (500 BSA)
3 V Eastwood (500 Matchless)
4 W Gwynne (500 Matchless)
5 J Scott (500 BSA)
6 D Nicoll (500 Matchless)

In many ways the opening round set the tone for the early years of the Grandstand series, with Dave Bickers and Jeff Smith dominating the 250 and 500cc classes respectively and giants of the British motorcycle industry, such as BSA and AMC, fielding strong teams in the hope that success out on the race track would be reflected in sales in the showrooms. Smith recalls that BSA were always very keen to participate in the TV events:

> The management at BSA became particularly interested in the TV events. Success was seen as an affirmation of the superiority of BSA machines and at that time every department wanted to help the Competitions Department, it was a wonderful atmosphere for development.

Smith, who worked in the BSA factory, also remembers the effect BSA's involvement had on morale on the shop floor:

> There was palpable pride amongst the workers that they could see some of their products showing their quality on TV. After a particularly successful weekend people would applaud as we came back into the factory. It seemed that almost everyone watched the racing and knew the results.

However, those in the know would have noted how easily Bickers, on his privately owned Swedish Husqvarna, had stamped his authority on the lightweight races, a wakeup call that sadly was not heeded by the all too dormant British motorcycle industry. As Bickers himself told me:

> I don't think Greeves realised at the time how big it would be. I didn't realise, for me it was just another place to go on a Saturday or Sunday. I'd work during the week, as a mechanic in my dad's garage, and race my bike at the weekend. It was a lot of travelling and the vehicles we used were not very comfortable, but for me it was always another weekend away with my mates.

The Royal Enfield Project Bike

Over the years several prototype machines would see the light of day in the Grandstand series. Much was made in the motorcycle press of the day of Royal Enfield's venture into the world of motocross; the famous Redditch Motorcycle manufacturer, whilst very successful in the world of observed trials, had not traditionally been associated with racing on the rough stuff. An 'all-new' model was supposed to be launched at Hawkstone Park, but on the day, Welshman Bill Gwynne, a former Greeves factory runner, rode a 250 Crusader-engined four-stroke in a new chassis and was off the pace, finishing 12th in the Grandstand Trophy race.

Gwynne recalls, 'It was a real bitsa, because they took the forks from one model (a variation on the GP5 racer leading-link fork), the frame from another and the swinging arm was adapted from a third model.'

The Villiers Starmaker-engined 250 Royal Enfield would eventually see the light of day at round four of the series at Winchester, where Gwynne raced it to an impressive sixth place in the 250 Trophy race. Sadly, the new model, though looking very business-like, would do little to enhance Royal Enfield's reputation, as it would suffer a brief and largely ignominious spell on the racetracks. However, Gwynne did manage to add to his Grandstand points tally, when he again finished sixth on his native Welsh soil at Builth Wells in January 1964.

With hindsight, Bill believes that the Enfield had potential. 'It wasn't a bad little bike. Unfortunately, though, after a few laps of almost every race the clutch would start to slip. In the mud it was quite good, but if it was dry and bumpy I could hardly hang on to the handlebars, as it used to wobble all over the place! Sadly, they were just starting to sort it out when the doors closed at the factory.'

Bill Gwynne's pristine looking Villiers Starmaker-engined Royal Enfield, here in the paddock at Builth Wells, January 1964 (MC)

Round 2

Farleigh Castle, Wiltshire, October 19, 1963

The BBC were pulling no punches in their attempt to entice the viewing public, selecting another famous off-road venue for round two of the series. Farleigh Castle had been the scene of grass track events from as early as 1938 and the Wessex National, held in January 1947, placed it firmly on the scrambles' map. However, soon after that the land had been lost to the West Wilts Club and scrambling only returned there in May 1963, for the first running of the famous Maybug Scramble, whilst the tracks' glory days as a GP venue still lay some years ahead at this time.

Of course, the organising West Wilts Club, led by the industrious Ken Lywood, had already been instrumental in promoting the sport on TV with their efforts on their other scrambles circuit at Naish Hill. Leading ACU official of the day, Harold Taylor, was keen to repay their hard work and dedication and as such they were awarded the right to organise the second round of the new series.

Though Dave Bickers and Jeff Smith were favourites to repeat their opening day victories, they faced a stiff challenge in the shape of the Rickman brothers, Derek and Don from New Milton, Hampshire. The brothers, though super-talented riders, had been devoting most of their time and energy to establishing their motorcycle business that produced the world famous Métisse framesets. The Métisse, meaning 'mongrel' in French, had first appeared in 1959 as a Triumph-engined special and by the time they took to the track at Farleigh Castle in October 1963, they had a long waiting list for a product that had evolved into a pure thoroughbred.

Although the Rickmans had favoured British four-stroke power plants, especially the Triumph twin and Matchless single, Don Rickman had forged a strong bond with the Spanish Bultaco concern, following victory in the 1960 Barcelona GP on a factory Bultaco, and at Farleigh they would field a brace of Matchless Métisses and a 196cc Bultaco Métisse - the forerunner of the 'Petite Métisse', as the lightweight model would come to be known.

The presence of the Rickman brothers, racing in their native south of England on a near perfect track, virtually guaranteed good viewing for the *Grandstand* faithful, but the spectacle was marred by a succession of poor starts. Early in the meeting the elastic start rope was broken and officials had to resort to flagging the riders away, which resulted in very uneven starts and was clearly far from satisfactory.

However, it wasn't always that easy to false start, as John Burton told me:

I was racing at a TV meeting one day and my father was positioned so that he could see the TV monitor. We were all on the start line and when the image cut from the studio to a muddy field he gave me the signal to go. However, on that day the elastic was very strong and I failed to break it and when it went up I was taken unawares.

250 Trophy Race

The 250 Trophy race saw Don Rickman, on his super-fast Bultaco Métisse, get away first and open up a small gap on the rest of the field. However, Dave Bickers knew there was a long way to go, this being a 14-lap contest and one of the longest Grandstand Trophy races ever staged, and was content to follow his adversary in the opening laps. Then as the race entered its 5th lap, Bickers slipped past Rickman, but the Hampshireman fought back and the two stars then proceeded to trade places for several laps.

A super-sharp Malcolm Carling shot captures Don Rickman racing the Bultaco Métisse to the runner-up spot in the 250 Trophy race

This shot captures two excellent and contrasting examples of motocross machine development in the early 1960s; Jeff Smith on the lighter, and clearly more compact, 420 BSA, leads Don Rickman on the exquisitely crafted full-500 Matchless Métisse. The two filled the first two places in the 500 Trophy race in this order (GF)

Behind the leaders, Chris Horsfield, Alan Clough, Freddie Mayes, on his factory Cotton, and John Griffiths were fighting for the minor places until Horsfield's James quit on him and Griffiths took a big tumble. Unfortunately for Griffiths, teammate and Comp Shop manager, Pat Lamper, who was running close behind couldn't avoid the prone rider and ran over him.

Amidst all the confusion, Bickers assumed control of the race and eased away from Rickman, whilst Clough got the better of Mayes, Lamper and Bickers' travelling companion Pete Smith (Greeves) for 3rd place.

Griffiths remembers the incident well:

When I fell at Farleigh Castle, the doctor who treated me at the track came to see me in hospital and said, 'You're a lucky guy. I saw the accident and I ran because of the way you fell. I thought you'd broken your neck and I didn't want anyone to move you.' I've still got the scar up my back though, where Pat Lamper rode right over me!

500 Trophy Race

Sadly, due to TV programming decisions, the 500 Trophy race was drastically cut to just 5 laps, though it still provided plenty of action. It is interesting to note here that in general, more airtime was being devoted to the sport than in the years to come, as the five or six lap, 15 minute race would soon become the norm.

Don Rickman was really on top of his game, having won his heat from Smith, but it was fast-gating Andy Lee on another Matchless Métisse who led the charge from Smith and Don Rickman, just ahead of brother Derek, with Horsfield and Burton filling the points scoring positions. On the second lap, Don edged past Smith, but all that seemed to do was to motivate the BSA man more, as a lap later he had passed both Rickman and Lee. Smith remained at the head of things to the flag, holding a slim lead over Don, who had ousted Lee, with brother Derek following suit to annex third place. Lee eventually finished 4th, some way ahead of Burton, who won his private battle with Horsfield for 5th spot.

Supporting Races

The Unlimited races, sadly not televised, saw the 250s go head-to-head with the 500s for the first time in the series, though the fast, grassy Wiltshire circuit definitely favoured the big four-strokes. In fact, the First Unlimited saw Burton, on his full-500 Gold Star, putting one over his Armoury Road teammate Smith, on the 420, whilst Bickers wrung the Husqvarna's neck in a bold bid to catch Vic Eastwood, the Matchless man just holding on to take 3rd place.

Bickers won a heat of the Second Unlimited, but the final saw Don Rickman take a fully deserved win from factory Triumph runner, John Giles, and Burton, whilst the big-hitters failed to feature for very different reasons. Smith, who had taken to the line, was disgusted by yet another ragged start - riders got underway at the third time of asking - and soon quit in protest, whilst Bickers' Swedish lightweight found it was no match for its rider in this particular race, as the gearbox seized up as he was scything his way through the field.

…

So, with two rounds down, Bickers and Smith had consolidated their leads. But did they face a serious threat to their trophy aspirations from Don Rickman? The answer was sadly no, as at the day's close, the Rickmans told *MCN* reporter Chris Carter that they would be 'hibernating' through the winter months.

In conversation with Derek recently, he explained the Rickman philosophy:

We didn't get too involved with the TV events. We felt that motocross was a summer sport and we didn't like the idea of driving all the way to Builth Wells or Yorkshire to ride in a muddy event.

The other thing that annoyed us, was that everything depended on the horse racing and we had to wait and wait for the start and we both felt that the races were simply run when the BBC needed something to fill a gap and we felt the BBC was taking advantage of us (those involved in the sport) when there was no horse racing because the weather was so bad. And of course, when the weather was so bad, the circuits were so bad. The other aspect is that in wintertime we used to ride in trials which we really enjoyed.

BSA Competition Manager, Brian Martin, is about to be interviewed by Murray Walker following a lap of the circuit with a BBC cameraman armed with a hand-held radio camera in the chair (MC)

Grandstand Trophy Race Results

250 Trophy
1 D Bickers (Husqvarna)
2 D J Rickman (200 Petite Métisse)
3 A Clough (Greeves)
4 F Mayes (Cotton)
5 P Lamper (Dot)
6 P Smith (Greeves)

500 Trophy:
1 J Smith (420 BSA)
2 D J Rickman (500 Matchless Métisse)
3 D E Rickman (500 Matchless Métisse)
4 A Lee (500 Matchless Métisse)
5 J Burton (500 BSA)
6 C Horsfield (500 Matchless)

Round 3
Beeston, Cheshire, November 2, 1963

Held in the shadows of the picturesque Beeston Castle, the third round saw Bickers march relentlessly on, whilst Arthur Lampkin provided teammate Jeff Smith with his stiffest challenge to date. However, aside from the performances of the 'big three', as *MCN* reporter Chris Carter liked to refer to the seasoned GP runners, the racing was rather dull in comparison with the previous rounds and was criticised for being too processional.

In their defence, the BBC always tried their best to select tracks that would provide good conditions both for racing and filming, as producer Brian Johnson explains:

Each meeting was planned well in advance; first the location was agreed with the Club and the ACU's Harold Taylor. I would arrange about a week before the show to visit the location with Taylor, the BBC engineering manager of the Outside Broadcast (OB) unit and a works rider, usually Jeff Smith or Arthur Lampkin. The rider would ride round the course and we would watch and the engineer and I would plot the positions of the cameras; usually four, with a radio camera if available. The engineer would also book the required links to get the show into the BBC network. I usually asked the rider for his opinion of the course, and the difficult parts.

On one of these early location meetings, a very wet day, Arthur Lampkin who had been riding a works Gold Star, and was soaked through, said, as we prepared to depart, 'I think the BBC should have a go.' and pushed the bike towards me. I attempted to bump start it (there was no kick start) in the hope it would not start, but it fired at once and round I went. I fell off once or twice, but managed to get round. Lampkin said nothing, but was always friendly after that.

With the TV antennae dominating the landscape, local man John Done leads this pack of riders during the 250 Trophy race (MC)

Above, basking in the sun, Dave Bickers completed a hat-trick of Grandstand Trophy race victories in the 250 event at Beeston (MC)

Left, BSA's Arthur Lampkin was in fine form at Beeston. Here he rolls the throttle off as he flies the factory 420 uphill (MC)

250 Trophy Race

In the 250 Trophy race Dave Bickers racked up his third straight win, though he was hounded till half distance by leading West Country ace and factory Greeves runner, Bryan Goss, who scored his first Grandstand Trophy points. However, Goss feels that he could have won the race if his luck had held.

I had the beating of Bickers, but I jarred the handlebars coming down off a jump and first I had to knock them straight and then I had to ride carefully to get the points.

Bickers eventually ran out an easy winner from Goss, whilst Alan Clough came through the field for 3rd place ahead of Chris Horsfield, Pat Lamper and another young rider making his mark on the Grandstand Trophy, Gloucester's Malcolm Davis. Most unfortunate rider on the day had to be local youngster John Done, on his factory Dot. Done, who lived just 20 miles away from the circuit in Pickmere, was lying 5th in the 250 Trophy race when his Dot seized up as he was about to start the final lap.

500 Trophy Race

The 500 Trophy race, which was a marathon 14-lap encounter, saw Arthur Lampkin surge to the front followed by teammates John Burton and Smith, with the Lutterworth, Leicestershire, rider keeping Smith at bay for five laps. This was fairly typical for Lampkin as Jeff Smith recalls. 'Arthur won many a pound note off me by betting he would be first into the first corner and he usually was!' However, as Lampkin I'm sure would tell you, Smith was more often than not ahead when it really counted - when he crossed the finish line.

By the time Smith had eventually found a way past Burton, Lampkin had a seemingly unassailable lead. However, by lap eleven, Smith had reeled in the Yorkshireman and stormed past on the final circuit to win, with Burton finishing third to confirm BSA's dominance. They may well have had even more success, had Wigan youngster Dick Clayton, on his ex-John Harris Gold Star not slipped off on the last lap whilst trying to oust AMC's teenaged star, Dave Nicoll, from 4th place. However, he still remounted in time to salvage 5th ahead of the second Matchless of Vic Eastwood.

Supporting Races

The highlight of the day though, was undoubtedly the televised Invitation race, which saw Bickers and Smith go head-to-head for bragging rights on BBC television. One man who wanted to usurp them both, however, was Lampkin, no stranger to the limelight of television himself. Arthur got the start again and narrowly led Smith and Bickers until the final lap, the three stars of the European motocross scene battling it out until the flag, when Smith pounced to deny his teammate for a second time, with Lampkin just holding off the irrepressible Bickers.

Poor Dick Clayton, having got himself into the points in the 500 Trophy race, was reminded of the dangers of motocross racing when he suffered a big fall in the Invitation event.

I had a problem with my Gold Star and I was racing a borrowed bike and I'd had a poor start and I was trying to ride up the outside of a group of riders when one of them stepped out and I shaved this tree and crashed in a big way.

Clayton shattered his elbow and fractured a scaphoid, though this was only discovered much later and by that time he needed a bone graft.

It kept me out for all of 1964 and most of 65 and it took me a long time to get back to where I'd been.

Grandstand Trophy Race Results

250 Trophy
1 D Bickers (Husqvarna)
2 B Goss (Greeves)
3 A Clough (Greeves)
4 C Horsfield (James)
5 P Lamper (Dot)
6 M Davis (Greeves)

500 Trophy
1 J Smith (420 BSA)
2 A J Lampkin (420 BSA)
3 J Burton (500 BSA)
4 D Nicoll (500 Matchless)
5 R Clayton (500 BSA)
6 V Eastwood (500 Matchless)

In other news, the BBC were preparing to launch another new series, this time a new Sci-Fi programme about a rather excentric looking individual who travelled through time in a Police phone box. Who would have thought that Dr Who would catch on, let alone still be going strong 50 years on?

Bryan Goss showed that he had the speed to match Dave Bickers in the 250 Trophy race (MC)

It was a day of contrasts for promising youngster, Dick Clayton. He finished in the points in the 500 Trophy race but suffered a season-ending fall in the Invitation race (MC)

Round 4

Winchester, Hampshire, November 30, 1963

When the televised scrambles circus moved on to Hankom Bottom near Winchester, the world was still in shock following the assassination of the American President, John Kennedy, in Dallas the previous week. But for the organisers, riders and TV crew alike, it was a case of: 'the show must go on'.

Hankom Bottom was a venue that would become synonymous with televised scrambles. The circuit had already been used by Southern TV, and the BBC, who had held a meeting there in very wintry conditions in January 1963, were eager to use the venue again. In late November, the going was pretty soft underfoot, though a clear, bright, autumnal day greeted the riders. However, the organisers and the BBC were to face further controversy over false starting, though this time, the big guns, Dave Bickers and Jeff Smith, rode their luck and extended their winning runs.

250 Trophy Race

One rider who had good reason to feel aggrieved by a false start was Bryan Goss, who would go on to finish as runner-up to Bickers in the 250 Trophy race. When the elastic had been released, half its length was momentarily left in place, reducing the race to a virtual

Greeves' Alan Clough does what very few managed to do in 1963 and gets himself in front of Dave Bickers on the Husqvarna (CB)

handicap event, with potential front runners such as Arthur Lampkin and Vic Eastwood left on the line. Goss remembers this occasion well; 'Bickers knew that being a TV race they wouldn't call him back and he was away, gone!'

Indeed Bickers simply rode away from the field, leading from first lap to last to register his fourth win of the series from Goss, Chris Horsfield and Cotton factory rider, Billy Jackson. Had Bickers found it difficult adjusting his tactics from 40 minute GP races to the 10-15 minute Grandstand dashes? 'No, I didn't treat those races any differently at all. I just had to be determined to get to the front, I never paced myself, I'd just go for it!'

John Done, who had been laid up in bed with flu before the event, experienced better luck this time out, as he came through for 5th place ahead of Bill Gwynne, who gave the Villiers Starmaker-engined Royal Enfield a very promising debut, both riders scoring their first points in the 250 Trophy.

One young rider who also took full advantage of the ragged start was 16 year-old Londoner, Len Neve, who found himself thrust into the limelight as he chased double European champion, Bickers, his image being broadcast live on national TV. Sadly, for young Len, his moment of glory was short lived as the more experienced riders moved through the pack, though he did fight on gamely, finishing 11th at the flag.

John Burton makes a few adjustments before Jeff Smith takes to the track with a 'state of the art' radio camera. Looking on are Murray Walker (left) and a rather bemused factory Triumph ace, John Giles (GF)

Two greats from the AMC stable; Dave Curtis (left), who came out of retirement to race selected BBC rounds, duels with rising star Vic Eastwood (CB)

500 Trophy Race

An exciting race saw Smith also add win number four in the 500 Trophy, but only after a tantalising dice with Eastwood, who was debuting a new 'lightweight' Matchless which tipped the scales with a dry weight of 290 lbs!

Jerry Scott from Poole, Dorset, on his Eric Cheney Gold Star introduced himself to *Grandstand* viewers by snatching the start, but Smith and Eastwood breezed past on the opening lap. Eastwood, the rising star of the AMC team, tenaciously held on to Smith on his 420 BSA in the early stages, not giving the Streetly man a chance to settle, though by the flag Smith had eked out his lead to win by 100 yards. Further back, Lampkin had got the better of Scott, though the privateer held off the third factory 420 BSA of John Harris to claim 4th spot, with Horsfield claiming the last point-scoring position in 6th place.

Grandstand Trophy Race Results:

250 Trophy
1 D Bickers (Husqvarna)
2 B Goss (Greeves)
3 C Horsfield (James)
4 B Jackson (Cotton)
5 J Done (Dot)
6 B Gwynne (Royal Enfield)

500 Trophy
1 J Smith (420 BSA)
2 V Eastwood (500 Matchless)
3 A J Lampkin (420 BSA)
4 J Scott (500 BSA)
5 J Harris (420 BSA)
6 C Horsfield (500 Matchless)

Round 5

Caerleon, Monmouthshire, December 14, 1963

As the Grandstand Trophy series entered winter, so it encountered the inclement British weather, with round five being run in the worse conditions to date. It also marked the day when Jeff Smith's stranglehold on the 500 Trophy series would be broken and the first time that a round of the Grandstand series was held outside of England.

Caerleon, a small town situated on the outskirts of Newport, South Wales, was steeped in history. Believed by many to be the home of King Arthur's Camelot, it had also played home to one of three permanent Roman Legionary Fortresses, along with York and Chester. In motorcycling history it would go on to become the most frequently used venue over the course of the Grandstand Trophy series.

500 Trophy Race

Arthur Lampkin was a rider coming into top form and one who was never unduly worried by adverse riding conditions. When the 500 Trophy race got underway Arthur shot into the lead, pursued by Dave Nicoll, Andy Lee and former holder of the ACU Scrambles Drivers' Star, Dave Curtis, making a rare TV appearance. But where was Smith? Soon after the start he had taken an excursion through the ropes, but had recovered to 6th place

Arthur Lampkin enjoyed his day out in South Wales, winning the 500 Trophy race and finishing third in the 250 Trophy race (MC)

Andy Lee, who would go on to finish the series as the top privateer, racing the Matcless-engined Bowman special (MC)

by the end of the opening lap. However, fully aware that his 100 percent record was in jeopardy, Smith pushed on a little too hard and fell again after tangling with Curtis and his race was run when the BSA refused to re-start.

Lampkin steadily increased his lead until the last lap, when he allowed Nicoll to close to within 50 yards, but the race was effectively already won, with Lee finishing 3rd, whilst AMC's young pretender, Vic Eastwood, got the better of former factory favourite, Curtis. Another Yorkshireman to make his mark in the series at Caerleon was Terry Silvester from Huddersfield on his Gold Star, who finished 6th to claim his first point.

Chris Carter remembers the impact Silvester had on the series:

Terry Silvester, was a hard-riding privateer, who rose above and beyond himself on many occasion over the winter of 1963-64. Of course, the factory BSA lads weren't happy about that. How dare this nobody come along and take the spotlight and publicity, not to mention the money, away from them!

250 Trophy Race

Having taken the 500 Trophy race and inflicted a rare defeat on Dave Bickers in one of the 250 Trophy heats, the question on everybody's lips was, could Lampkin stop Bickers in the 250 final? It didn't take long for an answer to appear, with Bickers stamping his mark on yet another 250 Trophy race, taking the lead and steadily extending it lap-by-lap over Bryan Goss, who in finishing as runner-up to Bickers for the third consecutive race was establishing himself as his closest challenger. Goss in turn finished well clear of Lampkin, Malcolm Davis, Freddie Mayes and Greeves man, Ken Sedgley.

Grandstand Trophy Race Results

250 Trophy
1 D Bickers (Husqvarna)
2 B Goss (Greeves)
3 A J Lampkin (BSA)
4 M Davis (Greeves)
5 F Mayes (Cotton)
6 K Sedgley (Greeves)

500 Trophy
1 A J Lampkin (420 BSA)
2 D Nicoll (500 Matchless)
3 A Lee (500 Matchless Métisse)
4 V Eastwood (500 Matchless)
5 D Curtis (500 Matchless)
6 T Silvester (500 BSA)

Below, Bryan Goss continued his fine run of form, finishing as runner-up to Dave Bickers for the third round in succession (MC)

Above, Dave Nicoll had his best Grandstand Trophy finish to date with an excellent runner-up spot in the 500 race (MC)

Round 6

Naish Hill, Wiltshire, December 28, 1963

The series reached its midway point between Christmas and New Year, when the BBC cameras returned to the Avon Tyre Company's dumping ground at Naish Hill. With good racing conditions, a strong field, and efficient organisation by the West Wilts Club, *Grandstand* viewers were treated to some excellent racing and a week after the fearsome 'Daleks' had made their TV debut, it was BSA who were doing the 'exterminating'!

250 Trophy Race

First up was the 250 Trophy, which saw Arthur Lampkin receive a late Christmas present. In company with Bryan Goss and Dave Bickers, he contested the opening laps until Bickers uncharacteristically slipped off the Husky and was relegated to 4th place by Alan Clough. With Bickers on the deck, Lampkin needed no invitation to push on, distancing himself

Making history, Arthur Lampkin follows his victory in the 500 Trophy at Caerleon with a win in the 250 Trophy at Naish Hill to become the first man to win races in both competitions (CB)

from Goss in the process and recording a comfortable win - BSA's first of the 250 series. In doing so, he also made history by becoming the first rider to have won races in both 250 and 500 Grandstand Trophy categories. Bickers tried to close down Clough, but another error on the closing lap meant he could finish no higher than 4th ahead of Freddie Mayes and Malcolm Davis.

500 Trophy Race

The 500 Trophy race saw Jeff Smith bounce back to record his fifth win of the series, taking the start from Lampkin and Jerry Scott, who had made another of his electrifying starts on his very rapid Cheney Gold Star. Whilst Smith edged away from his good friend Lampkin, Scott's race was run when his chain broke, allowing Dave Nicoll and his Matchless to prevent a BSA whitewash, as Alan Lampkin, Arthur's younger brother, who would become better known to *Grandstand* viewers as 'Sid', scored his first Grandstand points from 4th place on a 353 BSA, ahead of Terry Silvester, and another 353 BSA in the hands of Bernie Andrews.

In 1963 Greeves signed 19-year-old Malcolm Davis to ride in trials and scrambles. Having won the 250 Cup in the Scottish Six Day Trial, he shows his versatility at Naish Hill with 6th place in the 250 Trophy race (CB)

Anyone For A Pacemaker?

Of special note at the Naish Hill meeting was Dave Bickers' appearance on a 351cc Cotton special owned by Coventry engine tuner, Jack Heath. The engine consisted of a Heath barrel, featuring detachable transfer ports, and a special piston, on a Stepha Alpha bottom-end and was housed in a standard Cotton frame.

Sadly, however, the bike, ambitiously named the 'Pacemaker', did not live up to its name, even in the hands of a rider of Bickers' quality. Having said that, Bickers managed to qualify for the final by claiming sixth place in one of the heats of the 500 Trophy race. Bickers recalls, 'I used it a couple of times. It wasn't a factory Cotton, Jack Heath brought it along. I never liked the look of the Cotton, but it seemed to handle OK. It was better than I expected.'

In the final though, the experimental machine shed its exhaust mid-race and Bickers had to retire. However, it would appear from Bickers' exploits in the Invitation races that had his 250 Husqvarna been eligible, he would have fared much better than he did on the big Cotton.

Bickers would go on to ride the Pacemaker in the subsequent Grandstand Trophy rounds in the New Year at Tweseldown and Clifton, where he even managed to get amongst the points in the 500 Trophy race (see p67).

Dave Bickers debuted Jack Heath's 351cc Cotton Pacemaker at Naish Hill. Here he is pictured racing the special at Clifton in January, where he finished 5th in the 500 Trophy race (MC)

Supporting Races

Once again, though, it was the Invitation races that provided the day's best racing. In the first, Arthur Lampkin narrowly defeated Bickers, the 420 BSA just having the edge on the Husky, though it was the Second invitation that really saw some fireworks. Arthur was the man rocketing off into the lead, though Smith and Bickers were hard on his heels like a pair of Jumping Jacks. The three bright lights then proceeded to circulate at high speed and in close formation, until the race entered the last two laps when Smith and Bickers flew past Lampkin, bringing armchair viewers to the edge of their seats. For the first time in the day, Lampkin's challenge seemed to fizzle out, but Bickers fought Smith all the way to the line, where the BSA man grabbed a dramatic half-a-bike length victory.

Grandstand Trophy Race Results

250 Trophy
1 A J Lampkin (BSA)
2 B Goss (Greeves)
3 A Clough (Greeves)
4 D Bickers (Husqvarna)
5 F Mayes (Cotton)
6 M Davis (Greeves)

500 Trophy
1 J Smith (420 BSA)
2 A J Lampkin (420 BSA)
3 D Nicoll (500 Matchless)
4 A R C Lampkin (353 BSA)
5 T Silvester (500 BSA)
6 G Andrews (353 BSA)

So with six races down, and a further six to play for in the series, the 250 and 500 Trophy positions were as shown below.

Grandstand Trophy Positions After 6 Rounds

250 Trophy

1	D Bickers	8 8 8 8 8 4	44 pts
2	B Goss	0 0 6 6 6 6	24 pts
3	A Clough	4 5 5 0 0 5	19 pts
4	C Horsfield	5 0 4 5 0 0	14 pts
5	A J Lampkin	0 0 0 0 5 8	13 pts
6	F Mayes	0 4 0 0 3 3	10 pts

500 Trophy

1	J Smith	8 8 8 8 0 8	40 pts
2	A J Lampkin	0 0 6 5 8 6	25 pts
3	V Eastwood	5 0 2 6 4 0	17 pts
4	D Nicoll	2 0 4 0 6 5	17 pts
5	J Burton	6 3 5 0 0 0	14 pts
6	A Lee	0 4 0 0 5 0	9 pts

Round 7

Tweseldown, Hampshire, January 4, 1964

In a month that saw the BBC launch its new pop music show, *Top of the Pops,* the New Year didn't usher in too many changes for *Grandstand* viewers, with Messrs Bickers and Smith hanging on to their number one spots in dominant fashion at a fog bound Tweseldown circuit, though some very significant changes at BSA lay just weeks ahead.

250 Trophy Race

The 250 Trophy race saw Arthur Lampkin, continuing his fine run of form, grab the lead, though that man Dave Bickers was right on his tail again! With just two laps down the 'Coddenham Flyer' was out front once more and the race effectively resolved. This left Lampkin a lonely second, whilst Cheshire neighbours, Alan Clough and John Griffiths, did battle over 3rd place, the verdict finally going to the Greeves man, with Freddie Mayes and John Done filling the final point scoring positions.

Just as he had in the 250 European Championship in 1961, Arthur Lampkin took the challenge to Dave Bickers in the 250 Trophy race (CB)

A fine study of Dot factory man, John Griffiths, who found himself amongst the points in the 250 Trophy race at Tweseldown (CB)

500 Trophy Race

In the 500 Trophy race there was more interest than usual, as Bickers again took to the line on the Cotton Pacemaker. However, following a brief spell when John Burton set the pace in the opening laps, normal service was soon resumed when Jeff Smith raced into the lead and eased away from his rivals. Vic Eastwood, who would emerge as Smith's strongest challenger in the second half of the series, got the better of Burton for 2nd place, with local ace John Clayton (Matchless Métisse), Jerry Scott and John Giles getting amongst the points. Bickers had to battle through the field following a terrible start, which saw him placed 20th at the end of the first lap. However, showing his usual grit he got stuck in and eventually crossed the line in 10th place.

Supporting Races

The organising North Hants Motor Cycle Club, which was running its first BBC meeting, coped well, though they also experienced their share of starting problems. In the Experts final, the starter suffered the same fate that his opposite number had in the 250 Trophy final at Hankom Bottom, when only half the elastic start rope was released. This time, however,

Vic Eastwood, on his highly modified 500 Matchless, took the runner-up spot in the 500 Trophy race. Here he leads his good friend and frequent travelling partner, John Giles who finished 6th (CB)

the riders were recalled to the start with the exception of two escapees! John Clayton and Bill Gwynne had flown the coop and as they were not shown a flag of any colour, naturally pushed on to the end, entertaining spectators with, as *MCN* correspondent Ralph Venables put it, 'The finest tussle seen at Tweseldown for many a day'.

However, Clayton and Gwynne were duly disqualified and the TV cameramen, who had been tipped the wink, focused on the battle between Bickers, on the Husky, and a trio of BSAs led, naturally enough, by Smith. But on the tight, twisty, Hampshire circuit, the Bickers-Husky combination was simply unstoppable, and try as they might, Smith, Burton and Scott could do nothing to catch him.

Grandstand Trophy Race Results

250 Trophy
1 D Bickers (Husqvarna)
2 A J Lampkin (BSA)
3 A Clough (Greeves)
4 J Griffiths (Dot)
5 F Mayes (Cotton)
6 J Done (Dot)

500 Trophy
1 J Smith (420 BSA)
2 V Eastwood (500 Matchless)
3 J Burton (500 BSA)
4 J Clayton (500 Métisse)
5 J Scott (500 BSA)
6 J Giles (500 Triumph)

Excellent camera work from Cecil Bailey captures Alan Clough getting the best from his factory Greeves, on his way to 3rd place in the 250 Trophy race

Round 8
Clifton, Derbyshire, January 11, 1964

A week later, the BBC entourage headed back up the M1 to Clifton, near Ashbourne, Derbyshire, where Dave Bickers would become the first holder of a Grandstand Trophy, as he notched up yet another victory. Not to be outdone, Jeff Smith also won his seventh race out of eight, though he would have to wait to claim his trophy, as there was still an outside mathematical chance that he could be caught by Arthur Lampkin.

However, the big news coming from the BSA camp concerned neither Smith nor Lampkin. John Burton, from Lutterworth, Leicestershire, who had been a factory BSA runner since 1959 and had finished 5th in the 1961 world championship, had announced to the motorcycle press that he was quitting the Birmingham concern, but that he fully intended to race on at the highest level as a privateer.

At 18 stone, Burton, who was affectionately referred to in scrambles circles as 'Burly', found the new lightweight 420 BSAs were not to his liking. 'Of course I'd tried it (the 420), but I just couldn't get on with the little bike, it always felt like I was sitting on it, not in it.' Burton raced on through the 1963 season on a factory Gold Star, but he was all too aware of the direction BSA were heading in and had decided to make his own plans for 1964.

He announced those plans to the nation, when he was interviewed at Clifton, live on the *Grandstand* programme, telling viewers that he would be racing a factory BSA for the last time that day and that in the future he would be competing on a Matchless Métisse.

Sadly, gearbox problems hastened the end of his BSA days in the Experts' race, but help was at hand and ace bike-builder, Roger Kyffin, put his 500 Triumph-engined Dot at Burton's disposal for the 500 Trophy race. Burton duly showed his class by jumping straight on the unfamiliar bike and racing it to 4th place in the final.

John Burton, looking far from comfortable on the 250 BSA, at Clifton in 1962. (MC)

Roger Kyffin's Triumph-engined Dot, the forerunner of the Kyffin Saffire, as raced by John Burton to an excellent 4th place in the 500 Trophy race (MC)

Dave Bickers' win at Clifton made him the first Grandstand Trophy winner, but it was the performance of his young East Anglian neighbour John Banks, on his factory Dot, which really caught the eye (MC)

Burton's decision to leave BSA proved to be just the tip of the iceberg, as within just six weeks John Harris and Arthur Lampkin would also leave the Small Heath competition department, fulfilling Brian Martin's prophecy that there would be just one BSA rider contesting the world championship in 1964, that honour falling to Jeff Smith. BSA were also quick to react, however, with Martin putting a 420 at the disposal of rising star, Jerry Scott.

If looks could kill! Jeff Smith gives the lady with the clipboard a withering glare (MC)

250 Trophy Race

The 10-lap 250 Trophy race at Clifton provided plenty of entertainment, with Bickers having to first battle his way past Chris Horsfield, and then Arthur Lampkin, to hit the front. Young John Banks, racing on his factory Dot, presented his credentials as a future TV star, by slipping past Horsfield before engaging in a great duel with Lampkin. Banks showed great patience, shadowing his more experienced rival until, with two laps left to go, he raced past to claim 2nd place, his best TV finish to date. Lampkin was 3rd ahead of Alan Clough, who was well clear of another battle between Cotton runner, Freddie Mayes, and local man, Gordon Beresford on a Dot, which was eventually decided in that order.

500 Trophy Race

The 500 Trophy race saw Smith take a comfortable win and edge closer to his first Grandstand Trophy. He finished the race well clear of Lampkin, with Horsfield snatching 3rd place from Burton, on the Roger Kyffin hybrid, whilst Bickers turned in an excellent 5th place on Jack Heath's 'Pacemaker', to register its '15 minutes of fame' on national TV, and stalwart Triumph campaigner, Johnny Giles, completed the point scoring positions.

Supporting Races

Once again the supporting 'Open' Experts race provided the best viewing for the TV punters with Bickers and Smith turning in another fine double-act. Confidence bolstered by his fine ride in the 250 race, John Banks tried everything he knew to hang on to the 'dynamic duo', but from mid-race on, it was all about the cream of British scrambling. Banks established himself in a distant 3rd place, comfortably ahead of Lampkin, privateer Silvester on his Gold Star and fellow factory Dot man, John Done. But all the excitement was up front, as Bickers and Smith spent the last lap trading places, before dashing, side-by-side, for the line where the extra horsepower of the BSA saw Smith home to a half-a-bike length victory - just the stuff that BBC's Head of Sport, Bryan Cowgil, must have prayed for!

Three wheels on my wagon! John Done on his factory Dot and Bill Gwynne on a Matchless Métisse, both looking unbelievably relaxed as they race side-by-side in the Experts Invitation in which Done finished 6th (MC)

Grandstand Trophy Race Results

250 Trophy
1 D Bickers (Husqvarna)
2 J Banks (Dot)
3 A J Lampkin (BSA)
4 A Clough (Greeves)
5 F Mayes (Cotton)
6 G Beresford (Dot)

500 Trophy
1 J Smith (420 BSA)
2 A J Lampkin (420 BSA)
3 C Horsfield (500 Matchless)
4 J Burton (500 Kyffin Dot)
5 D Bickers (351 Cotton)
6 J Giles (500 Triumph)

Round 9

Builth Wells, Breconshire, January 25, 1964

Two weeks later, Jeff Smith would claim the 500 Grandstand Trophy, coming from behind in a characteristically late charge to catch and pass the Matchless duo of 'Mud Maestro' (and there was plenty of mud) Dave Nicoll and Vic Eastwood, whilst Dave Bickers would record win number eight in the series. Added spice in Wales was provided by the re-appearance of Don Rickman, who brought along a new full-250 Bultaco Métisse that had arrived in the country 24 hours earlier, and former BSA men, John Burton and John Harris, making their TV debuts on their Matchless Métisse machines.

250 Trophy Race

Bickers had an eventful 250 Trophy race and he was not alone. The treacherously muddy circuit provided plenty of spills, with Rickman and Chris Horsfield being the most noteworthy victims. Sadly, the challenge from Rickman, who had beaten Bickers in an invitation race, never really materialised as he fell after just two laps and would play no further part in proceedings.

However, Jeff Smith, making a rare 250 appearance, was the 4-stroke 'cat' amongst the two-stroke 'pigeons' and as any cat worth its salt would do in that situation, he caused plenty of confusion! With Bickers clear and seemingly comfortable in the lead, Smith hounded Greeves' Alan Clough and, when Bickers slipped off in the deep mud and stalled the Husky, the two of them were suddenly back in the hunt.

But Bickers deftly restarted and held on to his lead, eventually pulling clear to finish 60 yards ahead of Clough, who staved off the attacks of Smith and claimed 2nd place for his efforts. Further back, Bryan Goss took his Greeves to 4th ahead of Cotton's Freddie Mayes, and Bill Gwynne, racing in his native Wales, who just managed to keep the Royal Enfield ahead of Lampkin.

Alan Clough split Dave Bickers and Jeff Smith to take the runner-up spot in a muddy 250 Trophy race (MC)

500 Trophy Race

Jeff Smith secured the 500 Grandstand Trophy with his eighth win of the series, after passing AMC teamsters Vic Eastwood and Dave Nicoll on the last lap (MC)

The 500 Trophy race looked likely to cause a few upsets as Nicoll rocketed to the front of the field and soon established a useful lead. All eyes naturally were on Smith, but the BSA rider, who appeared to be biding his time, was surprised when Eastwood stormed past to relegate him to 5th place.

In fact it was just the catalyst Smith needed, as he tracked Eastwood and the pair rapidly moved past Arthur Lampkin and Andy Lee, who was having a successful outing on the Matchless-engined Bowman special, originally built by John Adamson from Harold Wood near Romford. With the clock ticking down, Smith breezed past Eastwood and Nicoll on the last lap, to deny the young Essex rider his first Grandstand Trophy win.

Nicoll, who always seemed to go well in the mud, explains why this was:

My parents were close friends with the local farmer where we lived and I rode in muddy fields and lanes all the time in my early years, so mud riding became second nature to me.

Supporting Races

That man Bickers sprang yet another surprise in the Invitation race, when he took to the line on a 250 Cotton, fuelling speculation in the scrambling fraternity about his future. However, the little Gloucester-built two-stroke proved to be far from an equal to his regular Swedish Husqvarna, though Bickers turned in a very creditable 5th place finish in a race that was comfortably won by Smith ahead of a very spirited Goss. Eastwood finished 3rd ahead of Jerry Scott, who was starting to get the hang of the factory 420 BSA, whilst Bickers got the better of Nicoll.

Grandstand Trophy Race Results

250 Trophy
1 D Bickers (Husqvarna)
2 A Clough (Greeves)
3 J Smith (BSA)
4 B Goss (Greeves)
5 F Mayes (Cotton)
6 B Gwynne (Royal Enfield)

500 Trophy
1 J Smith (420 BSA)
2 D Nicoll (500 Matchless)
3 V Eastwood (500 Matchless)
4 A Lee (500 Bowman)
5 A J Lampkin (420 BSA)
6 T Silvester (500 BSA)

Racing on home soil, Welshman Bill Gwynne took the Royal Enfield to its best result in the Grandstand series with 6th place in the 250 Trophy race (MC)

MCN reporter Chris Carter remembers that Dave Bickers came to his aid when he was stuck for transportation down to South Wales, though for a moment he must have wondered whether he would even get out of sleepy Suffolk.

I remember borrowing a Ford Zodiac from Dave to drive down to Builth Wells. He drove me over to the guesthouse where I was staying and I remember there being thick ice on all the windows. As he set off down the hill this big Zodiac was zigzagging all over the road! We couldn't see a thing, so he got the driver's door open and next thing I know, he's leaning out and looking under the car as we go along. Well he pops back into the car and says, 'There aren't any punctures, so it must be ice!' That man was always destined to be a stuntman!

Dave Nicoll (11) blasts his factory Matchless out of the gate ahead of, left to right, Jeff Smith (4), Ken Covell (30), Andy Lee (31), John Giles (22), Arthur Lampkin (25), Vic Eastwood (3) and Terry Sleeman (18) who is flanked by Jerry Scott and John Lewis (34) (MC)

Round 10

High Hoyland, Yorkshire, February 15, 1964

Dave Bickers was conspicuous by his absence from round ten of the series and despite the fact that he'd just agreed terms with Greeves to ride the all-new Challenger in an attempt to win the 250 world championship, his whereabouts must have caused Bert Greeves some consternation.

Wakefield in February must have been a pretty cold place to be, though I would wager it was considerably colder where Bickers and his young travelling companion, John Banks, were. The Suffolk boys had made a long trip east, to the CZ factory in Strakonice, Czechoslovakia.

In company with rising star Joel Robert, Banks tried the 1964 factory CZs and was offered a ride. However, John, who was nothing if not ambitious, really wanted to get a factory ride on a big four-stroke. So he rejected CZ's offer, though he did negotiate the loan of a twin-port 250 engine to slot into a Dot frame. Banks tried the resulting hybrid during 1964, though never rode it on TV, as come the 1964-65 Grandstand Trophy series, he had achieved his short-term goal and was already a fully-fledged factory BSA runner.

Back in South Yorkshire, the racing, on a mist shrouded 'undulating' Wakefield circuit, as Denis Parkinson always described it, was spoilt once more by some very ragged starts, not least of all in the 500 Trophy race, and arguably the biggest victim on the day was none other than Jeff Smith.

250 Trophy Race

In Bickers' absence, the 250 Trophy race was up for grabs and Smith saw an opportunity for a win on his quarter-litre bike. However, the script writers had other ideas, as after a long delay at the start, Smith's BSA oiled a plug. So when the race eventually got underway Smith was still changing the offending plug and took off in pursuit of the pack like the proverbial scalded cat, with a deficit of one minute to make up in an 8-lap race!

Up front the on-form Goss and local man Lampkin were disputing the lead and were pulling clear of Greeves' men Davis, a surprisingly off-colour Clough, and local man Tony Cook. Smith, with his 'never-say-die' attitude was relentlessly picking off riders, eventually finishing 7th just a few yards behind Sprite runner, Brian Nadin, who held on to take the last point. Back at the front, Goss won his, and Greeves', first race of the series, though Lampkin kept him honest to the flag.

Goss remembers this race very clearly:

> *I was out of the gate and gone that day. I was on a Greeves with a road-race barrel and pipe. Not many liked them, as you had to keep the revs up, but it suited me at the time.*

Surprisingly though, given the result, Goss had not received ideal preparation for race day.

> *I travelled up with my sponsor, John Coombes, in his Zephyr and we were a bit late setting off. When we got there it was about 11 o'clock at night and we couldn't find a bed and breakfast anywhere, so we had to kip in the car. I remember he had a polythene cover over the seats and I just couldn't get comfortable!*

Bryan Goss races through the fog on his way to his first Grandstand race victory ahead of Arthur Lampkin in the 250 series (MC)

Like Bryan Goss, Vic Eastwood took his his first Grandstand race win, after holding off the inevitable late charge from Jeff Smith (MC)

An incident in the 250 race highlighted the dangers of scrambling in the depths of winter, when James' new boy, Freddie Mayes took an unexpected trip over the handlebars. Mayes remembers the incident all too well:

It was my first race on the James. I had ridden a Cotton in previous rounds of the series and I was on a run of 5th place finishes. I was in 5th position again in this race and making a last lap effort for 4th when I went too close to the edge of the track and hit a tree root that was sticking up. I spent the next week in Barnsley hospital lying flat on my back as I had broken a small bone in my lower back and, once home, I had to spend another 5 to 6 weeks in bed, so it was April before I rode again.

500 Trophy Race

Smith was also out of luck in the 500 Trophy race, when he was snared in at the start and once again had to battle through the field. But battle he did, ousting, amongst others, teammate Lampkin, the Matchless duo of Nicoll and Horsfield and local man, Terry Silvester, who after beating Nicoll in one of the heats was having his best ride of the series and, arguably, of his career.

As the race went into the final lap, only Vic Eastwood and his factory Matchless lay between Smith and his ninth win in the series. However, Eastwood, who had led from the start, knew there would be a late charge from Smith and had enough in reserve to hold off the BSA man. Like Goss, Eastwood registered his first win of the series ahead of Smith, whilst Horsfield just got the better of a tiring Silvester, and Lampkin, in turn, pipped Nicoll for 5th place.

Grandstand Trophy Race Results

250 Trophy
1 B Goss (Greeves)
2 A J Lampkin (BSA)
3 M Davis (Greeves)
4 A Clough (Greeves)
5 T Cook (Greeves)
6 B Nadin (Sprite)

500 Trophy
1 V Eastwood (500 Matchless)
2 J Smith (420 BSA)
3 C Horsfield (500 Matchless)
4 T Silvester (500 BSA)
5 A J Lampkin (420 BSA)
6 D Nicoll (500 Matchless)

Terry Silvester racing his Gold Star doesn't look too pleased with Jeff Smith's racing antics. The privateer from Holmfirth, Yorkshire rode consistently well throughout the series with 4th in the 500 Trophy race at Wakefield his best result (MC)

Round 11
Westleton, Suffolk, February 29, 1964

February 1964 was a time of great interest in the world of off-road racing. No sooner had news reached the public that Bickers would race the Greeves Challenger along with new recruit, John Griffiths, than Arthur Lampkin dropped the bombshell that he would be racing Cottons in 1964, in company with younger brother, Alan. In an agreement with BSA, for the remainder of the 1963-64 Grandstand series, the brothers would race their 420s in the 500 Trophy and Invitation races, though in the coming series Arthur would have a 500 Triumph-powered Cotton at his disposal.

250 Trophy Race

Teammates Arthur Lampkin and Jeff Smith often enjoyed there TV tussles as they did at Westleton. Here they are giving no quarter in the previous round at High Hoyland (MC)

Both Bickers and Lampkin made their TV debuts on their new bikes in the 250 Trophy race at the Mummberry Hills track, with greatly contrasting success. Whilst Lampkin struggled to come to terms with the Cotton, eventually finishing 8th, Bickers won first time out on the new Greeves, taking his ninth win in the series, though only after a battle which warmed the hearts of the partisan Suffolk crowd that had braved the elements.

It was local heroes to the fore, as John Banks got his Dot out front and led Bickers for several laps until he got out of shape on one of the tricky descents and rode through the

Dave Bickers, pictured here a week later at the final round at Cuerden Park, took the Greeves Challenger to a Grandstand debut win in his native Suffolk (MC)

ropes. Bickers didn't need a second invitation and raced into the lead, but in a week that saw Cilla Black at number one in the pop charts with *Anyone Who Had a Heart*, Banks proved that he had plenty of heart, as he extricated the Dot from the ropes and quickly re-joined the race without losing any further positions. He then gamely gave chase to Bickers, but could make no impression on him as the more experienced man grew in confidence on his new machine.

At the flag Bickers won comfortably from Banks, with Alan Clough and Malcolm Davis, on the 'old' Greeves, taking 3rd and 4th places. Surprise package in the race was new BSA teamster, Jerry Scott, who had briefly held 3rd place and turned a few heads as he raced on to finish 5th ahead of Horsfield on the factory James.

500 Trophy Race

In the 500 Trophy race it was business as usual for Jeff Smith, as he continued to match Bickers race for race, adding win number nine for the series. Also, like Bickers, he had to work for his win, after Horsfield got the big Matchless out front for the opening three laps. However, the tight, technical course was far better suited to the smaller, lighter, 420 BSAs and Lampkin, shadowed by Smith, soon overhauled the man from Hampton Lucy. Smith held station behind his close friend until the 5th lap, when he breezed past and raced away to yet another win. Eastwood, who had also been making good progress, ousted his teammate Horsfield to finish 3rd, with John Giles and Andy Lee filling the final, point scoring positions.

Lee, who had briefly ridden the ex-Brian Stonebridge factory Matchless as a youngster and had subsequently received support from local dealers for many years, was racing as a privateer, initially on a Matchless Métisse and latterly on the Bowman special. Though he would miss the final round in Lancashire, the Cambridge man would finish the inaugural Grandstand Trophy series as top privateer, edging out Huddersfield's Terry Silvester, by virtue of some excellent rides earlier in the series, the pick being his 3rd place at Caerleon in December, which was the best placing by a privateer in the series.

John Banks, seen here earlier in the series at Beeston, led Bickers in the early stages and survived a scare to finish as runner-up in the 250 Trophy race (MC)

Grandstand Trophy Race Results

250 Trophy
1 D Bickers (Greeves)
2 J Banks (Dot)
3 A Clough (Greeves)
4 M Davis (Greeves)
5 J Scott (BSA)
6 C Horsfield (James)

500 Trophy
1 J Smith (420 BSA)
2 A J Lampkin (420 BSA)
3 V Eastwood (500 Matchless)
4 C Horsfield (500 Matchless)
5 J Giles (500 Triumph)
6 A Lee (500 Fenman)

Round 12

Cuerden Park, Lancashire, March 7, 1964

The final round of the inaugural Grandstand Trophy series was on another famous circuit, Cuerden Park, home to the Lancashire GN event. Conditions on the day were good, as was the organization, though there was one slight hiccup, but more of that later.

250 Trophy Race

The 250 Trophy race held a lot of promise, with Alan Clough winning one of the heats ahead of Banks, and Bickers and Goss both looking on good form. The final didn't disappoint, with Goss on his elderly Greeves jumping into the lead, hotly pursued by Bickers and Clough on the new Challengers, Lampkin on the Cotton and Banks on the Dot. Goss was setting a frantic pace at the front and Banks, in his efforts to couple onto the Bickers-Clough train, overdid things and derailed.

Win number ten for Dave Bickers in the 250 series and his second on the Greeves Challenger (MC)

Left, Arthur Lampkin never really looked comfortable on the 250 Cotton. Right, lookeing far more at ease on the ex-factory 420 BSA (MC)

On successive laps the pressure told on Goss, as he yielded first to Bickers and then Clough, but worse was to come when he cruelly lost his chain on lap four. Lampkin was having a much better ride on the Cotton and managed to stay in touch with the leaders and when Clough spun around whilst trying to pass Bickers, Lampkin was up to 2nd place. However, Clough had both the time and composure to recover his position, though there was no chance of closing down Bickers, who moved into double figures - 10 wins for the series.

500 Trophy Race

The 500 Trophy race was once again a battle between the 420 BSAs and the heavier, but more powerful, 500 Matchless machines. With Lampkin and Smith getting the start, Horsfield then slotted into 3rd place, but teammate Eastwood had to do things the hard way. Vic's performance in this 9-lap race was typical of the tenacity he showed throughout his long career in the sport. Lying 6th on the opening lap he rapidly moved up through the field, finally passing Horsfield, whose bike was down on power, mid-race to reach 3rd. He then set about closing down Lampkin, who had been passed by Smith, but try as he might, all he could do at that stage was to hold station.

Smith once again matched Bickers to claim his 10th series win ahead of Lampkin, who, in finishing in front of Eastwood, assured a BSA one-two in the series, whilst Eastwood finished 3rd in the race and took the same place in the series. Horsfield held on to finish 4th ahead of teammate Nicoll, with former factory BSA rider John Harris, who earlier in the day had finished 4th in the 250 race, closing the top six on his Vale-Onslow sponsored Matchless Métisse.

Supporting Races

The organizational problem alluded to earlier came in the Invitation race. The BBC apparently had a contract with the organising clubs to televise a minimum of three races. Sadly, the *Grandstand* faithful were denied the best race of the day, when a heat of the Invitation race, rather than the final was televised.

However, those that were in the crowd at Preston to see the final were in for a real treat. Eastwood got the start and gave Smith and Lampkin a real run for their money. Smith closed a little, lap by lap, and slipped past at half race distance, but Eastwood stuck to his task, and the rear wheel of the BSA, and chased him all the way to the flag. Lampkin finished in a comfortable 3rd place easing clear of the 250s of Clough and Banks, with a battling Terry Silvester holding off a charging Horsfield for 6th place.

Like Dave Bickers, Jeff Smith also registered his tenth win of the 500 series, outpacing teammate Arthur Lampkin and Vic Eastwood on the factory Matchless (MC)

Grandstand Trophy Race Results

250 Trophy
1 D Bickers (Greeves)
2 A Clough (Greeves)
3 A J Lampkin (Cotton)
4 J Harris (Vale-Onslow Métisse)
5 J Done (Dot)
6 C Horsfield (James)

500 Trophy
1 J Smith (420 BSA)
2 A J Lampkin (420 BSA)
3 V Eastwood (500 Matchless)
4 C Horsfield (500 Matchless)
5 D Nicoll (500 Matchless)
6 J Harris (500 Matchless Métisse)

1963/64 Grandstand Trophy Series Final Standings

250 Trophy

1	D Bickers	8 8 8 8 8 4 8 8 8 0 8 8	84 pts
2	A Clough	4 5 5 0 0 5 5 4 6 4 5 6	49 pts
3	B Goss	0 0 6 6 6 6 0 0 4 8 0 0	36 pts
4	A J Lampkin	0 0 0 0 5 8 6 5 0 6 0 5	35 pts
5	F Mayes	0 4 0 0 3 3 3 3 3 0 0 0	19 pts
6	C Horsfield	5 0 4 5 0 0 0 0 0 0 2 2	18 pts

500 Trophy

1	J Smith	8 8 8 8 0 8 8 8 8 6 8 8	86 pts
2	A J Lampkin	0 0 6 5 8 6 0 6 3 3 6 6	49 pts
3	V Eastwood	5 0 2 6 4 0 6 0 5 8 5 5	46 pts
4	D Nicoll	2 0 4 0 6 5 0 0 6 2 0 3	28 pts
5	J Burton	6 3 5 0 0 0 5 4 0 0 0 0	23 pts
6	C Horsfield	0 2 0 2 0 0 0 5 0 5 4 4	22 pts

The king holding court! Jeff Smith shares a joke with Chris Horsfield and former BSA teammate John Harris (MC)

So ended the first series. Dave Bickers and Jeff Smith had shown TV sports fans that they were the undisputed kings of British motocross, whilst the likes of Clough, Goss, Lampkin, Eastwood, Horsfield and Nicoll had demonstrated that they were ready to pick up the gauntlet should the Grandstand Trophy winners falter.

With viewing figures at around the 8 million mark, the BBC also had a huge success on their hands and the second series that would kick off at Clifton in October, was eagerly anticipated.

Three weeks after the inaugural Grandstand Trophy series came to a successful conclusion at Cuerden Park, an International Team Relay meeting was staged by the BBC and the Mid-Bucks MCC at Muswell Hill Farm, Brill. This was a three-way contest between the three giants of motocross during its formative years; Great Britain, Belgium and Sweden (see *p294*).

1964-65
The Times They Are A-changin'

*Chris Horsfield, Somerleyton,
24th October 1964 (MC)*

Setting The Scene

Following a long arduous campaign which saw his fortunes fluctuate, Jeff Smith was on top of the world, as he took the 500cc world championship with victory in the final GP of the 1964 season at San Sebastian, Spain, in September. After a steady start to the series, Smith and his 420 BSA had proved to be the winning combination, chalking up seven GP wins to pip his great rival, Rolf Tibblin, on his 500 Hedlund.

He also retained his ACU Drivers' Star (his seventh win) wrapping things up with his third straight win of the series at Hatherton Hall, Nantwich, in April, to finish comfortably ahead of the AMC pair, Vic Eastwood and Chris Horsfield.

Dave Bickers won the 250 ACU Star clinching victory at the final round at Farleigh Castle in October, though the result was never really in any doubt. Teammate Alan Clough was runner-up, whilst Dot runner Ernie Greer, who won the fourth round of the series, finished an excellent 3rd in the final standings.

On The Move

Earlier in the year John Griffiths had made the switch from Dot to Greeves, in order to contest the 250 world championship with Dave Bickers. The campaign started promisingly, with 3rd overall in the season opener at Barcelona in April, behind Torsten Hallman and Don Rickman, but ahead of Bickers. However, his efforts were curtailed by a fall at the Swiss GP which resulted in a broken collarbone. He also showed what he was capable of on the Greeves when he finished third overall behind Joel Robert and Alan Clough at the Thirsk International in September.

Jerry Scott became a member of the BSA team in March 1964, though he seemed to fluctuate between the Armoury Road prepared factory bikes and Eric Cheney's immaculate Gold Stars all season long. In June he raced a factory 250 at Longleat, Wiltshire, but he openly expressed his preference for the full-500 over the 420. In September he was back on the Cheney Gold Star for the Spanish GP, where he finished eighth overall, but at the Kidston Grand National (GN) later that month he'd returned to the official 420 BSA.

In June, 20 year-old John Banks, a rider with a very bright future ahead of him, was also contracted by Brian Martin at BSA, who was looking to strengthen his squad. Fellow East Anglian Freddie Mayes was racing a factory James in the early part of the year, but by August he was to be seen on a Greeves Challenger provided by Cambridge dealer Claude Scott.

In The News

AMC runners Vic Eastwood and Dave Nicoll made their mark on the GP scene, Eastwood taking 4th overall in the Austrian GP, whilst Nicoll's best finish was fifth overall in Denmark. Privateers Jerry Scott and Andy Lee also found themselves in the points, Scott taking his Cheney Gold Star to 4th overall in Luxembourg and Lee, riding a Matchless Métisse, to 6th overall in France and Spain.

Having wrapped up the world title in Spain in September, Jeff Smith was looking for a brief respite before the 1965 season began in earnest as he explains:

After the hurley burley of that 1964 season I was ready for a rest. So I pretty well disregarded the end of season events. After I won the world championship in 1964, Rolf Tibblin's local club put on a motocross exhibition and Rolf and I were invited to ride. I can't remember now if I took a machine along or if the intention was for me to ride a 4-stroke Husky (which he did). There was nothing sinister in my visit, it was just a sporting gesture from Rolf, with whom I got on really well.

As a memento of the trip they presented me with a beautifully rendered pastoral drawing of me on the BSA. The legend reads 'Rolf Tibblin and Nils Hedlund congratulate Jeff Smith on winning the championship'. It hangs proudly in my house to this day.

Into The 1964-65 Series

Over the course of the second Grandstand series, Britain would see a shift in the political balance following several high-profile scandals and those who tuned in to the BBC's flagship sports programme would also note some shifts in power, though thankfully, there was little scandal to report.

As the world's finest athletes assembled for the opening ceremony of the 18th Olympic Games in Tokyo, 6,000 miles away, on a desolate hillside in Derbyshire, Britain's finest rough riders gathered for the first round of the 1964 Grandstand Trophy Series.

By the autumn of 1964, the Greeves Challenger, here being put to good use by Alan Clough at Clifton in October, was the bike that the nation's clubmen aspired to (MC)

Round 1

Clifton, Derbyshire, October 10, 1964

Arthur Lampkin quite rightly stole the headlines at Clifton, with three wins on his new Triumph-engined Cotton, though I would wager that the Cotton management would have been a whole lot happier had he won the 250 race on their production Villiers-engined lightweight, which could be found in showrooms nationwide.

The 500 race also served to highlight how popular the Rickman brothers' Métisse machines had become, as despite the absence of the creators at the event, Métisse framed machines filled four of the top six places - a nice spot of TV 'advertising' for Don and Derek!

250 Trophy Race

There were few surprises in the opening 250 Trophy race, as Dave Bickers picked up where he had finished the previous series. Winning on the Greeves Challenger, seemingly at will. Bickers led a Greeves factory excursion, as he established a comfortable lead over Alan Clough, who also maintained a small lead over his close friend John Griffiths, on the third works Challenger. Further down the field, Freddie Mayes, on a private Challenger, got the better of John Banks, who was getting acquainted with the two-fifty BSA, and Dot rider Ernie Greer completed the point scoring positions.

Alan Clough (left) overcame the challenge from close friend and fellow Greeves factory rider, John Griffiths, to claim the runner-up spot in the 250 Trophy race (MC)

True to form, Dave Bickers started the series in winning style with a comfortable victory in Derbyshire (MC)

500 Trophy Race

It was the 500 Trophy race that brought a few surprises, as some of the 'smaller fish in the pond' created a few ripples; and in the week that the BBC launched its ground breaking *Wednesday Play* there was also plenty of drama to be witnessed on *Grandstand*.

With Jeff Smith away racing in Sweden, the only other factory BSA rider present, John Banks, was yet to really hit top form on his factory 420. However, it was two ex-BSA men who were entertaining the TV viewers, as Lampkin and John Burton, on his Matchless Métisse, went head-to-head.

Lampkin took the lead from the start, but Burton was in hot pursuit of his ex-teammate and, at one stage, as the big man from Lutterworth, Leicestershire, got alongside his rival, the two riders dramatically tangled. In the *mêlée*, Burton's machine was knocked out of gear and he momentarily lost contact. However, he came storming back and challenged Lampkin for the lead again, though it seemed that no matter what he tried, Arthur had an answer for it.

Indeed, Lampkin held out to win a thrilling 'photo' finish, providing the watching millions with further proof of just how exciting the sport could be. Behind them, Chris Horsfield, riding a bike reported in *MCN* as being a Matchless Métisse (see *Horsfield's Special p132*) eventually took 3rd place after deposing surprise package, Mike Peach, a youngster from

Arthur Lampkin sprung a surprise at Clifton, winning the 500 Trophy race on this Triumph-engined Cotton, built and owned by Cornishman, Aly Clift. (MC)

Big man on a big bike; John Burton pushed Lampkin all the way in a thrilling 500 Trophy race on his 500 Matchless Métisse (MC)

Eastbourne, on a Triumph Métisse who withstood the challenge from factory AMC rider Vic Eastwood and experienced campaigner, Brian Nadin, on another Triumph Métisse.

Supporting Races

An unexpected bonus was in store for scrambles fans on the day, as the BBC were experiencing relay problems from Tokyo and for that reason they televised the two Grandstand Trophy races live and also showed two pre-recorded invitation races. Oh, what joy!

Bickers, who was heading off to Belgium to race the following day, did not compete in the invitation races, leaving the door open for Lampkin. Indeed, the big bike riders dominated proceedings, with only Alan Clough presenting any serious challenge to their supremacy. Lampkin won the first from Burton, with Clough third, whilst in the second, Horsfield did his best to inflict a defeat on Lampkin, eventually failing by just two seconds, with Clough charging through the field after a poor start to snatch another 3rd place.

Grandstand Trophy Race Results

250 Trophy
1 D Bickers (Greeves)
2 A Clough (Greeves)
3 J Griffiths (Greeves)
4 F Mayes (Greeves)
5 J Banks (BSA)
6 E Greer (Dot)

500 Trophy
1 A J Lampkin (500 Triumph Cotton)
2 J Burton (500 Matchless Métisse)
3 C Horsfield (500 Matchless)
4 M Peach (500 Triumph Métisse)
5 V Eastwood (500 Matchless)
6 B Nadin (500 Triumph Métisse)

Round 2
Somerleyton, Lowestoft, October 24, 1964

Two weeks later, as the Olympic Games were drawing to a close and Britain was adjusting to a new Prime Minister following Labour's sweeping victory in the general election, the second round of the Grandstand Trophy came from the Herringfleet Hills track, near the Suffolk coast.

The track, with its tight turns and steep hills, was in fine fettle and Dave Bickers, who had helped the Lowestoft Invaders Club set out the circuit for their first scramble there in 1962, was to be the star of the meeting. Once again, Jeff Smith was a notable absentee, as he was in Prague being presented with his FIM gold medal to commemorate his victory in the 1964 world championship, which left the door open to his challengers.

I flew to the FIM congress in Prague to collect my gold medal, which, by the way, is real gold. Irene (Smith's wife) couldn't make the trip because she was pregnant, so my mother and father went with me for the weekend. Harold Taylor was there as ACU delegate and helped us to understand what was happening.

Curiously enough in the same week that Jeff Smith received his medal, his athletic training partner, steeple chaser Maurice Herriott, who also worked at the BSA factory in Birmingham, ran the race of his life to claim a silver medal in the Olympic final in Tokyo.

250 Trophy Race

Back in Suffolk, Bickers set the tone for the day as he effortlessly rode to another victory in the 250 Trophy race, his fourth consecutive win in Grandstand Trophy races on the

Dave Bickers out on his own in the 250 Trophy race (MC)

Local man Pete Smith passes in front of the BBC cameraman on his 250 Greeves at Somerleyton Hall (MC)

Challenger. One of the unsung heroes of the day, Birmingham's Ernie Greer, held 2nd berth until the plug on his Dot whiskered, allowing John Griffiths on his factory Greeves to pursue Bickers, with teammate, Bryan Goss, in tow. In fact, had it not been for Chris Horsfield on the James, it would have been a Greeves benefit, as he split Freddie Mayes and Malcolm Davis on their Challengers.

500 Trophy Race

Like Bickers, Horsfield was to have a good day, taking his first victory in the Grandstand series as he prevailed in a thrilling battle with local man John Banks on his 420 BSA in the 500 Trophy race. Horsfield got a great start, closely followed by series leader, Arthur Lampkin, and Banks. Lampkin's challenge was short lived, however, as he was sidelined when he lost his rear brake.

However, much to the delight of the Suffolk crowd, Banks, who was really flying, caught and passed Horsfield and led the Midlander for two laps. But the more experienced Horsfield slipped back into the lead and just managed to hold off the young gun. However, the drama was not over yet, as no sooner had they crossed the line than Horsfield was lying in a tangled heap on the ground. In his haste to grab the win, Banks had caught his sleeve on Chris' handlebar and sent him tumbling!

Chris Horsfield racing the Métisse-framed Matchless special to victory in the 500 Trophy race (MC)

Behind the leaders, another local ace, Jim Aim on his Tom Kirby prepared Matchless Métisse, claimed his first Grandstand Trophy series points from 3rd spot ahead of the in-form Mike Peach, factory Triumph runner Roy Peplow, making a rare appearance on our screens, and Brian Nadin.

Supporting Races

The Invitation races resulted in a win apiece for Bickers and Lampkin, the Yorkshireman taking the first, but only just, from Bickers and Griffiths on their Greeves, whilst Bickers comfortably claimed the second from Aim and Nadin and Greer finally had something to show for his day's efforts from 4th place.

John Burton didn't have much luck at Somerleyton either. A victim of false starts in the earlier races, the former BSA star deliberately broke the elastic start gate for the Second Invitation race. His reason for doing this was to protest about the position of the officials on false starting and disqualification of the offending riders. The race was duly stopped and Burton promptly false started again, this time without any reprimand. Chris Carter reporting in *MCN* noted:

> *The general feeling among competitors is that until an official does disqualify someone jumping the start then the starts will get worse.*

One rider who was seemingly detuned on the day was Vic Eastwood, who was making his final appearance on a factory Matchless before joining the powerful BSA team. Maybe the occasion was too much for him, but the best he could manage was a brace of 5th place finishes in the Invitation races.

John Banks had a good day on the factory 420 BSA, only narrowly beaten in the 500 Trophy race by Chris Horsfield (MC)

Grandstand Trophy Race Results

250 Trophy
1 D Bickers (Greeves)
2 J Griffiths (Greeves)
3 B Goss (Greeves)
4 F Mayes (Greeves)
5 C Horsfield (James)
6 M Davis (Greeves)

500 Trophy
1 C Horsfield (500 Matchless)
2 J Banks (420 BSA)
3 J Aim (500 Kirby Métisse)
4 M Peach (500 Triumph Métisse)
5 R Peplow (500 Triumph)
6 B Nadin (500 Triumph Métisse)

Another great Malcolm Carling shot of John Griffiths, racing to the runner up spot in the 250 Trophy race on the second factory Challenger (MC)

Round 3

Nantwich, Cheshire, November 7, 1964

Alan Clough, who lived some 40 miles from the Hatherton Hall circuit, always went well there, and the third round of the Grandstand Trophy series proved to be no exception, as he would break Dave Bickers' stranglehold on the 250 series. The meeting would also mark Jeff Smith's return to televised racing and his appearance seemed to galvanise his BSA teammates, who turned in some solid performances.

500 Trophy Race

The 500 Trophy race saw Smith's former teammate John Harris on his Triumph Métisse hit the front first, though he was soon overhauled by Chris Horsfield. Meanwhile, Smith, who had suffered a poor start, was steadily moving through the pack and, by mid-race distance, he eased past Horsfield and soon put some distance between himself and the Matchless runner. Former BSA man, John Burton, then moved up to challenge Horsfield, and Vic Eastwood and teammate John Banks also usurped Harris.

After missing the opening two rounds, Jeff Smith made a victorious return to the Grandstand series in the 500 Trophy race at Hatherton Hall (MC)

250 Trophy race winner, Alan Clough, racing over an especially bumpy downhill section of the Hatherton Hall circuit (MC)

BSA debutant Eastwood was the man on the move though and he soon passed Burton and was homing in on Horsfield when the BSA's motor cried enough. With Eastwood out, the first two places were safe and Banks eventually claimed 3rd ahead of Burton, whilst Jerry Scott on another 420 BSA came through to take 5th spot ahead of the consistent Brian Nadin.

250 Trophy Race

Alan Clough demonstrated in the 250 Trophy race that on his day he was a match for Bickers. But it was the Coddenham man, who always liked to control races from the front, who soon settled into his customary place at the head of the field, though he was being shadowed by his teammate from Cheadle Hulme. Clough bided his time and moved to the front with two laps to go, easing clear to take the chequered flag and record a well-deserved first win in the Grandstand Trophy series.

Behind him though, Bickers' race wasn't run. On the last lap and in sight of the flag, the Greeves died on him and he had to push uphill to the finishing line. Bryan Goss then slipped ahead of Jeff Smith and they both flashed past the hapless Bickers before he could cross the line. An exhausted Bickers eventually pushed over for 4th ahead of John Griffiths and Ernie Greer.

The TV cameras may have missed Halstead's Jim Aim in the Televised Invitation race, but Malcolm Carling caught him in determined mood on his Matchless Métisse

Supporting Races

However, the closest race of the day was undoubtedly the Unlimited Invitation, which saw Bickers harrying Smith all the way from start to finish though, try as he might, he just didn't have the horses to get past the factory BSA. Behind them Clough won a private battle with Goss, whilst Andy Lee on his Matchless claimed 4th spot.

Lee, at that time a motorcycle dealer from Ely, Cambridgeshire, had every right to feel aggrieved with the BBC's coverage of the racing. In the televised 500cc Invitation race, he and fellow East Anglian, Jim Aim, ran away with the race, finishing in that order but, sadly for them, the BBC producer had told the cameramen to focus on Smith, who had spun his BSA on the first lap and was roaring through the field.

Jim's wife, Sue, was at teacher training college in Warrington at the time and vividly recalls tuning in to *Grandstand* to watch her then boyfriend with her roommates:

Unfortunately the cameramen weren't following Jim and Andy and Murray Walker kept saying, 'Let's get back to Jeff Smith'.

Smith's progress was meteoric, but he could finish no higher than fourth at the flag, behind fellow BSA man Scott, and Lee and Aim effectively missed out on their 15 minutes of fame.

Grandstand Trophy Race Results

250 Trophy
1 A Clough (Greeves)
2 B Goss (Greeves)
3 J Smith (BSA)
4 D Bickers (Greeves)
5 J Griffiths (Greeves)
6 E Greer (Dot)

500 Trophy
1 J Smith (420 BSA)
2 C Horsfield (500 Matchless)
3 J Banks (420 BSA)
4 J Burton (500 Matchless Métisse)
5 J Scott (420 BSA)
6 B Nadin (500 Triumph Métisse)

The BBC were using a hand-held 'radio' camera at Nantwich. Here the two-man crew captures Jerry Scott (420 BSA) and Brian Nadin (500 Triumph Métisse) racing through (MC)

Vic Eastwood's TV debut on a factory BSA was not a happy one, when he was sidelined with engine trouble whilst running 3rd in the 500 Trophy race (MC)

Round 4
Frome, Somerset, November 14, 1964

What a difference a week makes. Following the dry, near perfect conditions riders had faced at Nantwich, this was the first muddy scramble of this series and the conditions at Asham Woods, Leighton, naturally provided plenty of thrills and spills as the fortunes of the leading riders fluctuated wildly.

500 Trophy Race

Following the heats for the Unlimited race came the 500 Trophy race which saw BSA new boy, Vic Eastwood, take his first win of the series and his second Grandstand Trophy race win. But controversy shrouded the start and the disqualification of world champion, Jeff Smith. On his way up to the startline, Smith discovered that a footrest was loose. He promptly returned to the paddock, tightened the offending peg and was on his way back to the start when the starter let the race go. After half a lap, he had carved his way past 18 of the 36 starters but, as he crossed the line, he was black flagged and had to pull out of the race.

Vic Eastwood bounced back from the disappointment at Nantwich, by winning the 500 Trophy race at Asham Woods (GF)

Meanwhile, at the sharp end of things, Eastwood had made the best start, initially pursued by John Burton. But Burton was soon struggling to free his Matchless Métisse after being pushed into the ropes by a wayward back marker. That left Eastwood's erstwhile AMC teammates, Chris Horsfield and Dave Nicoll, to dispute 2nd place with Horsfield prevailing and easing away from his younger rival.

There was still time for a little drama in this 9-lap race, however, as Eastwood managed to slip off on the penultimate lap, allowing Horsfield to close in. But after the disappointment of Nantwich, Eastwood was not in the mood to let this one slip away, rapidly restarting the BSA and riding a faultless final lap. Behind Horsfield and Nicoll came former Dot and Greeves factory star Joe Johnson, now on a Triumph Métisse and making a rare but welcome appearance on our TV screens, John Giles on his 'factory' Triumph and local man Terry Cox on another Triumph Métisse.

250 Trophy Race

The 250 Trophy race saw another win for Dave Bickers, though he really had to battle for this one. Early leader was Roger Snoad from Eastleigh, Hants, on his private Greeves, who made a great start, whilst Bickers got himself boxed in and found himself in a rather uncharacteristic 9th place on the first lap. However, Snoad's moment of glory was short lived as he soon ran to ground and the man in form, Alan Clough, slipped through into the lead. But Clough also took a tumble on the third lap, when he seemed to be in control of the race, allowing Bickers, who had rapidly moved up through the field, to take up the running.

The crowd's hopes were raised when local hero Bryan Goss moved into 2nd place, but in such sticky conditions he could make up very little ground on Bickers. At the finish, Bickers took a comfortable win over Goss, with Smith, enjoying a canter on his two-fifty, getting the better of Freddie Mayes, Billy Jackson and Pat Lamper.

Supporting race

The Invitation race was a real cracker, which developed into a three-way battle between the BSAs of Eastwood and Smith and Goss on his 250 Greeves, which kept the crowd on their toes. Enjoying his day out in the muddy West of England, Eastwood took up the running, though he was soon passed by Smith, who no doubt wanted to put his younger teammate in his place.

Goss, riding superbly, coupled on to the BSA train. Then, as the race reached the mid-way point, he boldly passed them both on a tricky downhill section. However, Smith was not to be denied and two laps later he regained the lead and was never headed again. All the action was taking place behind him, however, as first Eastwood and then Goss took tumbles, Eastwood dropping to 4th as Burton rode past. But at the flag it was Smith from Goss, whilst the resolute Eastwood reclaimed third place on the last lap from Burton.

Eastwood's former AMC teammate Chris Horsfield took the runner-up spot in the 500 Trophy race to consolidate his lead in the series (CB)

Former Dot and Greeves factory runner, Joe Johnson graced the TV screens, taking 4th place in the 500 Trophy race on this potent Triumph Métisse (CB)

Local rider Bryan Goss had a good day out at Leighton, finishing as runner-up to Dave Bickers in the 250 Trophy race and to Jeff Smith in the Invitation (CB)

Gordon Francis captures the action, as Jeff Smith leads the 250 race, shadowed by Arthur Lampkin (partially hidden) and Alan Clough (2). Also prominent are Bryan Goss (extreme left), Dave Bickers (1) and Freddie Mayes (8)

Grandstand Trophy Race Results

250 Trophy
1 D Bickers (Greeves)
2 B Goss (Greeves)
3 J Smith (BSA)
4 F Mayes (Greeves)
5 W Jackson (Cotton)
6 P Lamper (Dot)

500 Trophy
1 V Eastwood (420 BSA)
2 C Horsfield (500 Matchless)
3 D Nicoll (500 Matchless)
4 J Johnson (500 Matchless Métisse)
5 J Giles (500 Triumph)
6 T Cox (500 Triumph Métisse)

Round 5

Caerleon, Monmouthshire, November 28, 1964

With the BBC on the eve of launching their new comedy show 'Not only ... but also' with Dudley Moore and Peter Cook, the TV circus made its way to South Wales for the fifth round of the series, where the riders provided plenty of entertainment for the viewers and a few comic moments of their own. There were also plenty of surprises in store for the series leaders, Dave Bickers and Chris Horsfield, who had to settle for supporting roles in the day's live performances.

250 Trophy Race

The track at Caerleon, so often waterlogged, was in surprisingly good condition and the 250 Trophy race saw Greeves, after several near misses, finally run amok and fill all the point scoring positions. At the head of things, Bryan Goss took off like the proverbial 'scalded cat' and was never seriously challenged. Bickers, racing Dutchman Frits Selling's Greeves after experiencing problems with his own bike in practice, found himself in a battle for the runner-up spot with teammate John Griffiths and Freddie Mayes, whose recent performances hadn't escaped the watchful eye of Greeves' mercurial Derry Preston Cobb.

Gradually, as he became more comfortable on the borrowed bike, Bickers eased himself into a safe 2nd place, whilst Griffiths eventually got the better of Mayes in their race-long battle for 3rd. Behind them Pat Lamper managed to relegate a rather subdued Alan Clough to 6th place at the flag.

500 Trophy Race

If the result of the 250 Trophy race had been a surprise, the 500 Trophy race threw up a bigger one, at least for the millions of Saturday afternoon scrambles fans who had tuned in for their ration of thrills and spills. Andy Lee had long been one of the country's top riders, though he generally preferred to ply his trade on the race tracks of France and Belgium, where he would regularly compete in 30 international events a year.

The continental crowds have always been very knowledgeable and it is testament to Lee's riding ability that he was affectionately known there as the 'King of France'. Lee, who had been the protégé of Brian Stonebridge in his early days, went on to learn about the art of racing on the continent from Les Archer; no wonder he turned out to be so good, with such pedigree mentoring him!

In the opening Grandstand Trophy series the previous year, he had finished seventh overall and first private runner in the 500 class, and at Caerleon he would make history by becoming the first privateer to win a Grandstand Trophy race.

Lee, who was always a very good starter, took off on his Matchless special and was never headed. Behind him Horsfield, who was taking advantage of Jeff Smith's absence (he was riding in the British Experts trial some 60 miles away in Llandrindnod Wells), was literally battling John Harris for 2nd place. They clashed at one stage and Chris received a three-inch gash on his forearm. However, Harris began to slip downfield and Arthur Lampkin dropped out whilst running 3rd, allowing Lee's travelling companion, Dave Nicoll, to complete an all Matchless top three at the finish.

Bryan Goss was one of the day's stars at Caerleon. Here he races to a dominant 250 Trophy race win (MC)

Also worthy of note was Keith Hickman's ride, during his first season racing a Gold Star for Eric Cheney. The young man from Cumnor near Oxford, who would go on to become a factory BSA star, claimed his first Grandstand Trophy points from an excellent fourth place finish as he got the better of seasoned campaigners John Giles and John Harris.

Supporting Races

The day's Invitation final brought 250 and 500 Trophy race winners together and it was Goss and Lee who dominated proceedings. Again Lee was first out of the trap and again nobody could get near him. Goss worked his way up through the field, picking off opponents with great ease until he became embroiled in a scrap with BSA factory riders, Vic Eastwood, trying to make amends for his 7th place in the 500 Trophy race, and Jerry Scott. Goss eventually prevailed, as Eastwood fell and Joe Johnson eased past Scott for 3rd place, whilst Brian Nadin won his personal duel with John Giles to decide 5th and 6th places.

Big winner on the day, Andy Lee guns his 'hack' bike, a Matchless-engined BSA, to victory in the 500 Trophy race. He also won the invitation race from Goss (MC)

Grandstand Trophy Race Results

250 Trophy
1 B Goss (Greeves)
2 D Bickers (Greeves)
3 J Griffiths (Greeves)
4 F Mayes (Greeves)
5 P Lamper (Greeves)
6 A Clough (Greeves)

500 Trophy
1 A Lee (500 Matchless Métisse)
2 C Horsfield (500 Matchless)
3 D Nicoll (Matchless)
4 K Hickman (500 Cheney BSA)
5 J Giles (500 Triumph)
6 J Harris (500 Matchless Métisse)

Future BSA GP runner Keith Hickman scored his first Grandstand points in the 500 Trophy race, where he finished 4th on the Cheney Gold Star (MC)

I recently asked Jeff Smith why he had chosen to ride the British Experts Trial rather than race in the Grandstand Trophy.

I was completely drained by the end of the world championship events and needed a change of pace and the British Experts Trial was the single most important trial in those days. I had won it three times already and a fourth win would have been great, but mainly I wanted some time away from being the 'target for tonight'.

For the record, Tony Davis, Malcolm's older brother, a top trials rider and occasional TV scrambles rider, turned in the best performance on the day, but Sammy Miller, having his last ride on a factory Ariel, was declared the winner following a protest. Tony recalls:

I started on my Greeves, but had a problem and switched to Don Smith's spare bike. Unfortunately, for me, Sammy got wind of this and registered a protest.

Chris Horsfield never lacked bravery; here he soars through the air on his Matchless special on the, appropriately named, Soarbrook Farm circuit (MC)

Round 6

Tweseldown, Hampshire, December 19, 1964

In the week that saw the BBC launch a new sit-com that followed the exploits of two young men from Newcastle, *The Likely Lads*, there were plenty of likely lads present at Tweseldown racecourse, looking for an opportunity to make a name for themselves.

Saturday morning found the tight, twisty Hampshire circuit in a treacherous state following a severe overnight frost and over the day's racing there were plenty of tumbles. The most spectacular of these involved AMC youngster Mick Andrews, who enlisted the help of a gorse bush to break his fall when the throttle stuck open on his factory Matchless!

Factory Greeves man Alan Clough scored his second win in the 250 Trophy series to move level in the point standings with teammate John Griffiths in 3rd place (CB)

250 Trophy Race

The 250 Trophy race saw northerner Alan Clough record his second win of the series as Dave Bickers was forced out when the clutch bearing went on his Greeves when he was lying 4th behind Clough, Bryan Goss and Jeff Smith. Behind the leading trio, factory Greeves man John Griffiths had another battle on his hands, this time with two talented young riders who were looking to impress; Roger Snoad, who had enjoyed a brief spell in the limelight at Asham Woods and Arthur Browning, a 20 year-old from Great Barr, Birmingham, who was destined for great things.

Clough built a commanding lead early in the race, but Goss and Smith were closing in fast. Then Goss fell, dropping him back to 5th place and, try as he might, Smith couldn't catch Clough who eased away to victory. Behind them a typically determined late push from Goss saw him pass Snoad, Browning having been eliminated by a holed crankcase on his Villiers Métisse, though teammate John Griffiths still remained tantalisingly out of reach.

Local expert, Roger Snoad finished 5th in the 250 Trophy race. Here he leads Bryan Goss, Ernie Greer and Malcolm Davis (BH)

500 Trophy Race

Following two wins in the Invitation races, the first from Goss and Vic Eastwood, the second from John Banks and Joe Johnson, Smith sealed a hat-trick of wins with victory in the 500 Trophy race, without doubt the best race of the day. Smith, who was racing

Despite stern opposition, Jeff Smith raced the new 440 BSA to a winning debut in the 500 Trophy race (MC)

Rising star Arthur Browning, from Great Barr, Birmingham, was well placed in the 250 Trophy race on his Villiers Métisse, but was eliminated by a mechanical problem (CB)

the new 440 BSA, was the undisputed star, but it was the supporting cast that provided most of the entertainment.

A tremendous battle raged in the closing stages, with Banks lying second just ahead of series leader Chris Horsfield, Andy Lee, maintaining his recent good form, and Eastwood. One bystander who was truly impressed with the racing was *MCN* reporter Chris Carter, who takes up the action:

> As they started that last lap Chris swooped past Banks, but Banks went by once more and as the pair careered downhill, John bounced off Chris, through a Motor Cycle News course banner, scattering spectators left and right. But he refused to shut off!
>
> Horsfield started the uphill climb, and missed a gear. Once again they were side by side, but the Matchless had the legs of the BSA up the hill, and John relaxed a trifle, resigned to third spot.

The battle had carried them to within sight of Smith, at one time ten seconds clear. Horsfield was second, but Eastwood, gaining on them all the time, made a final effort over the line. Banks sensed the challenge, looked over his shoulder and wound the BSA up, but Eastwood just had the edge.

Horsfield, meantime, had slowed up, a tail ender was in the way, and for several anxious seconds it looked as if all four would crash heavily. Somehow, both Banks and Eastwood avoided them and braked hard - a heart stopping end to one of the finest races I've ever seen.

Carter's report suggests the race had an element of pantomime about it - 'Look out, he's behind you!' - it was the season for panto after all! But unlike pantomime, the racing was totally unrehearsed and deadly serious. 'Oh, yes it was!'

Grandstand Trophy Race Results

250 Trophy
1 A Clough (Greeves)
2 J Smith (BSA)
3 J Griffiths (Greeves)
4 B Goss (Greeves)
5 R Snoad (Greeves)
6 M Davis (Greeves)

500 Trophy
1 J Smith (440 BSA)
2 C Horsfield (500 Matchless)
3 V Eastwood (420 BSA)
4 J Banks (420 BSA)
5 A Lee (500 Matchless Métisse)
6 J Scott (500 Cheney BSA)

So, as 1964 drew to a close and the second BBC Grandstand series reached its halfway stage, the leading positions were as follows:-

Grandstand Trophy Positions After 6 Rounds

250 Trophy

1	D Bickers	8 8 4 8 6 0	34pts
2	B Goss	0 5 6 6 8 4	29pts
3	A Clough	6 0 8 0 2 8	24pts
4	J Griffiths	5 6 3 0 5 5	24pts
5	J Smith	0 0 5 5 0 6	16pts
6	F Mayes	4 4 0 4 4 0	16pts

500 Trophy

1	C Horsfield	5 8 6 6 6 6	37pts
2	J Smith	0 0 8 0 0 8	16pts
3	V Eastwood	3 0 0 8 0 5	16pts
4	D Nicoll	0 0 0 5 5 0	10pts
5	J Burton	6 0 4 0 0 0	10pts
6	A J Lampkin	8 0 0 0 0 0	8pts

Round 7

Yeovil, Somerset, January 16, 1965

1965 began with more of a 'splat' than a 'bang' in the Grandstand Trophy, with a ridiculously muddy meeting being televised from Westbury Farm, Little Norton, near Yeovil, organised by the Yeo Vale Motor Cycling Club, whose members must have worked tirelessly to keep things running.

However, for one rider, the year couldn't have had a better start. After a largely disappointing time riding for Cotton, Arthur Lampkin, along with his younger brother Alan, had returned to the fold at BSA for the 1965 season and he didn't have long to wait for his first successes on the Small Heath bikes.

Lampkin's first wins did in fact come on television, but not on the BBC, as they were at an ITV meeting from High Hoyland near Wakefield. Racing a well-used 420 model, with brother Alan's motor hastily fitted after a blow up on the Saturday, Lampkin stole the headlines after twice beating the 250 world champion, Joel Robert, on his 1964 specification 250 CZ.

Cecil Bailey is on hand to catch the moment as the moral victor of the 250 GT race, Alan Clough, pushes his stricken Greeves to the line (CB)

250 Trophy Race

First up at Westbury Farm, however, was the 250 Trophy race, where Lampkin was to receive a belated Christmas present. And what a race it was, with drama a-plenty. Jeff Smith was the first rider to show, but his lead was short lived as he fell after just half a lap. Alan Clough took up the running, acting as the engine in a Greeves locomotive, as Dave Bickers and Bryan Goss followed closely. For Greeves, though, it was a train that would ultimately be derailed.

After another lap, Bickers hit the front as Goss fell to earth and Arthur Browning on his Villiers Métisse, who was beginning to turn a few heads, moved up to 3rd place behind Clough. But Bickers lasted about as long as his great rival Smith had at the front, slithering to ground and allowing Clough to take up the lead for a second time. Bickers restarted and just stayed ahead of Billy Jackson, who was having a good race on the ex-Lampkin factory Cotton and had just displaced Browning.

Where was Lampkin? Well, at this stage he was lying 5th, but then he really started to motor, putting his vast trials riding experience to good use and passing Browning and Jackson before taking up 2nd spot when the engine of Bickers' Greeves seized up. But Clough had a lead of half a minute going into the last lap and it seemed impossible for Lampkin to catch him.

Arthur Lampkin, who took the first Grandstand double - winning both 250 and 500 Trophy races on the same day - passes side-lined teammate Jeff Smith (CB)

Making one of his rare BBC appearances, Derek Rickman finished runner-up to Lampkin in the 500 Trophy race on his own creation, the Matchless Métisse (CB)

But then fate stepped in, when within sight of the finish the gearbox on Clough's Challenger seized solid. Clough, who stood to gain points on Bickers and Goss, was soon off the Greeves and pushing with all his might. However, the line didn't come up quickly enough, as Lampkin swept down off the last hill to take a most unexpected victory. An exhausted Clough pushed in for 2nd place just before Browning flashed across the line for a very impressive 3rd spot ahead of Freddie Mayes, who was now a factory Greeves rider.

500 Trophy Race

With his confidence on a high, Lampkin simply rode away from the entire field in the 500 Trophy race, delivering a master class on how to ride in such truly atrocious conditions. Lap by lap he steadily built on his lead, initially over Jerry Scott, who was showing well on the big Cheney Gold Star, and in the closing laps ahead of Derek Rickman, who was making a rare appearance in the BBC series.

At the finish line, Lampkin had a 25-second lead over Rickman, as another top trials man, John Giles, came through to claim 3rd place ahead of Scott, John Burton and Dave Nicoll. What of Jeff Smith? Well, Jeff was definitely having one of his rare off days, as he fell again in this race and could manage no better than 8th place at the flag. The only consolation for Smith was that series leader, Chris Horsfield, now riding the factory Matchless G85 as opposed to his Métisse-framed special, had also fallen and had failed to add points.

In winning his second race of the day, Lampkin made his own little piece of Grandstand Trophy history, by becoming the first rider to win both the 250 and 500 Trophy races on the same day.

Third in the 500 Trophy race was Triumph factory runner John Giles. As a top trials rider, Giles coped admirably with the cloying Somerset mud (CB)

Grandstand Trophy Race Results

250 Trophy
1 A J Lampkin (BSA)
2 A Clough (Greeves)
3 A Browning (Métisse)
4 F Mayes (Greeves)
5 W Jackson (Cotton)
6 C Horsfield (James)

500 Trophy
1 A J Lampkin (420 BSA)
2 D E Rickman (500 Matchless Métisse)
3 J Giles (500 Triumph)
4 J Scott (500 Cheney BSA)
5 J Burton (500 Matchless Métisse)
6 D Nicoll (500 Matchless)

The performances of young Arthur Browning in the last two rounds didn't escape the notice of legendary *Motor Cycle News* scribe, Ralph Venables. Writing in the 10th February, 1965, edition, he opened his column, *The Sporting Scene*, with the headline *Tip for the top - the red haired racer from Great Barr* and went on to describe Browning as 'the most improved rider of 1965 - with a very bright future. As bright as his red hair!'

Round 8

Bewdley, Worcestershire, January 23, 1965

If conditions had been grim at Yeovil, things were simply diabolical at Bewdley, arguably the worst conditions ever in the series - but in keeping with the spirit of the day it was unanimously decided that 'the show must go on!' How ironic, though, that the BBC and the ACU chose this particular day to introduce sidecars to the race programme. It was also the eve of the death of Sir Winston Churchill, who I'm sure would also have expected the show to go on.

250 Trophy Race

Indeed conditions were so bad that even in the opening 250 Trophy race, only four riders went the full distance. Dave Bickers, not a man to let a waterlogged circuit spoil his day's racing, was simply too good for his rivals, though Alan Clough, who led briefly, at least managed to keep him in sight. Billy Jackson, who had finished runner-up to Chris Horsfield in an invitation race at Yeovil, maintained his form in Worcestershire and held 3rd place

Dave Bickers returned to his winning ways in the atrocious conditions at Palmer's Farm. Here he is pictured in the previous round at Little Norton, Yeovil (CB)

until the final lap when John Griffiths slithered past him to complete a Greeves 1-2-3. The other point scorers were young Randy Owen from Hereford on a second Cotton, a lap adrift, and Ernie Greer, who finished two laps down on Bickers.

Supporting Races

Next up were the 'charioteers', and it was the veteran sidecar exponent, Bill Turner from Reading, who set the pace in the opening laps. However, a spill wrecked his chances and Dave Elvidge then took up the running. However, the sidecar crews were having a terrible time trying to get up the steepest hill and a tow rope had to be deployed to get the fittest and most determined runners to the top. Entering the last lap, Dave Treleaven held a slim lead over Nick Thompson, but both outfits spun to a halt on the hill. However, Thompson, showing the determination which would see him become a multi-British champion, managed to keep going and was first to the flag, ahead of Treleaven, Elvidge and John Turner, son of Bill.

Jeff Smith, whose bike had given up in the 250 race whilst he was lying 4th, took some consolation in winning the Invitation race. Initially he was pursued by John Harris on his Matchless Métisse, but the former BSA factory rider was struggling to stay on the pace and was rapidly passed by both Lampkin and Eastwood. The BSA trio then held station to mark a 1-2-3 for the Small Heath concern, ahead of Harris, John Giles and Jerry Scott.

In the 500 Trophy race, Vic Eastwood scored his second series win on the 420 BSA. Like Bickers, he is also pictured at the previous round, where he suffered a torrid time (CB)

500 Trophy Race

By the time the 500 Trophy race began, the track, which had been a sea of mud prior to the sidecar race, was now a veritable ocean! However, In spite of the conditions a tremendous race ensued, with the lead changing hands three times on the first lap alone.

Jerry Scott took the start on the big Cheney, but Eastwood was right on his tail and soon took up the running, only to be passed in turn by Smith. Smith and Eastwood traded places another couple of times before the senior BSA man seized the initiative and pulled out a seemingly invincible lead. But then fate stepped in and handed the race to Eastwood when Smith's throttle stuck open, pitching him off at the same time.

So it was Eastwood who took the flag first, to claim his second win of the series, ahead of Andy Lee, who had quietly got on with things, and Chris Horsfield, who had fallen earlier and stubbornly fought back to claim 3rd place and five more valuable points. John Giles was next home, just in front of Smith, who had picked himself up and managed to limp home on the 440, with Dave Nicoll completing the top six.

Though for most of the riders and many scrambles enthusiasts, this racing was simply the antithesis of what the sport was all about, ironically the TV punters lapped up all the thrills and spills and the slapstick-like routines that they witnessed on their TV screens. They simply couldn't get enough of it!

Grandstand Trophy Race Results

250 Trophy
1 D Bickers (Greeves)
2 A Clough (Greeves)
3 J Griffiths (Greeves)
4 W Jackson (Cotton)
5 R Owen (Cotton)
6 E Greer (Dot)

500 Trophy
1 V Eastwood (420 BSA)
2 A Lee (500 Matchless Mètisse)
3 C Horsfield
4 J Giles (500 Triumph)
5 J V Smith (440 BSA)
6 D Nicoll (500 Matchless)

Round 9

Canada Heights, Kent, February 27, 1965

This particular round of the Grandstand Trophy has been bestowed with legendary status, thanks in part to the BBC, but mainly due to YouTube and the internet. In the mid-80s the BBC ran a programme entitled *100 Great Sporting Moments*. I don't recall now if it was a top 100 counting down to number one, but one of the featured clips was the Invitation race from this meeting, which produced probably the closest finish ever to a TV scramble.

250 Trophy Race

But let's backtrack a little bit, as before a wheel had turned in the Invitation race, there was the serious business of two Grandstand Trophy races to be run. Following his return to winning form at Bewdley, after a minor blip, Dave Bickers was the hot favourite for the 250 Trophy race, though a lot of attention was also focused on Bryan Goss who was making his TV debut on the 250 Husqvarna and Don Rickman on the Bultaco Métisse.

Whilst Bickers was racing to a start-to-finish win, Goss was floundering towards the back of the pack after an uncustomarily poor start and the hapless Rickman fared even worse, falling out of the running on the first lap. Behind Bickers, teammate Alan Clough initially held 2nd spot, but he was being chased hard by Jeff Smith, having another outing on his lightweight 250, and as the race approached its midpoint, Smith swept past the Greeves man. Meanwhile, Goss was really motoring through the pack, though he was rapidly running out of time. At the flag he finished 4th behind Dot's Ernie Greer, with Roger Snoad completing the point scoring positions.

Bryan Goss was getting the hang of his new 250 Husqvarna at the Heights. 5th in the 250 Trophy race, he improved to 4th in the TV Invitation (BH)

500 Trophy Race

Next on the programme was the 500 Trophy race, which saw Smith back to winning form. Jerry Scott made one of his lightning starts on the Cheney, before Smith blasted past him to lead to the flag. Scott, however, was having a really good ride and fended off the attacks of the works BSAs of Arthur Lampkin and Vic Eastwood, racing on his local track, for several laps. But then it was all change, as Lampkin slipped past Scott for second spot, Eastwood retired, after falling twice, and Horsfield and Don Rickman ousted John Giles from 4th place and the finishing positions had been decided.

Supporting Races

So the score after two races was Bickers 1 – Smith 1, which brings us back to the most exciting invitation race ever, which would decide who was top gun on the day. But in whose favour?

Bickers stormed the start from Giles and Smith and it only seems fit to let BBC race commentator, Murray Walker, take over from here:

Look at this, Bickers leads! The 250 leading all the 500s and the other 250s as well ... then Peach, Scott, Nicoll and Eastwood.

Birmingham's Ernie Greer was a regular competitor in the early Grandstand series and at Canada Heights he enjoyed one of his best races, finishing 4th in the 250 Trophy race (BH)

Bickers rapidly built a four-second lead over Smith, Giles, Scott, Eastwood and Horsfield with the 250s of Clough and Goss in 8th and 9th. By the third lap Bickers had lapped Andy Lee, who was having teething problems with his latest creation, and now held a seven-second lead over Smith. Back to Murray:

> *Here is Dave Bickers in the lead, leaping sideways through the air, but it looks like Smith is gaining on him now. Let's wait here now and see this tremendous scrap for third place ... and there's the battle for third and look at it! Jerry Scott on the BSA, number 3, Vic Eastwood, who's just ahead, and number 7 is Alan Clough ... and Vic Eastwood really loses it in a big way, but he's perfectly alright. Number 26, John Giles, coming up and through, Bryan Goss on the Husqvarna just behind him, number 56 is Chris Horsfield, number 57 is Derek Rickman and number 16 going through is Joe Johnson with the pack right behind them. Vic Eastwood getting back into the battle. Well done Vic!*

By lap six, just like the riders on the screen, Murray was truly getting into his stride on the mic:

> *Smith playing his usual waiting game, I wonder if he's left it too late?*

And a little later:

> *Smith has been watching Bickers all through this race and he's gaining on him in the closing stages. Bickers and Smith together. Number 11 the Greeves, number 6 the BSA. Downhill into the left-hander, up the hill into the right-hander, downhill into the left-hander to start lap seven.*

Dave Bickers won the 250 Trophy race, but his major triumph came in the TV Invitation, when he fought back to snatch victory from Jeff Smith on the finish line, which he crossed virtually travelling sideways (BH)

There's Bickers, up (over a jump) ... and away. Down goes Bickers and up goes Smith.

As the race entered its closing stages, Murray's commentary built to a crescendo:

There's the last lap flag and the interval now is still one second. Over the skyline they go, Dave Bickers, Jeff Smith, two-fifty Greeves, four-forty BSA, the world champion on the BSA, the ex-European champion on the Greeves. Watch this jump now, they're going to hit it almost together, uphill. Bickers ... Smith, away uphill, Bickers, Smith ... and the crowd, as you can see for yourself, really waving these two on.

And Dave Bickers is going to win this, I think, because there's only about 500 yards in it now. Let's see, into the left hander, Bickers looks around his shoulder, there's Smith behind him. Bickers hits the throttle Jeff Smith does the same. They're coming up the last hill together, into the right-hander together, Smith's done it, Smith's ahead! Jeff Smith's gonna win this race, into the downhill section ... is Bickers gonna try and take him? And Bickers has rounded him, Bickers has done it! Oh my goodness, what a fantastic race!

As everybody caught their breath after a truly spectacular race and unbelievable finish Walker added:

I'm accused of getting over excited in these scrambling spots, but no wonder, what an incredible race. Dave Bickers hit that throttle, got into a terrific broadside and rode round the outside of Jeff Smith!

Murray Walker has always been known for his infectious style of commentary, as illustrated above, and he was good enough to tell me his personal philosophy on commentating.

Jerry Scott was in fine form, here he leads eventual winner Jeff Smith in the 500 Trophy race (BH)

Your job as a commentator is to interpret the pictures that the viewer is looking at and to do so informatively and hopefully entertainingly as well. I always regarded my remit as being not just to inform, because anybody could do that, I was always conscious of the fact that it was show business and you're after the maximum audience and I always wanted to say to people, in effect, 'This is my sport, it's a fantastic sport and I love it and I want you to love it too'.

There is little doubt in my mind that Murray Walker's 'interpretation of the pictures' played a huge role in popularising the sport for TV viewers and anyone who has ever listened to his commentary will surely attest that he always kept them both informed and entertained. As former Formula 1 world champion Jackie Stewart, an avid motorcycling fan in his youth, once remarked, 'He (Walker) coloured the pictures.'

After being bestowed the honour of featuring in the BBC's *100 Great Sporting Moments* programme in the mid-80s, this race has reached 'cult' status with the advent of the internet. To date (April 2013) more than 100,000 people have taken to their computers to watch this classic race on YouTube!

Of course, the riders very rarely got to see the races, so they generally welcome an opportunity to re-live those moments again, though this isn't always the case, as Jeff Smith told me:

We, the riders, never saw the racing because it was live TV and there were no repeats. There are maybe two or three of the BBC Grandstand races available on the internet. I thoroughly enjoy watching them except the one where David Bickers wins by a back wheel!

Bickers told me:

When I was with Smithy in America, all the time we'd get - 'I remember you two in that TV race where Dave won all crossed up on the line.' - and Smithy told people, 'I don't want to talk about it!' To him you see it wasn't that he'd lost a race, but that he'd lost a few quid. He used to joke, 'It's not about the race, it's about taking the bread off my table.' On the finish itself, Dave had this to say. 'On the last lap I got held up by Brian Leask and I thought to myself "you want to take it a bit easier on the last lap", and just then Smithy came along and passed me! But it all ended up alright, I suppose!'

One has to spare a thought for the poor sidecar boys, who had to take to the track after such a breath-taking race. Naturally, it was an impossible act to follow but some of the country's leading charioteers did their best, with Rufus Rose prevailing ahead of Nick Thompson and Dave Elvidge.

Grandstand Trophy Race Results

250 Trophy
1 D Bickers (Greeves)
2 J Smith (BSA)
3 A Clough (Greeves)
4 E Greer (Dot)
5 B Goss (Husqvarna)
6 R Snoad (Greeves)

500 Trophy
1 J Smith (440 BSA)
2 A J Lampkin (420 BSA)
3 J Scott (500 Cheney BSA)
4 C Horsfield (500 Matchless)
5 D J Rickman (500 Matchless Métisse)
6 J Giles (500 Triumph)

Round 10

Ripon, Yorkshire, March 6, 1965

This was the BBC's first visit to this track situated midway between the Yorkshire Dales and the North Yorkshire Moors on the site of a former medieval castle. But the Ripon Motor Club had previously played host to several ABC Television scrambles and despite an entry that lacked the typical strength in depth that marked these events, the organisation was excellent and the racing left little to be desired.

250 Trophy Race

Dave Bickers was really coming to form and in the 250 Trophy race, he was simply too strong for his adversaries. Despite the frozen surface of the track, the 'Coddenham Flyer' took off from the start and was never challenged during the 11-lap race. Fellow East Anglian, Freddie Mayes, initially held 2nd place, but a slipping clutch on the Greeves saw Freddie slipping down the field.

Jeff Smith, having another great ride on the 250 took up 2nd spot and at the flag split the factory Greeves of Bickers and Clough for the second week in succession. Mayes held on for 4th place, with 20 year-old Alan Lampkin, racing just 30 miles from the family home in Silsden, making his mark in the Grandstand series by scoring his first points from 5th place ahead of another youngster, John Done, on the factory Dot.

Freddie Mayes ran second in the early laps, but his progress was hindered by a slipping clutch on the Greeves and he eventually finished 4th (MC)

Dave Bickers grabbed the lead in the 250 Trophy race and was never headed. Freddie Mayes (8), Bryan Goss (19), Jeff Smith (obscured behind Bickers) and John Griffiths (17) give chase (MC)

500 Trophy Race

In sharp contrast to his kid brother, Arthur Lampkin had a day to forget. He had only lasted one lap in the 250 race, before the ignition failed on his BSA, and his fortunes were not to improve in the 500 Trophy race. There was drama on the startline in this race, as series leader Chris Horsfield's Matchless engine mysteriously died and despite frenzied efforts to change spark plugs it wouldn't restart and Chris was reduced to the role of a spectator.

Jeff Smith seized his opportunity to close the gap on Horsfield and turned in a majestic performance, leading from start to finish. Arthur Lampkin was holding a comfortable 2nd place until his 420 also gave up the ghost, allowing Dave Nicoll to take up the chase with 'Sid' Lampkin proving his worth and improving on the 250 race to claim an excellent 3rd place ahead of a below par Vic Eastwood. Such was Smith's dominance, that he lapped all the riders down to 4th place, including the other point scorers, George Hodge, the visiting Scottish Scrambles champion on his Matchless, and local favourite Dickie Preston riding his faithful Gold Star BSA.

Supporting Races

The question on everybody's lips now must have been 'Can we expect a re-run of the invitation race at Canada Heights?' The answer, quite simply, was no. But once again, it did provide the most exciting race of the day. As the race got away, two BSAs leapt to the front, with Arthur Lampkin heading Eastwood, closely followed by Bickers and Smith. Lampkin's lead was short lived, however, as for the third time that day his BSA let him

Vic Eastwood's luck was out at Ripon, when, having forced his way back past Jeff Smith in the TV Invitation, his 420 BSA ran out of petrol (MC)

down. Eastwood was now clear at the front and made a bid for freedom not unlike that of 'Goldie', the golden eagle, which had escaped from its enclosure at London Zoo on February 28th and had taken up residence in nearby Regent's Park.

The man from Kent had also flown the coop, apparently leaving Bickers and Smith to fight for 2nd place. However, having taken the 500 Trophy race and reduced Horsfield's lead in the series to 11 points, Smith was in just the mood for a challenge. He passed Bickers for 2nd on the fourth lap and set about catching his teammate. Lap by lap, Smith was narrowing the gap to Eastwood and with two laps to go, the world champion hit the front of the race. But Eastwood wasn't prepared to just lie down and on the final lap he battled past Smith to regain the lead.

But there was still one last cruel twist in this race, as within sight of the finish Eastwood's BSA stopped abruptly, a ruptured petrol tank causing the bike to run out of petrol. So at the flag, Smith took his second win of the day, ahead of the Greeves of Bickers and John Griffths.

Grandstand Trophy Race Results

250 Trophy
1 D Bickers (Greeves)
2 J Smith (BSA)
3 A Clough (Greeves)
4 F Mayes (Greeves)
5 A R C Lampkin (BSA)
6 J Done (Dot)

500 Trophy
1 J Smith (440 BSA)
2 D Nicoll (500 Matchless)
3 A R C Lampkin (420 BSA)
4 V Eastwood (420 BSA)
5 G Hodge (500 Matchless)
6 R Preston (500 BSA)

Big Dave Nicoll had his best ride of the series bringing the factory Matchless home in 2nd place in the 500 Trophy race (MC)

Local man Alan Lampkin was on form at Ripon, here he is pictured on his way to 3rd spot in the 500 Trophy race (MC)

An unusual view of Jeff Smith from the camera of Malcolm Carling, but one that most of his competitors were used to seeing

Round 11

Bulford Camp, Wiltshire, March 20, 1965

A fortnight later the action moved to Bulford Camp on the edge of Salisbury Plain, where the racing was run off with military precision by the Kiwi MCC. By this stage of the series, Dave Bickers was virtually guaranteed his second 250 Grandstand Trophy after winning the previous three rounds, needing to score a solitary point in Wiltshire to do so. But the 500 Trophy series was starting to hot up, with Chris Horsfield's lead being slashed from 21 points at the mid-point to 11, with two rounds to play for.

250 Trophy Race

Had Welsh singer Tom Jones been present at Bulford Camp, he may well have broken into *It's Not Unusual*, as Dave Bickers made light work of winning his second BBC Grandstand Trophy, by taking the 250 Trophy race with yet another unchallenged start-to-finish win.

Seemingly unphased by the difficult conditions, the chalky hillside track being treacherous in places, Bickers stormed to victory, as the only rider who looked capable of

Dave Bickers, racing past the Swarfega banner, 'cleaned up' at Bulford Camp, to secure his second 250 Grandstand Trophy win (CB)

Factory Cotton man Billy Jackson sprung a surprise. Thriving in the tricky conditions, he took the TV Invitation from Vic Eastwood, seen here, and Jerry Scott (CB)

bothering him, Bryan Goss, slipped down the field when his Husqvarna began to lose power. Alan Clough inherited a safe 2nd place from Goss and the third Greeves factory runner, John Griffiths, pipped Goss on the line to claim 3rd place. Billy Jackson, who was in fine form on the day, took 5th spot on the factory Cotton with Roger Snoad completing the top six.

Supporting Races

The next race on the programme was the First Unlimited race, which threw up several surprises, not least of all, the race winner. Having shown his paces in the 250 race, Jackson went out and wrested this race from the grip of first Jerry Scott, then Vic Eastwood, to ease away from the BSA factory runner for a memorable win. Jackson remembers the race fondly:

> Oh yes, it was extremely wet that day and there was a part of the track, just before a steep downhill section, that I was jumping and nobody else was. So I was making up a lot of ground on the field.

500 Trophy Race

So to the 500 Trophy race, which found the leading players under a lot of pressure to perform. Out of the blue raced Horsfield's young teammate, and top trials star, Mick Andrews, who was revelling in the sticky going and led the field for the opening laps until Scott and Eastwood forced themselves by to renew their battle from the Unlimited race.

And what of the title protagonists? Horsfield was back in 5th place, with Smith even further adrift and off the leaderboard. Smith needed to get ahead of Horsfield to have any chance of retaining his trophy and he tried all he knew to do just that.

But Horsfield was holding all the cards and when Smith fell on the last lap, in a last ditch effort to get past the Stratford rider, he slipped back to 9th place, thus surrendering his hold on the Grandstand Trophy. Horsfield recalls:

Smithy wasn't very happy about it and we had words back in the paddock. But I have always been taught that if you give it out, you have got to take it too, and Jeff certainly knew how to dish it out!

So at the close of the race, Jerry Scott had won his, and Eric Cheney's, first Grandstand Trophy race ahead of Eastwood, Andrews had scored his first Grandstand Trophy points from an excellent 3rd place, and John Giles had ridden a steady race to take 4th spot. But the big winner on the day was Horsfield, who in finishing 5th, added three points to his total and took the Grandstand Trophy with one round to spare.

Reflecting on his TV triumph, Horsfield told me:

The main reason why I won the Grandstand Trophy was my fitness. When I was at James, I'd get up at 5 am and go for a 3-mile run, home for a slice of toast and a cup of tea, then drive to Greet where I'd clock in at 8 o'clock. Then I'd work till one, when I'd run down to the BSA track and run around there and up Spark Hill with Smithy, then we'd go into the baths. I'd get home at about 7 in the evening and before I ate anything, I'd go for another

Like Bickers, Chris Horsfield also guaranteed himself a Grandstand Trophy in Wiltshire, a calculated race on the factory Matchless bringing him 5th place and enough points to put him beyond the reach of Jeff Smith (CB)

3-mile run, week in, week out, and that stands you in good stead. Having said that, I couldn't have won it without the bike, it was the best 500 in the country at the time.

Grandstand Trophy Race Results

250 Trophy
1 D Bickers (Greeves)
2 A Clough (Greeves)
3 J Griffiths (Greeves)
4 B Goss (Husqvarna)
5 W Jackson (Cotton)
6 R Snoad (Greeves)

500 Trophy
1 J Scott (500 Cheney BSA)
2 V Eastwood (441 BSA)
3 M Andrews (500 Matchless)
4 J Giles (500 Triumph)
5 C Horsfield (500 Matchless)
6 D Nicoll (500 Matchless)

Every schoolboy enthusiast's dream: Dave Bickers' factory Greeves Challenger in the paddock at Bulford Camp (CB)

Round 12

Crowborough, Sussex, March 27, 1965

The final round of the series came a week later at Cross-in-Hand, giving scrambles fans in Sussex a rare chance to see the 'TV stars' at close quarters. The racing on the day may have lacked a little verve, as many of the top riders were down to race in the opening round of the ACU 500 Star at Hawkstone Park the following day.

However, nobody could doubt the youthful enthusiasm of Greeves' factory runner, Malcolm Davis, who had turned 21 the previous day. It would appear that Malcolm had received the 'key to the door', as he proved to be the surprise package of the meeting, cementing the idea that many off-road observers held, that he had a very bright future ahead of him.

250 Trophy Race

The 250 Trophy race definitely lacked a bit of sparkle, with Greeves' factory riders Dave Bickers and John Griffiths on a ferry boat bound for the first Grand Prix of the year in Spain. However, in the absence of his teammates, it was Alan Clough who waved the Greeves flag, taking the start and never being challenged for the entire race.

Alan Clough, had a comfortable win in the 250 Trophy race. His third success of the series secured him the runner-up place in the final standing behind Dave Bickers (BH)

Above left, 250 Trophy race action, as eventual runner-up, Freddie Mayes, leads Bryan Goss, Jeff Smith and Malcolm Davis (MC)

Above Right, a star is born! Malcolm Davis won both Invitation races at Cross-in-Hand, much to the delight of Greeves' mercurial Derry Preston Cobb (BH)

Behind Clough, Freddie Mayes headed Jeff Smith, Bryan Goss, Billy Jackson and Malcolm Davis. Cotton factory runner, Jackson, was enjoying some of the best form of his career and by lap two, he'd despatched both Bryan Goss and Jeff Smith, no mean achievement! Not content with that however, he was reeling in Mayes, when the Cotton's chain jumped its sprockets. Meanwhile, Goss, on the Husqvarna, had got past Smith and the pair of them were closing in on Mayes.

Then going into the last lap Goss slid off and suddenly Mayes' 2nd place was coming under pressure from Smith. However, while all eyes were on the battle for 2nd spot, seemingly undetected, Malcolm Davis caught the pair and took a wide birth to pass Smith in the run in to the line, though Mayes remained agonisingly out of reach. Davis' last lap charge cemented yet another 1-2-3 for Greeves and registered his best Grandstand finish to date.

500 Trophy Race

By contrast, the 500 Trophy race was like a stroll in the park for Smith. He gunned the 440 to the front and controlled the race from there. Behind him, it was a case of 'follow the leader', as most of the leading riders held their position. Vic Eastwood, who by then had a 440 of his own, albeit an ex-Smith bike, took up station in 2nd place ahead of his good friend and frequent travelling companion, John Giles, and his former AMC stablemate, Dave Nicoll.

There was a little action behind the leading trio, as new 500 Grandstand Trophy holder, Chris Horsfield, moved up from an indifferent start, to pass Peter Hole, on his hybrid Moto-Manx (a Norton engine housed in a Métisse frame), and Mike Peach, racing in his native Sussex. However, Chris, who Dave Bickers once told me was 'A very good rider, but he crashed too much', did just that, falling on the last lap and allowing Peach to move up to 5th spot.

Jeff Smith, employing some trials riding technique as he races to victory in the 500 Trophy race (MC)

From there on, Malcolm Davis' day just got better and better. The young man from Gloucester on the factory Greeves scored a double win in the Invitation races, taking the first from Roger Snoad and Dave Nicoll and the second from Horsfield, and Giles. No doubt that provided a real confidence boost for Malcolm and it certainly earmarked him as one of the bright hopes for the future of British motocross.

Spare a thought for ace photographer Malcolm Carling, who would have made a 500-mile round trip from Manchester, arriving home late on Saturday evening, before setting off again very early Sunday morning for the first round of the 500 ACU Star contest at Hawkstone Park. Following a full day of racing in Shropshire, he would have headed off home to develop all his films from the weekend, before rushing off to Manchester Piccadilly station to put them on an overnight train bound for the *MCN* office in Kettering!

Grandstand Trophy Race Results

250 Trophy
1 A Clough (Greeves)
2 F Mayes (Greeves)
3 M Davis (Greeves)
4 J Smith (BSA)
5 R Snoad (Greeves)
6 A Browning (Métisse)

500 Trophy
1 J Smith (440 BSA)
2 V Eastwood (440 BSA)
3 J Giles (500 Triumph)
4 D Nicoll (500 Matchless)
5 M Peach (500 Triumph Métisse)
6 C Horsfield (500 Matchless)

1964/65 Grandstand Trophy Series Final Standings

250 Trophy

1	D Bickers	8 8 4 8 6 0 0 8 8 8 8 0	66pts
2	A Clough	6 0 8 0 2 8 6 6 5 5 6 8	60pts
3	B Goss	0 5 6 6 8 4 0 0 3 0 4 0	36pts
4	J Griffiths	5 6 3 0 5 5 0 5 0 0 5 0	34pts
5	J Smith	0 0 5 5 0 6 0 0 6 6 0 4	32pts
6	F Mayes	4 4 0 4 4 0 4 0 0 4 0 6	30pts

500 Trophy

1	C Horsfield	5 8 6 6 6 6 0 5 4 0 3 2	51pts
2	J Smith	0 0 8 0 0 8 0 3 8 8 0 8	43pts
3	V Eastwood	3 0 0 8 0 5 0 8 0 4 6 6	40pts
4	D Nicoll	0 0 0 5 5 0 2 2 0 6 2 4	26pts
5	J Giles	0 0 0 3 3 0 5 4 2 0 4 5	26pts
6	A J Lampkin	8 0 0 0 0 0 8 0 6 0 0 0	22pts

131

Chris Horsfield's 'Special' Matchless

When Chris Horsfield took to the line for the opening round of the 500cc Grandstand Trophy series at Clifton in October 1964, he was armed with what he has described to me as 'a very special Matchless'. Chris would go on to win the 500 series, but he only raced his special bike until the end of the year, when the AMC top brass insisted that he ride a factory G85 bike. Below he tells us a little more about that exceptional bike.

'When I won the Grandstand Trophy I didn't win it on a Matchless, it was a hand-built bike with a special lightweight Métisse frame. I rode it right through the series until the round at Tweseldown, where they took it off me and wouldn't let me ride it anymore.

'But that bike was special. It was a lightweight Rickman frame, with AMC forks, the (Dave) Curtis motor in it, that had obviously been rebuilt, a special gearbox done by one of the Swedes, which came with two sets of gears, they'd shortened the gap between 2nd and 3rd and it went so much better. You could start it in 3rd gear every time and round Hawkstone, you'd never change out of 3rd. It was super.

'The gearbox was matched to a Manx clutch that the guys from Bracebridge Street (the Norton works, who by then were working in a corner of the James factory), did for me. It had a massive one and three quarter inch carb on it, as used on the road racers, and a guy from Amal used to come out every week to set it up. But it was so easy to ride. Bob Cooper put it together for me and everybody was sworn to secrecy or they'd have got the sack. We got it down to 268 lbs (the stock 500s weighed close to 350 lbs) and it was light enough and fast enough to win a world championship.'

Horsfield makes his TV debut on the new bike at Clifton in October 1964, where he took 3rd place in the 500 Grandstand Trophy race behind Arthur Lampkin and John Burton (MC)

Murray Walker catches up with Horsfield at the end of the 500 Grandstand Trophy race at Caerleon in late November 1964. I'm sure he had plenty of questions for Chris about his new steed that was proving to be not only very fast, but also very reliable (MC)

As Horsfield explained above, following the sixth round of the series at Tweseldown, where he rode the G85 Matchless in practice, he was instructed by Comp Shop manager, Hugh Viney, to race the factory product for the remainder of the series. Sadly, within two years AMC had lost all their leading riders as Vic Eastwood, having already departed to BSA, would be followed out the door by Horsfield, who raced a brace of CZs throughout the 1965-66 series, and Dave Nicoll, who also built up and raced his own private Matchless Métisse, before joining Eastwood on the BSA payroll.

The greatest irony of all is that the Rickman brothers had tried to sell their Métisse frameset to AMC in 1963. The Rickman's have always claimed that they were reluctant manufacturers; they were running a motor cycle shop and simply wanted to have more competitive machinery to race come the weekend, as Derek Rickman explains. 'We built the first Métisse because we wanted something to compete with the Swedes (at that time, the late 1950s, Swedish riders such as Sten Lundin, Bill Nilsson and Gunnar Johansson were the ones to beat, with their meticulously prepared machines, predominantly based on British components). When we first built the Mk3 Métisse frameset, we took it, complete with drawings, along to Matchless, Triumph and BSA and all three turned us down. So we decided there and then that we would have to become manufacturers ourselves. The strangest thing of all was that in a few years' time we were the only manufacturer left, as Matchless, Triumph and BSA had all gone.'

At Tweseldown, on December 19, 1964, AMC had told Horsfield that he was to race their latest G85 CS model for the remainder of the series. Chris is seen here posing with the pristine bike in the paddock, but tellingly it was the Métisse framed special that he raced to 2nd place in the 500 Trophy race. At the close of the meeting he had amassed 37 points, an incredible 21 point lead over his nearest challenger, Jeff Smith (CB)

1965-66
Normal Service Is Resumed

Jeff Smith, Asham Woods, 5th March, 1966 (CB)

Setting The Scene

In late July, Jeff Smith retained his 500 world championship crown, beating a young and relatively unknown East German, Paul Friedrichs, to the title. Racing in the deep sand of the Dutch GP at Berharen, Smith took a comfortable win in the first race and rode a calculated second, finishing 3rd behind Jef Teuwissen and Rolf Tibblin, which saw him clinch the title with his sixth GP win of the season.

He also racked up his eighth ACU Star, though Dave Bickers, who with Greeves' permission raced a 360 CZ for most of the season, and BSA teammate, Vic Eastwood, pushed him hard all season long. Wins at Hawkstone Park, the Cotswold Scramble and the final round at the Jackpot Scramble in October, where Bickers was out on the experimental 360 Greeves, brought Smith the title, with Bickers winning at the Cumberland GN meeting and Eastwood victorious at the Whitsun Bank Holiday Monday meeting at Hadleigh, Essex.

Eastwood, in his first GP season on a BSA, showed that he had the potential to be a world champion. He rode consistently well all season, with his best result being runner-up to teammate Smith in Sweden, though he also stood on the podium in Finland and in the home GP at Hawkstone Park. He eventually finished level on points with Rolf Tibblin, behind Smith and East German sensation, Paul Friedrichs.

Bickers had finished 3rd overall in the 250 world championship behind Torsten Hallman and Joel Robert, though he managed to win three GPs on the Greeves: the opening round in Spain, in Belgium and on home soil at Glastonbury, in July. However, he continued to dominate the 250 ACU Star contest, winning the opening two rounds, held over the Easter Bank Holiday weekend, at the Hants GN on the Friday and at the Cambridge GN two days later. This laid the foundations for Bickers to claim his fifth Star in six years and although Bryan Goss won the fourth round at Larkstoke on his Husqvarna and Alan Clough the final round at the Lancs GN, Bickers finished second on both occasions and took the title by a winning margin of 14 points over Goss.

On The Move

Bryan Goss surprised many by quitting Greeves to race a private Husqvarna and was in sensational form on the Swedish lightweight, whilst John Done like Alan Clough and John Griffiths before him, made the move from Dot to Greeves. Though he never really hit the heights, Done finished joint 5th in the 250 ACU Star with Don Rickman in 1965.

In The News

John Griffiths had a difficult season on the Greeves, but a highlight was 5th overall at the 250 Italian GP in April. In the 500 GPs, Chris Horsfield scored an excellent 4th overall in Austria, whilst his travelling companion, Jerry Scott, was runner-up to Smith in France, his best ever GP result.

Into The 1965-66 Series

At a time when staunch Conservative Mary Whitehouse was poised to establish the National Viewers' and Listeners' Association, following an indiscretion on the part of theatre critic Kenneth Tynan who famously used the 'F-word' on British television for the first time whilst appearing on the BBC's late night satirical show *BBC-3*, the third Grandstand Trophy series quietly got underway.

The Grandstand series showed viewers plenty of 'mucky scenes' over the years and I'm pretty sure a fair amount of four-letter words were uttered along the way, though thankfully, for Mary Whitehouse and her *Clean Up TV* campaign at least, the BBC sound engineers didn't seem to pick them up!

Round 1

Builth Wells, Breconshire, November 13, 1965

When the BBC entourage arrived in the mid-Wales market town of Builth Wells in mid-November, for the opening round of the 1965-66 Grandstand Trophy series, all eyes were focused on the reigning 500 Trophy holder, Chris Horsfield, following the sensational news that he had signed to race for the go-ahead Czechoslovakian manufacturer, CZ. As such, he would join the likes of 250 world champion Victor Arbekov and former world champions, Joel Robert (250) and Rolf Tibblin (500). The *MCN* headline for Wednesday 10th November 1965, light years before the concept of political correctness had been floated, simply read: 'HORSFIELD GOES FOREIGN'.

The accompanying article informed readers that Horsfield would became the first British rider to race under contract to a foreign manufacturer, Dave Bickers and Bryan Goss having previously raced Husqvarnas, but as privateers. Horsfield really came up trumps though, as he was signed to race both 250 and 360 models and also had a Czech mechanic at his disposal.

Also making news was a 250 BSA that Eric Cheney had built up specifically for Jeff Smith, who, let us not forget, had been busy over the summer securing his second world title. The stunning looking bike carried many of the Cheney hallmarks, such as lightweight hubs, a floating rear brake plate and, naturally, a beautifully crafted lightweight frame. The engine had also received a serious going-over in the Cheney workshop and the whole bike reputedly weighed some 25 lbs less than the factory 250s as raced by Smith and Lampkin.

Unfortunately, for Horsfield, the Builth Wells round came a week too soon.

When Sten (Polanka, Horsfield's Czech mechanic) brought the CZs over I was supposed to have a few days to get used to them, bearing in mind that the gear change was on the left-hand side. Sten turned up at 9 pm on the Friday night with the bikes and we went down to Builth Wells on the Saturday morning. The first time I saw them was when we got them out of the van to practice. Builth Wells was always pretty hairy, with lots of steep drops and jumps, and I remember going to brake and passing someone going through the air before crashing through the ropes.

250 Trophy Race

However, the CZs were good enough to allow Horsfield to make an instant impact in the 250 Trophy race, where despite his brief foray into the undergrowth, he would challenge the factory Greeves of Alan Clough and Dave Bickers. In next to no time, he had passed Bickers and set off in hot pursuit of Clough, who had stormed the start. It looked for a while as if he might make a winning debut on the two-fifty, but just as he was about to challenge Clough for the lead he crashed again and put himself out of the running.

Horsfield's fall from grace paved the way for the second of only two one-make clean sweeps in the Grandstand Trophy series, as Clough led home Bickers, Arthur Browning, Freddie Mayes, Malcolm Davis and Roger Snoad, all mounted on Greeves Challengers. I would wager that Greeves' Derry Preston Cobb must have gone to bed that night a very contented man.

Alan Clough picked up where he had finished the previous series, winning the opening round in Wales (MC)

500 Trophy Race

Horsfield, always a very tough rider, picked himself up, dusted himself down and readied himself for the 500 Trophy race. Jeff Smith who had failed to compete in the 250 race as he was still awaiting delivery of the experimental Cheney BSA, took the lead on his trusty 440 and was never headed, though it was far from being a comfortable win for the double world champion.

Initially Smith was pursued by Andy Lee on his Matchless Métisse and the factory Matchless of Dave Nicoll, but then it was the turn of the 360 two-strokes to take up the chase, in the hands of Clough, Horsfield and Bickers. Sadly, the East Anglian's challenge was over all too soon, when the Albion gearbox on his Greeves locked up. Try as he might, Clough could not contain Horsfield, who despite slipping off whilst narrowing the gap to Smith, still held on for 2nd place on his CZ debut. Behind Clough came Birmingham BSA rider Mick Bowers, scoring his first Grandstand Trophy points, Lee and Vic Eastwood, who had suffered a difficult race.

Supporting Races

The day's most interesting TV offering was arguably the Second Invitation race. Smith, who had added the First Invitation, was looking for a hat-trick of wins, but it was Johnny Giles, on a far from standard Triumph, who took the start from Lee, with Smith 3rd ahead of Clough. A lap later Clough was out, his Greeves having whiskered a plug, but next up was Horsfield,

Jeff Smith kicked off his 1965-66 campaign in fine style with a win, leading from start to finish (MC)

who rapidly began to hound Smith. However, this was also short lived, as Chris took yet another tumble from his new 360. Bickers, racing his 250, was right on Horsfield's tail and when the CZ man fell he spurted past a startled Smith to move into 3rd place.

Meanwhile, Lee had taken up the lead and Giles slipped further down the field when Bickers moved past, shadowed by Smith. Bickers, who was always happiest leading a race, soon sped past Lee to hit the front, but Smith could only annex 2nd place from the determined Fenman on the last lap, by which time Bickers had built a winning lead. At the flag it was Bickers from Smith, Lee, Giles, Alan Lampkin and Welsh champion, John Lewis on a factory Matchless.

Grandstand Trophy Race Results

250 Trophy
1 A Clough (Greeves)
2 D Bickers (Greeves)
3 A Browning (Greeves)
4 F Mayes (Greeves)
5 M Davis (Greeves)
6 R Snoad (Greeves)

500 Trophy
1 J Smith (440 BSA)
2 C Horsfield (360 CZ)
3 A Clough (360 Greeves)
4 M Bowers (440 BSA)
5 A Lee (500 Matchless Métisse)
6 V Eastwood (440 BSA)

Arthur Browning was in impressive form at the series opener, taking 3rd place in the 250 Trophy race. Here he leads fellow Greeves rider Freddie Mayes through a water splash (MC)

Bryan Wade, a young rider from Barnard Castle with a bright future ahead of him, made his Grandstand series debut at Builth Wells, though his lasting memory of this momentous occasion is not what you might have expected.

I remember Builth Wells, because in the hotel the night before we were messing about and we ended up sprinting down the High Street to see who was quickest. John Banks won, he was like greased lightning!

A week after the Builth Wells meeting, Saturday November 20th, the BBC staged a GB v USSR match race from Canada Heights (see p295).

Chris Horsfield really animated the meeting, where he raced his new CZs for the first time. Here, on the 360, he battles with Alan Clough on the 360 Greeves. They finished 2nd and 3rd respectively in the 500 Trophy (MC)

Round 2
Lyng, Norfolk, December 4, 1965

On the first Saturday of December, the track at Cadders Hill, which the organising Norwich Vikings MCC had been using since 1936 (and still uses to this day), was in tip-top condition and with its steep climbs, sharp drops and sandy surface it provided *Grandstand* viewers with some spectacular racing.

250 Trophy Race

First up was the 250 Trophy race, and what a cracker it was! The main protagonists were Dave Bickers and Chris Horsfield, who was really getting the hang of his new CZ. Poor Bryan Goss was left in the paddock when the race started, fixing a puncture he had picked up in the earlier Invitation race, won by Smith, and it was Bickers and Horsfield who raced away into the lead.

The leading pair traded places throughout the 10-lap race, much to the delight of the crowd and, I'm sure, the armchair viewers too, with neither rider ever establishing a clear advantage. At the flag, it was Horsfield who pulled off a narrow victory ahead of Bickers,

Chris Horsfield and Dave Bickers raced like this throughout the 250 Trophy race. However, body language suggests that Bickers had to work harder to maintain the pace than Horsfield (MC)

Two masters at work, as Malcolm Carling, behind the camera, catches Jeff Smith in full flow as he races to a hat-trick of wins in Norfolk

followed, by the now customary pack of Greeves riders led by Freddie Mayes ahead of Alan Clough, Malcolm Davis and Roger Snoad.

Mayes, who has always been a very modest man, feels his performance that day was overlooked.

> I remember the race at Lyng very clearly. I finished third, but was always within a few feet of the Bickers-Horsfield scrap for the win and I hardly got a mention on TV or the reports in the press.

500 Trophy Race

The 500 Trophy race resulted in a 1-2-3 for the BSA factory, but their riders had to work hard to achieve the result. Like Goss, Horsfield had experienced trouble in the opening Invitation race and he turned out on a borrowed BSA Victor for this race, though unfortunately he was never really on the pace.

Andy Lee on his very rapid Matchless Métisse was first out of the gate and led the race for the opening three laps, until Jeff Smith swept past and set about building a comfortable lead. But teammates Vic Eastwood and Arthur Lampkin were on the march and had other ideas. Eastwood was really in the groove and was closing Smith down, though the more experienced man still had a little in reserve and held on to take the win.

Lampkin had also got past Lee, but had not managed to shrug him off and the privateer made a bold attempt to pass Lampkin on the last lap, but ultimately had to settle for 4th place. Behind Lee came two more full-500s, in the hands of Dave Nicoll and Brian Nadin on his Triumph Métisse.

Supporting Races

The TV Invitation saw Smith complete his hat-trick in the style that TV motocross fans had become accustomed to. Eastwood led from the start, with Smith stationed some 25 yards behind, but tracking Vic's every move. Behind them Horsfield, on his 250 CZ, was enjoying a tussle with his ex-teammate, Nicoll, and Goss. Smith bided his time until, with a lap and a half to go, he made his move, passing Eastwood and easing clear for the win, with Horsfield, Nicoll, Goss and Nadin completing the top six.

So, with two rounds down, the 250 series was nicely balanced, with Bickers and Clough joint leaders, three points ahead of Mayes, with Horsfield looking a real threat in 4th place. In contrast, Smith already seemed to have a grip on the 500 series, with a maximum score of 16 points, 8 points clear of teammate Eastwood, with Lee 3rd on 7 points.

Grandstand Trophy Race Results

250 Trophy
1 C Horsfield (CZ)
2 D Bickers (Greeves)
3 F Mayes (Greeves)
4 A Clough (Greeves)
5 M Davis (Greeves)
6 R Snoad (Greeves)

500 Trophy
1 J Smith (440 BSA)
2 V Eastwood (440 BSA)
3 A J Lampkin (440 BSA)
4 A Lee (500 Matchless Métisse)
5 D Nicoll (500 Matchless)
6 B Nadin (500 Triumph Métisse)

Freddie Mayes kept the leading pair in sight throughout the 250 Trophy race, but simply could not close the gap (MC)

Vic Eastwood was really on the pace at Cadders Hill, taking 2nd in both the 500 Trophy race and the TV Invitation (MC)

Andy Lee has a clear lead as the field drops down the steep hill at the back of the circuit in the 500 Trophy race. Lee went on to finish 4th on his Matchless Métisse (MC)

Round 3
Belmont, Durham, December 18, 1965

The last BBC Grandstand meeting of 1965 took place at Belmont, just outside Durham, the furthest north the series had been at that time. The muddy going on the day failed to dampen the spirits of the riders and once again the viewers at home - curled up in front of a warm fire if they had any sense - would have found the racing very entertaining.

Indeed, they would have enjoyed more, had the BBC not decided to cut the Invitation races in order to accommodate the splash down of Gemini VII, which was televised live. I guess the crew were happy to return to earth, as having made 206 orbits in 14 days, the heads of astronauts Lovell and Borman must have been reeling.

250 Trophy Race

The 250 Trophy race had drama before it even started, as Dave Bickers raced against time to fit new piston rings to his Greeves. He made it with seconds to spare and took his place on the line just as the starter let the race go. But it was Horsfield, who had just returned from a 2,300 mile flying visit to the CZ factory, who got the jump on the others. Bickers slotted into 2nd place ahead of Goss, who was enjoying his first televised ride since returning to the fold at Greeves, and when the man from Suffolk took an uncharacteristic tumble, Goss was through in a flash.

Goss was really flying now, but he could make little impression on Horsfield, who was cruising to victory. Bickers was secure in 3rd place after Freddie Mayes had also succumbed

New Greeves factory recruit, John Done, grits his teeth as he races on to finish 5th in the 250 Trophy race (MC)

Jumping for joy; Chris Horsfield on the 250 twin-port CZ. The man from Hampton Lucy dominated the 250 Trophy race, leading from start to finish (MC)

TV Drama! Even double world champions make mistakes; Jeff Smith has stalled the factory BSA in the 500 Trophy race (MC)

to the conditions whilst challenging him, and Jeff Smith, still riding a factory 250, took 4th ahead of John Done, now on a factory Greeves, and Mayes who had remounted to finish 6th.

500 Trophy Race

Jeff Smith took his hat-trick of 500 Trophy race wins at Belmont, though once again he was made to work hard for his win. It was Horsfield on the CZ who got the start again and Smith, very uncharacteristically, stalled the 440 BSA whilst disputing the lead. This appeared to have gifted the race to the Stratford rider, who eased away from the field and built a good lead.

Behind Horsfield, Smith had a tussle on his hands with Andy Lee, who was really enjoying his first TV appearance on the Rickman brothers' ESO Métisse, and they were followed by Mick Andrews on the factory Matchless and Alan Lampkin, who was starting to find some form on his factory BSA. But then Horsfield took another tumble and slipped back to 6th spot.

From there on Smith managed to maintain a small lead, taking the win from Lee, with Dave Bickers storming through the field from nowhere to take 3rd on his 360 Greeves. Horsfield also fought back, ousting Lampkin and Andrews, who finished in that order to complete the top six.

Chris Carter, writing in the *MCN*, December 22nd, 1965, was full of praise for the performances of Horsfield:

Horsfield and his CZ are the biggest shake-up British Scrambling has had in months. Three rounds have gone in the 250cc Grandstand Trophy chase and reigning champion Dave

Bickers is still without a win. And though he leads at the moment only a major disaster looks as if it could stop Chris taking his crown. And if Horsfield can repeat Saturday's performance, he's going to worry Jeff Smith in the big class, too.

Carter had boldly made his predictions, but would they come true?

Grandstand Trophy Race Results

250 Trophy
1 C Horsfield (CZ)
2 B Goss (Greeves)
3 D Bickers (Greeves)
4 J Smith (BSA)
5 J Done (Greeves)
6 F Mayes (Greeves)

500 Trophy
1 J Smith (440 BSA)
2 A Lee (500 ESO Métisse)
3 D Bickers (360 Greeves)
4 C Horsfield (360 CZ)
5 A R C Lampkin (440 BSA)
6 M Andrews (500 Matchless)

On the 22nd December, 1965, Transport Minister, Tom Fraser, introduced a 70 mph speed limit, following a series of motorway pile-ups in foggy conditions during the autumn months. Originally seen as a temporary measure, it became permanent when Barbara Castle succeeded Fraser in 1967.

At Belmont, Andy Lee had his first outing on the very potent ESO Métisse. It proved to be a successful venture, Lee finishing as runner-up to Jeff Smith in the 500 Trophy race (MC)

Bryan Goss, now back on a Greeves, tried all he knew but was unable to reel in the flying Horsfield (MC)

Round 4

Caerleon, Monmouthshire, January 1, 1965

This should have been a good day for Alan Clough, as it marked his 27th birthday, but having driven some 180 miles from his home in Cheshire, no doubt dutifully keeping to the new speed restrictions, Alan had very little to celebrate out on the race track, as Lady Luck turned her back on the birthday boy.

Torrential overnight rain had left the South Wales track waterlogged and though the racing may have 'entertained' some of those who tuned in to watch, for many this was an advertisement for scrambling at its very worst.

So bad were conditions, that the 6th placed rider in the 500 Trophy race didn't even reach half race distance. Chris Carter's *MCN* report carried the headline: *The show must go on: It could only happen in scrambling* - a fitting reminder of just why the sport had proved so valuable to the BBC.

250 Trophy Race

The 250 Trophy race saw Chris Horsfield notch a hat-trick of race wins in the series. He took the lead on the first lap and was never headed, ploughing through the mud on the CZ and making it all look relatively easy. In his wake, came Dave Bickers, Clough, Malcolm Davis, now on a Bultaco, Randy Owen, on a private CZ, and Jeff Smith.

But Bryan Goss was already struggling after taking several runs at the first hill, and Clough's luck would run out mid-race when, having lost both his seat and his exhaust pipe, the engine seized on the factory Greeves. At the flag, only Horsfield, Bickers and Owen completed the full race distance. Billy Jackson came through to snatch 4th spot from Smith, with Colin Harrison on a Dot in 6th but three laps adrift!

Conditions were far from ideal in South Wales on New Year's Day, 1966. Murray Walker about to conduct an interview from the middle of a very large puddle in front of the Newport and Gwent Club's courtesy caravan! (MC)

The start of the 250 Trophy race with Chris Horsfield shutting out Dave Bickers (to the left of Horsfield). Also visible are Roger Snoad, who has made a great start, and birthday boy Alan Clough, on the extreme right (MC)

Below left, Randy Owen, from Hereford, was one of the first privateers to race a CZ. At Caerleon, he finished an excellent 3rd in the 250 Trophy race. (MC)

Below right, farmer's son Jim Aim, on the Tom Kirby Matchless, ploughs through the Caerleon mud on his way to a well-earned 4th place in the 500 Trophy race (MC)

500 Trophy Race

If the 250 race had been bad, the 500 Trophy race was dire. Vic Eastwood led the race for the opening five laps, but then fell, surrendering the lead to Smith and slipping rapidly down the field. Horsfield tried his best to stick with Smith, but after getting filled in with mud, he lost vital time cleaning his eyes so that he could continue. From there on it was simply a matter of how many riders would manage to get their bikes to the finish.

Whilst most competitors were cursing the conditions in South Wales, Chris Horsfield seemed to be positively enjoying himself in the 250 Trophy race (MC)

At the flag Smith won from Horsfield, with Andy Lee on the ESO Métisse 3rd, a lap down. Jim Aim on his Kirby Métisse was 4th, Tom Leadbitter from Rugeley, Staffordshire, was 5th on a Triumph Métisse and Brian Walker on a 440 BSA finished 6th, though he had only completed four laps of the nine-lap race!

Supporting Races

Horsfield, the man of the hour, won the First Invitation, catching and passing Alan Lampkin on the last lap. Lampkin, in his attempts to regain the lead, then slid off, but next man up was brother Arthur, who chaperoned him over the line for a fully deserved 2nd place. Despite being in Arthur's shadow for so many years, Alan Lampkin has nothing but praise for his big brother.

He gave us, (Alan and Martin), so much to aim for and he was the best brother you could have. He took us everywhere and he'd always look out for us.

The Second Invitation saw Arthur do the winning himself. Panic reigned when the starters let the race go with only half the riders lined up, Horsfield being one of the victims. Lampkin, taking full advantage of the situation, led a very processional race from start to finish, though he had to have his wits about him on the last lap, as teammate Eastwood was closing in fast. Smith unexpectedly stalled his BSA on the last lap, thereby gifting 3rd spot to Aim.

Grandstand Trophy Race Results

250 Trophy
1 C Horsfield (CZ)
2 D Bickers (Greeves)
3 R Owen (CZ)
4 W Jackson (Cotton)
5 J Smith (BSA)
6 C Harrison (Dot)

500 Trophy
1 J Smith (440 BSA)
2 C Horsfield (360 CZ)
3 A Lee (500 ESO Métisse)
4 J Aim (500 Kirby Métisse)
5 T Leadbitter (500 Triumph Métisse)
6 B Walker (440 BSA)

So, at the mid-point of the series, Chris Horsfield had edged ahead of Dave Bickers, who in sharp contrast to Horsfield had yet to win a 250 Trophy race in this series. Meanwhile, Jeff Smith was building a massive lead, with privateer Andy Lee surprisingly leading the challenge three points ahead of Horsfield.

Lee remembers the press suggesting that he should continue to ride in the New Year, as with a good run of results he could take the trophy, but he had another agenda altogether:

> I did an awful lot of the BBC meetings, but I never really took it that seriously, even when I was going well. I told them I had better things to be doing, and I did. I went away and built up my new bike for the season and got ready to go away (to France) in March.

Grandstand Trophy Positions After 4 Rounds

250 Trophy

1	C Horsfield	0 8 8 8	24 pts
2	D Bickers	6 6 5 6	23 pts
3	A Clough	8 4 0 0	12 pts
4	F Mayes	4 5 2 0	11 pts
5	J Smith	0 0 4 3	7 pts
6=	B Goss	0 0 6 0	6 pts
	M Davis	3 3 0 0	6 pts

500 Trophy

1	J Smith	8 8 8 8	32 pts
2	A Lee	3 4 6 5	18 pts
3	C Horsfield	6 0 3 6	15 pts
4	V Eastwood	2 6 4 0	12 pts
5=	D Bickers	0 0 5 0	5 pts
	A Clough	5 0 0 0	5 pts
	A J Lampkin	0 5 0 0	5 pts

What Chris Carter had not been privy to, or more likely had not been able to share with the *MCN*'s readership when he made his predictions for the Grandstand Trophy series, was that Bickers' days with Greeves were rapidly drawing to an end. From the humble beginning in 1957, when the management of the Thundersley, Essex, company had provided him with a complete

Dave Bickers on his way to his last GP win on a Greeves at Glastonbury Tor, in July 1965. However, by this time the writing was already on the wall for the Essex factory, as this was their last GP win and within six months Bickers would quit to race for CZ (CB)

rolling chassis in which to put the Villiers engine from his 197 Dot, through the glory days of the double European championship, Bickers' name had become synonymous with that of Greeves.

The darkest days for Bickers had been during the world championship campaign of 1963 accentuated by the glorious run of form he had on his privately owned Husqvarna. Bickers had dominated the lightweight racing scene in Britain for many years and as Greeves didn't have a large capacity bike of their own, they couldn't prevent him racing larger capacity bikes when the fancy took him. In 1962 he rode a factory Matchless in a handful of events, including the 500 GP at Hawkstone Park where he finished 5th overall, had a couple of rides on the 351 Cotton Pacemaker over the winter of 1963-64 and put a 360 CZ to very good use during the latter part of 1965. But then the Greeves factory started developing a 360 of its own, and the CZ had to be returned.

Bickers had ridden the Challenger in the 1965 250 GPs, but despite winning in Spain, Belgium and the home GP at Glastonbury, which proved to be Greeves' last GP success, he found the bike to be largely unreliable. It had also proved to be no match for the CZ that Chris Horsfield was campaigning in the Grandstand Trophy.

So it was that as the New Year began, and after much soul-searching, following three straight defeats at the hands of Horsfield on the factory CZ, Dave Bickers made the difficult decision to move on, thus ending one of the most successful associations ever in British motocross. His last race on a Greeves came a day after the Caerleon TV meeting, at the North v South Scramble at Brands Hatch on Sunday 2nd January, 1966, where the only riders to beat him were Jeff Smith and Horsfield for the Northern team.

A week later the BBC staged another International meeting between Britain and Belgium at Clifton, which marked Bickers' first competitive ride on a 250 CZ (see p296).

There was also bad news for lovers of Pirate Radio, as on Thursday 20th January, Radio Caroline's pirate radio ship the *Mi Amigo* ran aground on Frinton beach, Essex, during a heavy storm. As a result, the station, admired by many of the riders, including Bickers, who spent endless hours travelling was off the air for ten days. Legend has it that the last record broadcast that night was Barry McGuire singing *Eve of Destruction*!

Round 5

Nantwich, Cheshire, January 22, 1966

The fifth round at Hatherton Hall, Nantwich, was eagerly awaited by the estimated eight million viewers tuning in at home, desperate to see Dave Bickers take on Chris Horsfield with a CZ of his own. Horsfield had finally overhauled Bickers to take the lead in the series at the previous round at Caerleon, but this lead proved to be very short lived.

Further spice was added when the BBC cameras captured Bryan Goss re-signing to Greeves, with competition manager Bill Brooker in attendance and journalist Peter Arnold providing the commentary for the *Grandstand* viewers. Goss had returned to Greeves two rounds earlier, at Belmont, but he only signed the contract at Nantwich, which coincidentally, or not, marked Dave Bickers' first official ride on the CZ. The West Country ace was out of luck at Belmont, however, with 5th place in the First Invitation on the ex-Bickers 250 his best result.

But on the day, it was two still relatively unknown riders, Alan Lampkin and Arthur Browning, who blew up a storm, causing some of the biggest upsets since the series started back in October 1963. There was also more than a splash of drama, befitting of a BBC production, and never more evident than in the 250 Trophy race.

250 Trophy Race

Tension was high at the start and the starter, under direction from the BBC, let the line go as Chris Horsfield raced up to take his place at the gate. With hindsight it is easy to say that Horsfield panicked, but in his haste to make up lost ground, he rounded the second corner to find an abandoned bike in his path. Unable to stop, he rammed the prone bike, wrecking his front wheel in the process, and his race was run.

Bickers knew that a top-six finish would see him regain the lead, but he was never one to settle for anything less than his best effort and he set off in pursuit of young Arthur Browning, whose confidence was sky high after winning an Invitation race. Browning looked to be on his way to a comfortable maiden victory in a Grandstand Trophy race, but nothing is ever comfortable when you have Dave Bickers giving chase, especially on his TV debut on a CZ.

Bickers, who had moved up to 2nd place after Freddie Mayes had spun his Greeves, relentlessly closed in on the young Brummie lad and with two laps to go he slipped past and into the lead. However, Browning wasn't done just yet and the pair traded places on the last lap, with Bickers eventually taking the flag just a few yards ahead of his youthful challenger. Behind them Jeff Smith took 3rd ahead of Alan Clough, Malcolm Davis, scoring his first points on a Bultaco, and Mayes.

Smith rode a factory 250 at Nantwich, but the Cheney BSA eventually saw the light of day at this meeting, with Jerry Scott in the saddle. It would seem that Scott had little success at this juncture, but he would fare better at the seventh round at Leighton, when he rode Eric Cheney's latest masterpiece into the points.

A week after the Nantwich meeting, Bob Light wrote a profile of Browning for the *MCN*, titled the *Red-haired rocket*, in which Browning recalled his recent duel with Dave Bickers.

In front of the TV cameras, Bryan Goss re-signs to Greeves. He is flanked by journalist Peter Arnold (left) and Greeves' Competition Manager Bill Brooker (MC)

Arthur Browning came of age at Nantwich, beating Dave Bickers, who was having his first competitive race on a 250 CZ, into 2nd place in the opening Invitation race and finishing as runner-up to the master in the 250 Trophy race (MC)

Dave Bickers made a winning debut on the 250 CZ at Nantwich (MC)

It worried me blooming stiff, having him after me, I kept wondering when and where he would pass me and all this looking behind cost valuable time. But I reckoned if I had beaten Dave once already (he took the Second Invitation race - see below), then I stood a good chance this time.

500 Trophy Race

The 250 race may have been the more exciting spectacle, but it was the 500 Trophy race that served up the major surprise of the day. Going into this race, Jeff Smith had been invincible, racking up four straight wins, but he would leave Hatherton Hall as second best, after 21 year-old Alan Lampkin took an emphatic win. Lampkin the Younger, who was also a top-flight trials rider and would go on to win the Scott Trial and the Scottish Six-Day Trial the same year, revelled in the sticky conditions, keeping his feet firmly on the foot pegs and traversing the icy sections of the circuit with great aplomb.

First to show, however, was Jack Matthews, riding a 360 Lindstrom, though within a lap he had fallen, allowing BSA's John Banks to take up the running. Banks, who had not been having the best of times in this Grandstand series was pushing a little too hard and he was next to take a tumble. The next man to the fore stayed there though, as Lampkin hit the front and just cruised round for his first Grandstand Trophy win, followed home by Smith, while behind them chaos reigned.

Alan Lampkin remembers his moment of TV glory very well:

You had to be a trials rider really, as it was sheet ice everywhere, but it was one of those days when everything just clicked. I passed Jeff going up the start-finish straight and he looked a bit surprised as I went past!

Alan Clough eventually finished 3rd on his 360 Greeves, whilst BSA teamsters, Banks and Vic Eastwood, had more falls between them than they would care to remember. Poor Banks fell again, just a few hundred yards from the finishing line, whilst lying 4th, and kissed goodbye to the points as Arthur Lampkin, Matthews and Roy Peplow on his factory Triumph all swept past.

With the TV cameraman following Jeff Smith's progress, local ace Alan Clough races on to 3rd place in the 500 Trophy race on the factory 360 Greeves (MC)

Alan Lampkin emulated his brother, Arthur, at Hatherton Hall, passing teammate Jeff Smith before going on to win the 500 Trophy race (MC)

John Lewis on the factory Matchless goes handlebar to handlebar with Jack Matthews on his 360 Lindstrom (MC)

Supporting Races

Worthy of note was Browning's win in the Second Invitation race. The young Brummie lad had earned himself a reputation as being a demon in the muddy conditions that so often typified the TV scrambles, and at Nantwich, he left a quality field for dead, stretching away from Bickers to win by some 23 seconds.

It should also be noted that the first three riders home in this race were all on two-fifties, as Pat Lamper, in his first meeting on a West German Maico, took 3rd, ahead of Horsfield on his 360 CZ, Alan Lampkin and Matthews.

Grandstand Trophy Race Results

250 Trophy
1 D Bickers (CZ)
2 A Browning (Greeves)
3 J Smith (BSA)
4 A Clough (Greeves)
5 M Davis (Bultaco)
6 F Mayes (Greeves)

500 Trophy
1 A R C Lampkin (440 BSA)
2 J Smith (440 BSA)
3 A Clough (360 Greeves)
4 A J Lampkin (440 BSA)
5 J Matthews (360 Lindstrom)
6 R Peplow (500 Triumph)

Round 6
Biggin Hill, Kent, February 12th 1966

Jewels Hill Wood is situated less than a mile from Biggin Hill Airport, famous for its role in the Battle of Britain when it played home to a host of Spitfire and Hurricane squadrons that took to the air to defend London and the South East from the continuous bombing raids of the Luftwaffe.

On this occasion, flying over the Kent countryside was limited due to the incredibly muddy conditions that greeted riders for the sixth round of the Grandstand series. Indeed, the conditions were so bad that plans to televise a sidecar race had to be abandoned after a heat ground to a halt after just one lap. Jeff Smith may well have been picked up on the Biggin Hill radar though, as he flew to three race victories, one of which clinched his second 500 Grandstand Trophy with two rounds still to play for.

Supporting Race

Smith's first win came in the First Invitation race, when he quickly worked his way to the front on the opening lap chased by top all-rounder John Giles, who was campaigning a BSA Victor at the time. Poor Giles came an almighty purler down in the woods, which sent the bike cartwheeling down the track and the hapless rider high into the air.

Giles (who raced on into his eighties) suffered fused vertebrae, an injury which has affected him to this day and has served as a constant reminder of the fall.

It was getting muddier and muddier and I kept moving over onto drier lines all the time, but unbeknown to me, they'd dug a tree stump out in the hedgerow. So I was going right down the edge of the track on full chat in top gear and it just buried its nose in this hole, and it went over and over and threw me up about fifteen feet in the air.

When the bike landed the frame broke, taking the forks with it, and it hit me right in the middle of my back. I lay there for what seemed like ages and the medical people never got to me. I remember crawling up through the woods back to my car and I sat there and all I could think of was getting home. So that's what I did and nobody knew where I was.

The man who took up the challenge of catching Smith was Giles' close friend, Vic Eastwood, who raced through the field and was within striking distance of Smith at the flag, after the elder statesman of the BSA team picked up a rear wheel puncture.

The lot of a BBC cameraman was a solitary one and they were often totally exposed to the elements (BH)

Bryan Goss had a profitable day out in the Kent countryside, winning the 250 Trophy race and finishing 2nd to Jeff Smith in the 500 Trophy race (BH)

250 Trophy Race

Smith's luck deserted him in the 250 Trophy race, however, when the little Beezer stopped after just two laps, a missing plug washer being identified as the cause. Dave Bickers wasn't having much luck either, sliding off no less than three times in the treacherous conditions.

At the head of the race, Arthur Browning was following up on his brilliant performance at Nantwich by blazing the trail ahead of Goss and Clough. But his more experienced teammates stuck to their task and, by the fourth lap, they had both slipped past the junior member of the Greeves squad. However, Clough fell heavily exiting the bombhole and Browning, with Horsfield on his tail, took full advantage.

Horsfield who had been rapidly picking off riders got the better of Browning, but could make no impression on Goss, who was well ahead at the flag to take his first win of this campaign, though according to *MCN* reporter, Lionel Barlow, he still found time to complain about the Greeves' handlebars, which were not to his liking!

500 Trophy Race

Vic Eastwood, racing just 10 miles from his home in Otford, Kent, took control of the 500 Trophy race and stayed out front for seven laps till fate dealt him a cruel blow. In the opening laps it looked like being a three-way battle, as Eastwood led Smith and Horsfield, but Horsfield was the first to go, dropping the big CZ in the bombhole and damaging the forks and the handlebars.

Eastwood's race also came to an abrupt end when the BSA's chain broke, allowing Smith to inherit a huge lead over Goss, who was having his best ride to date on the 360 Greeves. Smith went on to win comfortably from Goss and clinch his second 500

Before his big spill, John Giles, on the 440 BSA the factory had loaned him, leads Dave Nicoll (BH)

Kent's finest; Vic Eastwood leads the charge at Jewels Hill in the 500 Trophy race. In attendance are Chris Horsfield (24), John Banks (35), Jeff Smith (1) with Alan Lampkin riding in tandem, Bryan Goss (32) and Dave Nicoll (10). Smith went on to win and regained the Grandstand Trophy (BH)

Grandstand Trophy with an unassailable lead of 28 points over Andy Lee, who didn't compete in this meeting. John Banks, having his best result in a disappointing campaign, took 3rd ahead of Alan Lampkin, who moved up to 4th in the points standing, Dave Nicoll and Clough completed the top six.

Supporting Race

The best race of the day was the last - the Second Invitation - which saw Eastwood, looking for some reward for his day's efforts, involved in a dog-fight with Jeff Smith throughout. Behind them Dave Bickers came storming through the field to renew old rivalries with Arthur Lampkin, who had been having a difficult day. With three laps to go, Bickers caught the Yorkshireman, but Lampkin's 440 just had the advantage over Bickers' 250 CZ in the glutinous mud. At the flag, Smith pipped Eastwood, Lampkin edged out Bickers, for yet another BSA 1-2-3 and Horsfield held off Browning.

With the 440 BSA's mudguard removed, John Banks scored his best result of the series with 3rd place in the 500 Trophy race (BH)

Grandstand Trophy Race Results

250 Trophy
1 B Goss (Greeves)
2 C Horsfield (CZ)
3 A Browning (Greeves)
4 A Clough (Greeves)
5 D Bickers (CZ)
6 W Jackson (Cotton)

500 Trophy
1 J Smith (440 BSA)
2 B Goss (360 Greeves)
3 J Banks (440 BSA)
4 A R C Lampkin (440 BSA)
5 D Nicoll (500 Matchless)
6 A Clough (360 Greeves)

A week later, the BBC crew headed north to Yorkshire for another match race, this time between Britain and Czechoslovakia, from Hutton Conyers, near Ripon (see p296).

Round 7
Frome, Somerset, March 5, 1966

In a week that saw the Beatles' John Lennon controversially proclaim, 'We're more popular than Jesus now', the Grandstand Trophy series, which was proving pretty popular itself, returned to the Frome Club's Asham Woods circuit where, much to the delight of the partisan crowd, local favourites Bryan Goss and Jerry Scott did the winning.

250 Trophy Race

First race of the day was the 250 Trophy race, which saw Malcolm Davis on the Bultaco Métisse take up the running, though he was soon ousted by the Greeves pair of Freddie Mayes and Bryan Goss. As always, Mayes was riding in his very neat and tidy style, but Goss was eager to press on and with three laps completed the man from Yetminster hit the front and was never headed.

Dave Bickers, who had been experiencing both highs and lows since moving onto CZ, lost his chain whilst well placed, and up to 3rd stormed Chris Horsfield, followed by Davis and Alan Clough, with Jerry Scott having a rare outing on Eric Cheney's 250 BSA in 6th place.

Horsfield, who was poised to regain the lead in the series at Bickers' expense, was left fuming when his CZ coasted to a stop. In the meantime, Scott had fought past Davis and caught and passed Clough on the last lap. So the finishing order was Goss, from Mayes, with Scott an excellent 3rd ahead of Clough, Davis and Jeff Smith, who completed the top six.

Malcolm Davis gets the Bultaco Métisse out front in the 250 Trophy race, with Freddie Mayes (right) and Chris Horsfield in close company (CB)

500 Trophy Race

The 500 Trophy race also provided plenty of thrills and spills. Blasting off the line, Rob Jordan on his very potent Triumph Wasp led the race to the first corner, but it was Scott on his equally rapid Cheney Gold Star who powered around the outside to take the lead, closely followed by Derek Rickman. BSA factory runner, John Banks, was left on the startline to rue his luck, with a length of start rope wound into his rear wheel and at the end of the first lap Chris Horsfield was also out, a victim of the same malaise.

Scott was motoring at the front, but lap by lap, Rickman was closing in on him. By mid-race distance, Rickman had hit the front, but his lead was short lived. The Rickman's machines were always immaculately prepared, but on this occasion, Derek had forgotten to tighten the end nut on the swinging arm and as a result the chain jumped its sprockets and the elder Rickman's race was run. The BSAs of Vic Eastwood and Arthur Lampkin then took up the chase, followed by Alan Clough and Bryan Goss on their 360 Greeves.

A big reshuffle then occurred, when Lampkin overshot a bend. Clough seized the initiative and Smith followed him through, demoting Eastwood and Lampkin to 4th and 5th places, whilst Don Rickman came through to fill 6th spot. And that's how it stayed to the flag, with Jerry Scott scoring his second Grandstand Trophy win on his first outing of the series.

Bryan Goss completed back-to-back wins in the 250 Trophy series at Asham Woods (CB)

Dave Bickers was out of luck at this round, but this photo perfectly illustrates a point he once made to me. 'The CZ was superb, even in the mud. If there were ruts, it was like going across on skis – you'd just slide through on the exhausts. The twin-port was not a disadvantage at all!' (GF)

Supporting Races

For a while, it looked like Scott, who was having a brilliant day, might add a second race win in the TV Invitation race. After another electric start, he led from Smith and Derek Rickman for three laps, but then Smith was through, taking advantage of a momentary lapse of concentration on the part of the man from Poole. The man on the move, though, was Dave Bickers on his 250 CZ who had been racing through the pack, towing Goss and Banks along with him. As Rickman lost his chain for a second time, Bickers took second behind Smith, and Scott held off the challenge from Goss to claim third place.

Derek Rickman was poised for his first Grandstand victory until a very rare oversight, in terms of maintenance, sidelined him (CB)

Grandstand Trophy Race Results

250 Trophy
1 B Goss (Greeves)
2 F Mayes (Greeves)
3 J Scott (Cheney BSA)
4 A Clough (Greeves)
5 M Davis (Bultaco Métisse)
6 J Smith (BSA)

500 Trophy
1 J Scott (500 Cheney BSA)
2 A Clough (360 Greeves)
3 J Smith (440 BSA)
4 V Eastwood (440 BSA)
5 A J Lampkin (440 BSA)
6 D J Rickman (500 Triumph Métisse)

Jerry Scott, who enjoyed a very successful day's racing, scored a popular victory at Leighton, his second in the Grandstand series (CB)

Below, continuing a fine run of form on the 360 Greeves, Alan Clough finished strongly to claim the runner-up spot in the 500 Trophy race (CB)

Two days before the Leighton round, the BBC had announced their plans to broadcast in colour for the first time. The chosen event was to be the Wimbledon Tennis fortnight, though the first broadcast was only on 1st July 1967 on BBC2 and it would be 15th November 1969, before BBC1 first aired in colour in company with ITV. It's interesting to note that at that time a Colour TV set cost about £250, quite expensive when you consider that you could buy a 175cc BSA Bantam Supreme commuter bike for £142, or the latest offering from Ford, the Mark 2 Cortina, for £750.

Round 8

Brill, Buckinghamshire, March 12, 1966

With Britain on the verge of a general election and the country buzzing in anticipation of the World Cup, which was just four months away, the third Grandstand Trophy reached its conclusion at Brill, just 50 miles away from Television Centre at the White City. And for the first time in its brief history, the winner of one of the Grandstand trophies would be decided by the final day's racing.

250 Trophy Race

Dave Bickers and Chris Horsfield had been the two outstanding riders in the 250 Grandstand Trophy. As always, much had been expected of Bickers, but he had struggled to match Horsfield, whose form on the 250 CZ was exceptional. The final round of the series saw Bickers go to the line with a four-point lead over the pretender to his title.

For the Suffolk man the task was simple: finish ahead of Horsfield and he would complete a hat-trick of Grandstand Trophy wins. Things were more complicated for the Stratford rider; he had to hope for a win, with Bickers finishing outside the first three. The odds were stacked against Horsfield, but Bickers had only scored three points in the

Chris Horsfield and Dave Bickers were never more than a couple of bike lengths apart throughout the dramatic, final 250 Trophy race (BH)

Back in the paddock, MCN reporter, Peter Howdle, shares a joke with Bryan Goss (MC)

previous two rounds and Greeves' factory runner, Bryan Goss, would go to Brill on a wave of confidence, having won the previous two rounds and looking for a hat-trick. The stage was set for a great finale!

Tension was high at the start of the 250 Trophy race and it was the man in form, Goss, who got the best start, but the race was all about the two CZ aces and they soon came to the fore. Once out front, Horsfield and Bickers traded places throughout the race, the irony being that the TV viewers were denied the dramatic finish as the TV transmission failed mid-race! However, spectators at Muswell Hill Farm were treated to a classic scrap between two of the most determined riders who ever raced a motorcycle.

It looked for a while as if Horsfield's race was run after he was hit in the face by a stray stone which temporarily hindered his vision. But he was soon back in the groove and closed Bickers down so quickly that going into the last lap he was putting pressure on the leader. Horsfield told me recently, 'David never came off'. However, he had a moment on the last lap that encouraged Horsfield to believe that he might still scoop the big prize.

On the last lap I knew at the top of the hill he'd got me, but as we went into the final corner he hit a molehill and went sideways and I thought, 'That's it, I've won it' and I shut off and was coasting and he came down, straightened up and rode straight past me! I'll never forget that.

So Bickers won the race, to record a hat-trick of 250 Grandstand Trophy wins, finishing eight points clear of runner-up Horsfield. Goss finished 3rd, leading home the Greeves pack, after Alan Clough 4th, Freddie Mayes 5th and Arthur Browning 6th, had all overhauled the 250 BSAs of Jeff Smith and Arthur Lampkin.

Having caught his breath, Murray Walker is eager to hear what the three-time Grandstand Trophy winner, Dave Bickers, has to say (MC)

500 Trophy Race

The 500 Trophy race saw Smith turn the tables on Clough, but only after a race-long duel was resolved on the last lap. BSA's Smith and Lampkin led for a lap, but then Clough, on the new single carburettor 360, swooped past both of them. Horsfield, having switched to his 360 CZ, moved up through the field and eventually ousted Lampkin for 3rd place, a position he held to the flag, where Smith edged out Clough for his sixth win of the series and Derek Rickman, in a late charge, pipped John Banks to decide 5th and 6th places.

Supporting Races

The organising Mid-Bucks MCC put on a full programme on the day, including televised invitation and sidecar races. Bryan Goss and Jerry Scott, the stars of the previous round at Leighton, renewed their rivalry in the invitation, after Goss had fitted new clutch plates to his two-fifty. It did the trick and Goss rode away from the pack to record another brilliant televised win. Scott, who was battling a dose of flu, as well as the rest of the field, held off Jeff Smith to claim 2nd spot, though it was a close run affair.

The Sidecar boys, taking advantage of some all too infrequent TV coverage, raced for seven laps and it was Dennis 'Wacker' Westwood who led for the first five, but he couldn't hold off Dave Treleaven or John Turner, who brushed him aside in the final laps. At the flag, Treleaven took the win from Turner, Westwood, veteran Bill Turner, Bob Norman and Bob Sadler. However, despite this success, this would be the last time that sidecars would appear in the Grandstand Trophy meetings. (*For more on the sidecar races turn to p298.*)

Alan Clough was really coming good on the 'big' Greeves by the end of the series. Here he leads eventual 500 Trophy race winner, Jeff Smith (BH)

Grandstand Trophy Race Results

250 Trophy
1 D Bickers (CZ)
2 C Horsfield (CZ)
3 B Goss (Greeves)
4 A Clough (Greeves)
5 F Mayes (Greeves)
6 A Browning (Greeves)

500 Trophy
1 J Smith (440 BSA)
2 A Clough (360 Greeves)
3 C Horsfield (360 CZ)
4 A J Lampkin (440 BSA)
5 D E Rickman (500 Matchless Métisse)
6 J Banks (440 BSA)

1965/66 Grandstand Trophy Series
Final Standings

250 Trophy:

1	D Bickers	6 6 5 6 8 3 0 8	42pts
2	C Horsfield	0 8 8 8 0 6 0 6	36pts
3	A Clough	8 4 0 0 4 4 4 4	28pts
4	B Goss	0 0 6 0 0 8 8 5	27pts
5	F Mayes	4 5 2 0 2 0 6 3	22pts
6	A Browning	5 0 0 0 6 5 0 2	18pts

500 Trophy:

1	J Smith	8 8 8 8 6 8 5 8	59pts
2	A Clough	5 0 0 0 5 2 6 6	24pts
3	C Horsfield	6 0 3 6 0 0 0 5	20pts
4	A Lee	3 4 6 5 0 0 0 0	18pts
5=	A J Lampkin	0 5 0 0 4 0 3 4	16pts
	V Eastwood	2 6 4 0 0 0 4 0	16pts

Alan Clough looks to be doing a screen test for the role of 'Swarfega Man' as he washes up after a hard day's racing (MC)

Brill race programme

Jerry Scott, 1939 - 1966

The final weekend of July 1966 brought mixed emotions for sports lovers in Britain. Football fans were ecstatic following the England team's thrilling 4-2 victory over the powerful West German team in the World Cup final at Wembley stadium on Saturday 30th, but just a few hours later, scrambles fans who had gathered to watch the North v South meeting at Boltby the following day were devastated by the tragic death of 27 year-old Jerry Scott, who was killed whilst racing for the Southern team. In the days that followed, motocross fans, not only in Britain but also across the whole of Europe, would mourn the passing of a highly talented and very likeable rider.

Scott, who had moved from his native Coventry to Parkstone, near Poole, Dorset, as a boy, had started racing as a young lad on a 150 Francis Barnett and soon caught the eye of former speedway star, 'Pop' Sharp, father of off-road all-rounders, Triss and Bryan. 'Pop' put a 250 Greeves at Jerry's disposal and on the Essex-

Jerry Scott (MC)

built two-stroke he soon graduated to Expert status. Impressed by his form on the Greeves, Cotton then offered him a semi-works ride on a 250. However, that didn't really work out for him and it was whilst racing a Gold Star at Beenham Park in 1963 that he first came to the attention of Eric Cheney.

Eric took him under his wing and first time out on the Cheney-prepared Gold Star, he managed to beat the Rickman brothers. From there on, things just got better and better. He soon established himself as one of the top riders in the Southern Centre, which at the time boasted the likes of the Rickmans, Ivor England and Ken Heanes, amongst others. He also began to make a name for himself nationally and contested the Grandstand Trophy series from day one at Hawkstone Park in October 1963, finishing amongst the points in 5th place.

Brian Martin at BSA soon recognised Jerry's talent and put a factory BSA at his disposal and by March 1964, he was a fully-fledged member of the factory team following John Burton's departure from the Birmingham concern. But despite some success on both the 250 and the 420, ironically, like Burton, he preferred the power of a full-500 and soon returned to the Cheney stable.

A teenaged Scott racing the 'Pop' Sharp 150 Francis Barnett, at Lulworth Castle, Dorset, May 1958 (GF)

Eric knew that Jerry had both the temperament and the talent to be a top rider and set about building his young jockey a thoroughbred machine. Armed with a super potent BSA engine, housed in a beautifully crafted frame weighing just 20lb, Scott headed off to Europe to compete in his first GP, the Austrian round of the 1964 world championship at Sittendorf. The Cheney bikes were always very quick, but Jerry surprised many motocross aficionados, when he led both races at the start and managed to finish 6th in the second leg on his GP debut. Later the same season, in only his second GP, he finished an excellent 4th overall at Ettelbruck, Luxembourg, to score his first world championship points.

Scott continued to improve and 1965 found him winning a Grandstand Trophy race at Bulford Camp, Wiltshire in March (see p125). Some excellent domestic results followed, such as his best ever ACU Star finish at the Cumberland GN meeting in April that year, when he finished third to Bickers on the 360 CZ and Alan Lampkin on a 420 BSA. He also finished as runner-up to Bickers in the main event of the day, the GN race. Then at Hadleigh, Essex, in June, he was in devastating form, winning both legs of the 500 Motocross, and both legs of the Up to 750cc race. Sadly, he could only manage 6th in the ACU Star race, thus missing out on the headlines in the motorcycle press as the winner of that race, Vic Eastwood, took the plaudits. He would go on to finish 4th in the season-long, 500 Star contest, behind Smith, Eastwood and Bickers.

But it was on the continental scene, a scene that Cheney himself knew so well, that he really started to blossom. At the Swiss GP at Wolhen in early April, he again finished 4th overall, but improved to runner-up position to Jeff Smith in the next round at Tarare, France, after finishing second in race one and third in the second outing. At that stage of the championship, with three rounds concluded, Scott was lying third in the overall standing to world champions, Jeff Smith and Sten Lundin. But despite such success, he found it difficult to regularly get entries in the GPs. His season also

Scott flying the big Gold Star BSA to 5th place at the opening round of the Grandstand Trophy series, Hawkstone Park, October 1963 (MC)

included a 6th overall in his home GP at Hawkstone Park in July and he was selected for the 1965 Motocross des Nations, where the British team were triumphant at the Belgian citadel circuit of Namur.

In March 1966, Scott took his second win in the 500 Grandstand Trophy at Leighton, Frome (see p161) and a month later, still on the Cheney, he won four finals at the same venue on Easter Monday, including the Leighton Scramble, with Cheney teammate Keith Hickman providing the stiffest opposition. That week, *MCN* carried a short news item simply titled 'Hoping for a ride' which stated that Scott and Chris Horsfield were to travel out to the first 500 GP of the season in Switzerland, though they were unsure as to whether they would actually get to ride! They did eventually ride, though neither one of them finished a race, so as the saying goes, I guess they 'chalked it up to experience'!

Scott returned to the factory BSA team in late May and had his first competitive ride on a 440 at the Maybug Scramble at Farleigh Castle, which played host to the third round of the new, 500cc British championship. Scott made one of his famous starts, to edge out Eastwood and Bickers at the first corner and as the race settled he was just ahead of Bickers, with Eastwood third. Bickers flew past him over one of the jumps and that was the last any of the following riders saw of him. Scott was struggling with a fault on the BSA's forks and he was passed in turn by teammates Eastwood and Banks, though he did hang on to finish 4th and net three championship points on his return to BSA.

A fortnight later he was really coming to grips with his new 'lightweight' at the West of England MCC's Patchquick Trophy Scramble at Thorns Cross, near Exeter. Dave Bickers on his 360 CZ proved invincible, but Scott was flying on the works bike, leading the first leg for seven laps before Bickers and Bryan Goss on his 250 Husqvarna stormed through. He also led the second leg away from the start and held it for the opening three laps, till Bickers again swept past to take control of the race. Scott rode on strongly

During his first spell on a factory BSA, Scott is pictured at the Kiwi Scramble at Tidworth, Hants, Easter Sunday 1964 (CB)

The bike that Eric built! Master bike creator, Eric Cheney, poses with Scott's machine for the 1965 season in the paddock at the final round of the 1964-65 Grandstand series at Cross-in-Hand, Sussex (MC)

to finish 2nd, comfortably ahead of BSA teammate Vic Eastwood. Indeed on the day he reversed his fortunes at the Maybug, by getting the better of both Eastwood and Banks.

Form such as this augured well for Scott on the BSA, but within three short weeks his life would have ended on that tragic day on the North Yorkshire moors at Boltby.

Chris Horsfield, who was Scott's travelling companion to the GPs, remembers the events of that weekend all too well:

> Jerry and I had been racing abroad and we'd been promised good money to come back and do it. Jerry was going to pick up his new Austin Cambridge diesel and we agreed to meet at my place. A few hours after I got home, we got a phone call to say his car was playing up and that we should go ahead. So, I went up with my father-in-law and Grant (Chris' eldest son) and it was dark when we got up there - I remember, because I couldn't find the paddock. Jerry only arrived after we'd finished practice, he and his father had spent the night in the pub just down the hill from Thirsk and had only got into their room at about six in the morning, so of course they'd overslept. As Jerry hadn't ridden it, I walked round with him and showed him the lines and said 'Watch yourself, because it's a rough course. Just take it easy for a couple of laps'.

The accident occurred on the fifth lap as Jeff Smith, Scott and Horsfield were closing in on the leading group of riders. Scott lost control of the BSA, fell and was hit by Smith who had no chance of avoiding him in the melee.

The race continued as the trackside medics worked on Scott and Smith, who broke a wrist and a collarbone in the accident. However, by the close of the first leg it was all too obvious that something was seriously wrong and an eerie silence befell the race track as Thirsk organiser, Colin Hutchinson, informed the public that Jerry had been fatally injured in the crash and that the decision had been made, by riders and organisers, to cancel the rest of the meeting as a mark of respect.

Anyone who ever saw Jerry Scott race will never forget his dashing style, his strong physique, his wavy fair hair and his cheerful demeanour. He was sorely missed, not least of all by the millions of TV viewers who had watched him take on the mighty BSA and Matchless concerns on his Cheney BSA and tuned in for the beginning of the 1966-67 Grandstand series only to be informed, by Murray Walker, of the sad news of his passing.

Great friends off the track, but rivals on it, Chris Horsfield gets cross-threaded in the ruts and Scott races past on the 250 Cheney BSA. The photo was taken at the Grandstand Trophy meeting at Asham Woods, Leighton in March 1966, where Scott went on to finish 3rd in the 250 race (CB)

1966-67
The Dave Bickers Spectacular!

Dave Bickers, East Meon, 31st December, 1966 (CB)

Setting The Scene

Jeff Smith gamely tried to secure a hat-trick of world titles in 1966, but had to cede to Paul Friedrichs and Rolf Tibblin on their factory CZs as he faded to third overall after a promising start. Dave Bickers raced the 500 GPs for the first time that year, having switched from Greeves to CZ for 1966, and finished 5th in the world championship at his first attempt. Smith would also see his stranglehold on the British championship eventually broken, following six consecutive wins.

Following five 250 championship titles, Bickers won the 500 British championship and came within a whisker of taking the double. With Jeff Smith spending much of the 1966 season sidelined by injury, Bickers dominated the season, winning at Hawkstone Park and Farleigh Castle and finishing 2nd to Smith, at the Cleveland GN, and to Vic Eastwood, the only man who could have beaten him to the title, in the final round at Cadwell Park.

However, Bickers was denied the double when former Greeves teammate Freddie Mayes, who raced consistently well all season, took the title. To do so, he had to survive a scare in the final round, when Bickers was on track to make history for a few laps. Mayes' win brought Greeves' total to six wins out of seven in the 250 championship, since its introduction in 1960.

On The Move

The big moves this season all seemed to involve Greeves. After returning to the fold in December 1965, Bryan Goss left again to start his second spell on a 250 Husqvarna and John Griffths returned to Dot following a largely disappointing spell on the factory Greeves, hindered by injury.

Moving in the opposite direction, following a frustrating summer of 500 GPs on an ageing CZ, was Chris Horsfield, who signed to the Essex factory which was naturally looking to strengthen its squad. Greeves also bolstered their squad by signing Bryan Wade, who had deputised for the injured Goss at the Spanish GP in March, where he finished an excellent 7th overall, a result that impressed Competition Shop manager, Bill Brooker, and helped earn him a full factory ride.

Into The 1966-67 Series

Having captured the 500 British championship in 1966, over the coming winter Dave Bickers would make a bold attempt to win both the 250 and the new 750 Grandstand Trophies for the first time, but could it be done?

This series was marked by the demise of the AMC factory. Since the start of the Grandstand Trophy series the factory James and Matchless machines had been prominent on our TV screens and just two years earlier, Chris Horsfield had won the 500 Trophy. Vic Eastwood had moved on to BSA in 1964 and Horsfield had, of course, secured factory support from CZ, so as the Grandstand series got underway AMC had no serious trophy contenders, with Dave Nicoll now campaigning a private 600 Matchless Métisse that he had built up the previous spring.

With the coming of the big two-stroke machines, not only from overseas but also from home manufacturers, most notably Greeves but also Dot, the BBC followed the lead of the FIM who had introduced the 750 *Coupe d' Europe*. However, whereas the FIM contest was for four-strokes only, the 750 Grandstand Trophy pitted oversized four-strokes against the 360 two-strokes and the full-500 BSAs. However, the days of the big four-stroke motocross bikes were coming to an end, as was Britain's once dominant motorcycle industry which was unable to move with the times.

On Saturday October 15th, a week before the Grandstand Trophy series kicked off, Canada Heights played host to a GB v Sweden International meeting (see p297).

However, all these developments paled into insignificance following the tragic events that beset the small Welsh mining community of Aberfan on the morning of Friday 21st October, 1966. Following several days of intense rain, a landslide hit the small village, when a spoil tip gave way. In the ensuing turmoil, a row of cottages, a farm and the Pantglas Junior School were all destroyed, resulting in the loss of 144 lives, including 116 children who were attending school on the last day before the half-term holiday.

By a strange quirk of fate, the 1966-67 Grandstand series would open the following day, less than 30 miles away at Caerleon, Newport. BBC producer Brian Johnson remembers the day well:

Naturally, because of the gravity of the situation, we lost our Outside Broadcast crew.

Bryan Wade, who would register his first points in the Grandstand Trophy at this meeting, struggles to recall the race, but clearly remembers the mood in the paddock:

There was a great deal about the disaster on the news and it all just seemed too horrible to believe.

At Caerleon, Dave Bickers was presented with his third 250 Grandstand Trophy, for the 1965-66 series. Here he is flanked by Murray Walker and Jeff Smith, who was still on the sick list following his accident at Cadwell Park in October (MC)

Round 1

Caerleon, Monmouthshire, October 22, 1966

A fair deal of mystery surrounds this round. As you've just read, BBC producer Brian Johnson recalls losing his OB Unit on the day, but Gavin Trippe reporting in the MCN referred to the TV races. I think the most likely scenario was that the racing was not televised, but the results still counted towards the series.

First Supporting Race

The first race of the day was a seven-lap 'TV' Invitation and flying away from the start went Dave Nicoll, on his very potent home-brewed 600 Matchless Métisse. Nicoll was more than happy with the BBC's decision to open up the larger capacity Trophy to 750cc. Gavin Trippe's 'Moto Cross Talk' two weeks prior to this event had carried the headline: MONSTER MOTO CROSS FOR TV, and avid big bike devotees, such as Andy Lee, the Rickman brothers and Nicoll, all naturally expressed their delight, with Nicoll telling readers, 'I really reckon my 600. It goes like a bomb and it's terrific in the mud. Let's see how the 360s cope.'

In the Invitation race at Caerleon, Nicoll was keen to prove his point, and there was plenty of mud there, but Vic Eastwood on a 'little' 494 BSA displaced him on the second

Bickers in the groove! The East Anglian ace started the new Grandstand series on a real high and was unstoppable in the 250 Trophy race (MC)

lap and was never headed. Dave Bickers was the leading 360 rider on his CZ and he also had the measure of Nicoll. Alan Lampkin rode through strongly in the closing laps to oust Nicoll from the top three. Behind the first four came two youngsters keen to make an impression: 20 year-old Bryan Wade, the 'Junior' member of the Greeves team on a 250, who had made the long trip down from Barnard Castle, and Terry Challinor from Pontesbury, near Shrewsbury, on a 250 Husqvarna.

250 Trophy Race

Bickers made one of his super-fast starts in the 250 Trophy race, squeezing out Chris Horsfield, now on a Greeves, and Roger Snoad, who would enjoy an excellent spell of form in the Grandstand series. However, it was British champion, Freddie Mayes, who took up the challenge and chased Bickers for all he was worth. Mayes did well to assert himself, as he was the first of no less than five Greeves, as Horsfield got the better of Arthur Browning in a battle for 3rd place and Wade, who was already developing a taste for the limelight, edged out Snoad.

750 Trophy Race

After his Invitation win, Eastwood blasted his BSA to the front in the 750 Grandstand race intent on opening his Grandstand account with a win. But before the first lap was over Bickers had raced into the lead and, following a brief interchange between the two, he cleared off for his second win of the day.

Things didn't go so smoothly for Eastwood, who stalled the BSA in a corner allowing Browning to take his 360 into 2nd place and he then came under pressure from Nicoll, who was having fun on his big banger. Horsfield's luck deserted him when he had a big fall just after the start and Eastwood's teammate, John Banks, was making up for a poor start on the injured Jeff Smith's 'Titan', picking off rider after rider to sneak into the points.

At the flag, it was Bickers, who took only the second Grandstand Trophy race double (Arthur Lampkin scored the first in January 1965), from Browning, Eastwood and Nicoll, with Ken Sedgley, out on a new 360 CZ, 5th ahead of Banks.

Without wishing to detract from Sedgley's performance, it serves, however, to illustrate a comment that Arthur Browning made to me, that if you put a top privateer on a CZ or Husky at that time, they had the speed to compete with the best factory riders in the country.

Second Supporting Race

To round off a very entertaining meeting came the Second TV Invitation, which like the Trophy races was an 8-lap affair. Bickers soon established himself at the head of the race, followed by Browning who looked very accomplished racing in the muddy conditions. Keith Hickman on Eric Cheney's BSA charged through the field and eventually split the Lampkin brothers, whilst Wade had another impressive ride bringing his 250 Greeves home in 6th place.

250 British champion, Freddie Mayes, was runner-up and the first of five Greeves riders to score points in the 250 Trophy race (MC)

Greeves' 'young guns', Arthur Browning and Bryan Wade, disputing the same patch of track in South Wales (MC)

Bickers completed a memorable double at Soarbrook Farm, by winning the inaugural 750 Grandstand Trophy race (MC)

Grandstand Trophy Race Results

250 Trophy
1 D Bickers (CZ)
2 F Mayes (Greeves)
3 C Horsfield (Greeves)
4 A Browning (Greeves)
5 B Wade (Greeves)
6 R Snoad (Greeves)

750 Trophy
1 D Bickers (360 CZ)
2 A Browning (360 Greeves)
3 V Eastwood (494 BSA)
4 D Nicoll (600 Métisse)
5 K Sedgley (360 CZ)
6 J Banks (494 BSA)

Round 2
Dodington Park, Glos, November 5, 1966

'Remember, remember, the fifth of November'. It was unlikely that Dave Bickers, who produced the fireworks on the day, would forget it, though his Eastern Centre companion Jim Aim could have been excused if he was a bit hazy on the events. Jim went down in the middle of a group of riders just yards from the start of the first race of the day, the non-televised Invitation, receiving a big bang on the head, which left him feeling a bit groggy and his Kirby Métisse was also a little worse for wear.

Supporting Race

In the first televised race, the Invitation, Vic Eastwood set out his stall, rapidly establishing himself at the head of the race ahead of Bickers and Dave Nicoll, on his 600 Matchless Métisse, after early leader Arthur Browning had taken a fall. Bickers tried his best, as always, but could do nothing about Eastwood and the man from Kent ran out as race winner.

750 Trophy Race

The 750 Trophy race was a different affair though, as Bickers stormed the start and was never headed in the six-lap contest. Behind him Browning rode equally well to secure his second straight runner-up spot in the 750 series, whilst Nicoll finished 3rd for the second

Magnanimous as always, Dave Bickers (left) congratulates Vic Eastwood after the BSA factory rider registered his second consecutive TV Invitation race win (CB)

Eastwood, seen here drifting the 494 BSA through a tricky corner, was in the thick of the action all day and finished 4th in the 750 Trophy race (CB)

time on the day after resisting the challenge of Eastwood. Jeff Smith rode into 5th spot, on his second ride back from injury, as Alan Lampkin dropped his 440 BSA and John Banks on another 440 also took advantage of 'Sid's' mishap to round off the top six.

Second Supporting Race

A second TV Invitation saw Eastwood, Alan Lampkin and Nicoll involved in a three-way scrap in the opening laps, but whilst Eastwood and Lampkin both slipped off, Nicoll was rock steady, as was the big Métisse which never missed a beat. Eastwood fought back to pass teammate Banks and Browning, but he could make no impression on Nicoll.

In contrast, the Essex-based privateer, who had been gaining experience racing on the continent with Andy Lee, was making a big impression on watching BSA Competition shop manager, Brian Martin. Martin was so enthralled with Nicoll's riding on the day that he sought him out in the paddock and offered him the loan of a 440 BSA for the rest of the year. At the flag, Nicoll took the win from Eastwood, Browning, Banks and Lampkin with Mayes, giving his new 360 Greeves an outing, taking 6th place.

250 Trophy Race

The 250 Trophy race saw Bickers produce a virtual carbon copy of the 750 race, as he was quite simply in a league of his own. As Bickers sped away into the distance, showering his would-be challengers in mud, Greeves teamsters Alan Clough and Browning entered into their own private battle for the runner-up spot. They traded places a few times till Clough suffered a spill, which left him in the clutches of Mayes, and Browning secure in 2nd place.

Behind them came two more Greeves, in the hands of Southampton's Roger Snoad and factory runner, Chris Horsfield. On the final lap, Mayes slipped past a weary Clough, and Horsfield did just enough to pip Snoad to settle the points.

So with two rounds down, Bickers remained right on target for the double, with maximum scores in both the 250 and 750 Trophies.

Always entertaining, Arthur Browning pushing on hard on his 360 Greeves in pursuit of the elusive Mr Bickers (CB)

Bickers tries in vain to see where the opposition is, as he heads for a very comfortable win in the 750 series (CB)

Grandstand Trophy Race Results

250 Trophy
1 D Bickers (CZ)
2 A Browning (Greeves)
3 F Mayes (Greeves)
4 A Clough (Greeves)
5 C Horsfield (Greeves)
6 R Snoad (Greeves)

750 Trophy
1 D Bickers (360 CZ)
2 A Browning (360 Greeves)
3 D Nicoll (600 Métisse)
4 V Eastwood (494 BSA)
5 J Smith (494 BSA)
6 J Banks (440 BSA)

Two weeks later, on 19th November, the BBC televised another International match race, this time from Hatherton Hall, Nantwich, where the Great Britain team took on the Belgians (see p296).

Essex man, Dave Nicoll, was on top form at Dodington and capped his day with his first race win during the Grandstand series. Here he expertly negotiates a tricky downhill jump on his 600 Matchless Métisse, as he heads for victory in the second TV Invitation (CB)

Round 3

Hawkstone Park, Shropshire, December 10, 1966

This meeting arguably showed Hawkstone Park at its worst, despite the sterling efforts of the Salop Motor Club, led, as always, by their President, Cuth Bate. Torrential rain had reduced the circuit to a mudbath and following the 250 Trophy race, where only the first six riders finished, Hawkstone's famous hill had to be cut for the rest of the programme. How ironic it was that Hawkstone Park had lost its GP status the previous summer, following on-going complaints about poor visibility due to dust at the circuit!

250 Trophy Race

One man who had no problems with visibility, or the conditions in general, was Dave Bickers. In the 250 Trophy race he soon took the lead and stormed the hill closely followed by Bryan Goss on his Husqvarna. However, these two riders were the only ones to crest

Unstoppable! Dave Bickers racked up his fifth and sixth race wins of the series at Hawkstone Park. Here Malcolm Carling captures him on his way to another unchallenged victory in the 250 Trophy series

With Bickers vanishing in the distance, Bryan Wade came out on top in a thrilling three-way battle with teammate Arthur Browning and John Banks in the 750 Trophy race (MC)

Banks maintained a consistent run in the 750 series with 3rd place at Hawkstone Park (MC)

the hill at their first attempt and when the others finally began to trickle through it was obvious that some of the big guns were already missing.

Gone were Alan Clough and Chris Horsfield and, as Bickers disappeared over the top of the hill for a second time, Goss' challenge slithered to a halt; try as he might, Goss just couldn't get the Husky up the hill and he joined the growing list of retirees. Bickers endured a very lonely race out front, eventually taking the flag more than half a lap ahead of Freddie Mayes and Arthur Browning. Roger Snoad was next, just edging Malcolm Davis, whilst local man John Done, who had returned to Dot, finished 6th. All three were a lap adrift of Bickers.

750 Trophy Race

In the 750 Trophy race, with the big hill sensibly by-passed, Bickers again took a start-to-finish win, oblivious to the hectic racing going on behind him. Browning had settled into 2nd place, but he then came under pressure from teammate Bryan Wade, having his first ride on a new 360, and BSA's John Banks.

Soon the three 'young guns' were involved in a captivating struggle for 2nd spot. The pressure finally told on Browning, who made a slip that let Wade through, and on the last lap Browning had Wade in his sights again. But in his efforts to catch his teammate he failed to defend 3rd place and was pipped on the line by Banks. Behind these three, Clough made it three 360 Greeves in the first five and Eastwood grabbed the final points for 6th place.

Wade, who scored his first Grandstand points from a magnificent 2nd behind Bickers, recalls his success on the big Greeves:

> *The good thing about Hawkstone, was that it was a hell of a lot easier to ride in the winter than places like Nantwich, which were a total slop. Jumping onto the 360 was like riding a 250 with a turbo. We'd been mixing it with the 500s (on 250s in the invitation races) and now we basically had the same bike with more get up and go.*

Supporting Races

To crown Bickers' day, he took a third win in the Invitation, though this time he actually had to pass someone, taking early leader Browning as he came down off the hill on the first lap! Once out front the result was never in doubt, though Browning held on for another impressive 2nd place, followed home by Alan Lampkin and big brother Arthur, whilst Horsfield held off Eastwood to take 5th place.

Grandstand Trophy Race Results

250 Trophy
1 D Bickers (CZ)
2 F Mayes (Greeves)
3 A Browning (Greeves)
4 R Snoad (Greeves)
5 M Davis (Bultaco)
6 J Done (Dot)

750 Trophy
1 D Bickers (400 CZ)
2 B Wade (360 Greeves)
3 J Banks (440 BSA)
4 A Browning (360 Greeves)
5 A Clough (360 Greeves)
6 V Eastwood (494 BSA)

Round 4

Tweseldown, Hampshire, December 24, 1966

Conditions weren't much better when racing reconvened at Tweseldown, two weeks later. However, unlike Hawkstone Park, the Hampshire circuit had very little change in altitude, so despite being very wet, it was infinitely more rideable.

250 Trophy Race

The 250 Trophy race kicked things off and Dave Bickers maintained his 100 percent start to the series, registering his fourth straight win with another masterful display in the tricky conditions. Surprise of the race was local man, Roger Snoad. The semi-supported Greeves rider put all his knowledge of the narrow, twisty track to good use, holding off Arthur Browning until the sixth lap. Even then he wasn't done, fighting back past the growing star of the Greeves team to take a well-earned runner-up spot to Bickers, his best ever Grandstand Trophy finish. Browning didn't fare so well, slipping back through the field in

Wherever the BBC went, a lot of heavy equipment went too. The Bedford in the foreground is a radio links truck with a folding mast that was used to connect the Outside Broadcast unit to the BBC studio (BH)

With the BBC engineers setting up, Murray Walker takes Brian Johnson's C15T BSA for a lap of the circuit and, from the expression on his face, he thoroughly enjoyed it (BH)

This beautifully crafted Eric Cheney special featured a BSA gearbox grafted onto a Greeves engine and a dummy petrol tank, the fuel actually being stored under the seat. Bryan Goss tried it in practice, but although he thought it handled like a dream, he also found it to be a bit of a nightmare in terms of power output (BH)

the closing laps, as first Greeves teammates Bryan Wade and Freddie Mayes moved past, before Bryan Goss further demoted the Birmingham youngster to 6th at the flag.

Now the question on everybody's lips was, 'Could Dave Bickers reach the half-way mark of the series unbeaten?' One thing was for sure, in typical TV fashion we wouldn't have to wait long to get an answer.

Eastwood became only the second race winner of the series to date, as Bickers 'slumped' to an unaccustomed 3rd place in the 750 race (BH)

750 Trophy Race

The 750 Trophy race provided the best racing of the day despite the incessant rain. TV viewers were soon aware that Bickers would have to fight very hard if he was to secure win number eight, as he found himself chasing not only Browning, but also the BSA pair of Vic Eastwood and Jeff Smith, who was starting to look more like his old self again. The leading quartet had broken away from the rest of the field and as the race neared its conclusion they bunched up so tightly that the proverbial handkerchief could have covered them!

Bickers, aware that time was running out for him, burst past Smith and set about closing down Eastwood. However, the Kent ace simultaneously made his move, passing poor Browning, who had led from the start and had seemed destined to win his first Grandstand Trophy race, and the three riders dashed for the line in very close formation. The final verdict went to Eastwood, who just edged Browning, with Bickers 3rd. Smith finished some way clear of John Banks, now armed with a 494 BSA of his own, and Wade, who filled the last point scoring position on his 360.

Supporting Races

The 8-lap TV Invitation saw Bickers struggling to come to terms with the full-500 BSAs of Smith and Eastwood again. Smith led for the first couple of laps, but Eastwood, who was on top form and was the fitter of the two at this stage of the season, would not be denied, passing his senior teammate and going on to record his second TV win of the day. Smith used all his guile to fend off Bickers, with Wade, Arthur Lampkin and Freddie Mayes, having another canter on his 360 Greeves, completing the top six.

Arthur Browning led the 750 race until the last lap, when Vic Eastwood passed him. Here Browning defends a slender lead over the BSA man (BH)

Grandstand Trophy Race Results

250 Trophy
1 D Bickers (CZ)
2 R Snoad (Greeves)
3 B Wade (Greeves)
4 F Mayes (Greeves)
5 B Goss (Husqvarna)
6 A Browning (Greeves)

750 Trophy
1 V Eastwood (494 BSA)
2 A Browning (360 Greeves)
3 D Bickers (400 CZ)
4 J Smith (494 BSA)
5 J Banks (494 BSA)
6 B Wade (360 Greeves)

So at the mid-point of the series Bickers still had a stranglehold on the 250 Trophy, but Eastwood and Browning had proved that he could be beaten in the 750 series. But would either of these riders, or anyone else for that matter, be able to mount a serious challenge for the trophy?

Grandstand Trophy Positions After 4 Rounds

250 Trophy

1	D Bickers	8 8 8 8	32pts
2	F Mayes	6 5 6 4	21pts
3	A Browning	4 6 5 2	17pts
4	R Snoad	2 3 4 6	15pts
5	C Horsfield	5 3 0 0	8pts
6	B Wade	3 0 0 5	8pts

750 Trophy

1	D Bickers	8 8 8 5	29pts
2	A Browning	6 6 4 6	22pts
3	V Eastwood	5 4 2 8	19pts
4	J Banks	2 2 5 3	12pts
5	D Nicoll	4 5 0 0	9pts
6	B Wade	0 0 6 2	8pts

Local ace, Roger Snoad, had by far his best TV campaign in the 1966-67 series and at Tweseldown he scored his best ever Grandstand result, when he finished as runner-up to Dave Bickers in the 250 Trophy race (BH)

Round 5

East Meon, Hampshire, December 31, 1966

Time, tide and, it would appear, *Grandstand*, wait for no man! On New Year's Eve 1966, when the majority of the population would have been enjoying a nice, relaxing day, the country's leading scrambling aces were gathering at Garston Farm, near the Hampshire village of East Meon, a settlement which dates back to the Bronze Age, for the fifth round of the series.

This meeting saw several riders ringing the changes for the New Year, most notably Malcolm Davis, who was returning to Greeves after a spell on a Bultaco and 250 British champion Freddie Mayes, who was having his last ride on a Greeves before joining Norton Villiers. It was also an event that resulted in vastly contrasting fortunes for the Lampkin brothers.

Once again, the weather contrived to defeat our heroes, with heavy downpours greeting the riders in Saturday morning practice. But as always the meeting went ahead

On the slopes of the South Downs, BSA's latest recruit, Dave Nicoll, was the first to show in the opening 750 Trophy race on New Year's Eve (CB)

When Nicoll faltered, teammate Arthur Lampkin took up the running. Here he is hotly pursued by Dave Bickers (CB)

and despite the very muddy conditions there was some excellent racing to keep the Grandstand punters happy. Indeed, *MCN* staffman, Gavin Trippe, hailed it as 'one of the best BBC Grandstand meetings yet'.

Supporting Races

The first race of the day saw a young man who was rapidly making a name for himself win the qualifying race on his newly acquired 250 CZ. Within two months, Andy Roberton, an 18 year-old from Knighton, Powys, would have earned himself a factory ride and would go on to become a British champion in 1972. Although he didn't feature in the televised races that day, it would not be too long before he would do so.

750 Trophy Race

The 750 Trophy race was the first televised event and there was plenty of action even before the first lap had been completed. BSA new boy, Dave Nicoll, sped into the lead on his ageing 440 BSA, whilst behind him chaos reigned.

First to fall were new teammates Jeff Smith and John Banks, who went down in a heap with Bryan Wade. This was followed by another collision, which again took out two BSA runners and a Greeves factory man, as Vic Eastwood, Alan Lampkin and Arthur Browning all came together. Lampkin was the only rider who couldn't continue, sadly ambulanced away to the local infirmary for observation.

Nicoll was really enjoying himself out front, until a mistake allowed Arthur Lampkin through into the lead. Arthur wound on for a couple of laps and was never headed again, going on to register his first Grandstand win in almost two years. Nicoll then came under pressure from Dave Bickers, and when the younger man stalled, Bickers ran into the back

Conditions on the day were very difficult as illustrated in this shot, as even riders of the calibre of Bickers, Smith and Nicoll struggle in the cloying mud (BH)

With Bickers away out front on his own, Freddie Mayes led the followers home. Here he heads Arthur Browning past a BBC cameraman, as they all bask in a little midwinter sun (BH)

of him and they were both momentarily out of the running. Bickers was soon off and running again, but by the time Nicoll had restarted the BSA, Smith and Chris Horsfield on the 360 Greeves had moved in front of him.

At the flag, it was Lampkin from Bickers, Smith, Horsfield, Nicoll and Wade who had made a great recovery from his first lap spill. Even more impressive was Smith's ride, until it was brought to the attention of the organisers that he had taken a shortcut and he was promptly disqualified!

250 Trophy Race

The 250 Trophy race proved to be another Dave Bickers exhibition, as he led the race from start to finish to keep his 100% record in this class intact - five races and five wins! Behind him, Horsfield led a Greeves posse of Mayes, Browning, Roger Snoad, who had been credited with 6th place in the 750 race following Smith's disqualification, and Wade.

Horsfield, in his efforts to close on Bickers, then fell allowing Mayes to take 2nd. Ironically this was Mayes' best result in the series at that time, in what would be his last competitive outing on a factory Greeves, as he was due to join Norton Villiers in the New Year. Browning held on for third, whilst Wade eventually got the better of Roger Snoad and Davis finished in the points to mark his return to Greeves, no doubt much to the delight of Derry Preston Cobb.

Supporting Races

The Invitation race was an entertaining affair, with the unlucky Eastwood leading the opening laps, hotly pursued by Smith, Nicoll and Bickers. But by half distance, Bickers had passed Smith, and Browning, who was on a charge, had dislodged Nicoll.

Eastwood then spilled letting Bickers and Smith through and though he restarted 3rd, he had Browning all over him, like the proverbial 'bad rash'. As Bickers took the race ahead of Smith, Browning swept past Eastwood, and Nicoll came in 5th behind one former Matchless teammate, and ahead of another, Chris Horsfield.

Spare a thought for poor Alan Lampkin who missed out on any New Year's Eve celebrations and spent New Year's Day, not to mention the following week, under observation in a hospital bed in Portsmouth. The stoic Lampkin told me, 'These things happened, it was an occupational hazard'. Whilst incarcerated on the south coast, he no doubt read the Queens New Year's Honours list, where he would have noted that England's World Cup winning manager, Alf Ramsey, and captain, Bobby Moore, had received a knighthood and an OBE respectively.

Grandstand Trophy Race Results

250 Trophy
1 D Bickers (CZ)
2 F Mayes (Greeves)
3 A Browning (Greeves)
4 B Wade (Greeves)
5 R Snoad (Greeves)
6 M Davis (Greeves)

750 Trophy
1 A J Lampkin (440 BSA)
2 D Bickers (400 CZ)
3 C Horsfield (360 Greeves)
4 D Nicoll (440 BSA)
5 B Wade (360 Greeves)
6 R Snoad (360 Greeves)

With the New Year just a few days old, BBC viewers watched in horror as Donald Campbell, the holder of both land and water speed records, met his death whilst trying to better his water speed record on Lake Coniston on 4th January. After successfully completing his first run, Campbell's boat, Bluebird K7 flipped over and broke up whilst travelling in excess of 300mph as he approached the finish of his second run.

Round 6

Cuerden Park, Lancashire, January 14, 1967

A week before the Grandstand Trophy reconvened, the BBC had launched its ambitious *Forsyte Saga*, which, as the name suggests, was an epic serialisation of a period drama in 26 episodes that would run right through to July. Hugely popular at the time, with a claimed audience of 18 million viewers, it was, however, hard pressed to match the drama of the Grandstand Trophy.

On the afternoon of Saturday 14th January, millions of armchair sports fans, especially the motorsport variety, tuned in to BBC1 for the latest live instalment of the 'Dave Bickers Spectacular', with the Ipswich motorcycle dealer looking to extend his unbeaten run in the 250 Trophy to six wins.

250 Trophy Race

Happy to oblige, Bickers immediately jumped into the lead in the 250 Trophy race chased by the factory Greeves of Arthur Browning, Alan Clough and Bryan Wade. Wade, who was to experience a torrid day, fell three times with the Greeves' throttle sticking open. The last of these, although failing to dampen Wade's enthusiasm, rendered his bike unrideable.

Man on a mission was Chris Horsfield, racing a new twin-port Greeves. He had raced through the pack passing all his teammates to take the battle to Bickers and for a fleeting moment it looked as if he might be the rider to end Bickers' run. But as Horsfield closed in on Bickers the Greeves' engine seized up and his race was run.

However, the race for the runner-up spot was still up for grabs. Browning succeeded Horsfield, but with the race drawing to a close a small mistake allowed Malcolm Davis and

Malcolm Davis, who had recently returned to Greeves, following a spell on a Bultaco Métisse, enjoyed an upturn in form with 3rd place in the 250 Trophy race. Note the absence of roping here - Malcolm is not riding through the paddock! (MC)

Freddie Mayes about to take the new Norton Villiers project bike out for its TV debut (MC)

Youthful exuberance from Andy Roberton, but the young Welshman held it all together and was rewarded with his first Grandstand points in the 250 Trophy race (MC)

Alan Clough, who had been having their own private duel, to slip by. The more experienced Clough then shadowed his teammate, before passing him on the last lap to claim 2nd spot.

Freddie Mayes debut on the Norton Villiers development bike started promisingly enough, when he was amongst the leaders in the early laps. But a missed gear dropped him off the leaderboard and he eventually finished just outside the points in seventh place.

So Bickers added win number six, Clough was second, Davis third and Browning fourth. Behind them young Andy Roberton brought his CZ home in 5th, for his first Grandstand series points and in doing so became the first Welshman to score points since Bill Gwynne in the opening series, and Roger Snoad completed the point scoring positions in 6th place.

750 Trophy Race

In the 750 Trophy race, it was advantage two-strokes on the first lap, as Bickers led Greeves' 'Terrible twins', Browning and Wade, with the BSA's of Jeff Smith, Vic Eastwood and Arthur Lampkin hanging on to their coat-tails. Browning, whose form had been improving from meeting to meeting, then swept past a surprised Bickers and into the lead. Bickers could never settle for second place though, following the Birmingham boy at close quarters, whilst behind them Eastwood was the man on the move, displacing Smith and Wade and establishing himself in 3rd place.

At the flag, the same six riders who had led on the first lap comprised the top six finishers, though the order was quite different. A delighted Browning took his first Grandstand Trophy race win, and Greeves' first in the 750 Trophy, ahead of Bickers who just hadn't been able to find a way past his tall, rangy, rival. Eastwood took a comfortable 3rd, whilst Smith rode into 4th place, when Wade contrived to slip off on the last corner. Fortunately, he still had time to pick himself up, dust himself down and get the Greeves home before Lampkin appeared.

For race winner Browning, this is one of the clearer memories he has from that period of his career:

> I had a right old battle with Bickers at Cuerden Park. It was a horrible wet day and I remember it because at that time it was rare that I'd find myself battling him. I think the Greeves also suited those conditions, as it was under-powered compared to a CZ and it didn't spin up the back wheel so much, so I'd get better traction out of the corners.

Supporting Races

The BSA boys gave a better account of themselves in the Invitation race. Smith took an immediate lead and was soon joined by Eastwood. Their task was made easier when Browning fell on the opening lap and John Banks on his 440 took up third place. After a race-long tussle, Eastwood got the better of Smith, whilst Chris Horsfield on his 360 Greeves came through strongly to take 3rd place. Arthur Lampkin got the better of Banks on the last lap and 6th place went to Tom Leadbitter on a 250 Husqvarna.

After consistently providing the sternest challenge to Dave Bickers supremacy in the Grandstand series, Arthur Browning finally got his just return, with a win in the 750 Trophy race at Cuerden Park (MC)

Grandstand Trophy Race Results

250 Trophy
1 D Bickers (CZ)
2 A Clough (Greeves)
3 M Davis (Greeves)
4 A Browning (Greeves)
5 A Roberton (CZ)
6 R Snoad (Greeves)

750 Trophy
1 A Browning (360 Greeves)
2 D Bickers (400 CZ)
3 V Eastwood (494 BSA)
4 J Smith (494 BSA)
5 B Wade (360 Greeves)
6 A J Lampkin (440 BSA)

Bryan Wade once told me that Murray Walker had been responsible for adding the 'Wild' tag to his name. With hindsight, it's not too difficult to see why. Wade, who had been establishing himself as a young rider with a great future ahead, fell no less than six times during the Cuerden Park meeting and from there on he was affectionately referred to by many as 'Wild Wade'.

In conversation with Wade I put it to him that the nickname didn't really seem to harm his reputation and that he might even have played on it:

Yeah, I reckon it was a package, and with the distinctive crash hat and the wild tag it was coming together, I just needed to learn to stay with my bike! All I can say is thank god my riding eventually caught up with my flamboyant antics, or I'd have looked a bit of a prat!

However, Wade's speed and riding skills were already impressing a lot of people in the sport. A fortnight after the action-packed event in Lancashire, Wade found himself representing Britain for the first time, when he was selected to race in the International match race against Czechoslovakia at Clifton on January 28th, where he repaid the faith the selectors' had placed in him (see *p296*).

Round 7

Naish Hill, Wiltshire, February 11, 1967

After a break of four weeks, the Grandstand series resumed at Naish Hill in mid-February, where there were plenty of surprises in store. There was a fair bit of paddock news as well, most notably Alan Clough's move to a brace of privately owned Husqvarnas, after more than four years representing Greeves. But teenaged sensation Andy Roberton was also attracting a lot of attention, having been snapped up to ride for Norton Villiers, where he would join Freddie Mayes.

250 Trophy Race

There was high drama at the start of the 250 Trophy race, when Dave Bickers' one-hundred per cent record went out the window. Bickers was struck by a wayward bike in the first corner, leaving him not only with dented pride, but also with a sore shoulder and a terminally damaged 250 CZ.

At the front of the race Freddie Mayes, who had been out of luck on his debut at Cuerden Park, was really on the pace on the Métisse-framed Norton Villiers, battling with his ex-Greeves teammates, Arthur Browning and Bryan Wade. Mayes led for the first five laps, but then a missed gear was the only invitation the Greeves duo needed to take up the running. A lap later, as he tried to make amends for his mistake, Mayes caught a tree root which unseated him and effectively ended his race.

Then the debutants began to make their presence felt, as Clough whistled through the pack on the lightweight Husky and zeroed in on Wade and Browning. Wade used this situation to his advantage, putting some distance between himself and Browning, who had a real fight on his hands with Clough. Meanwhile Roberton, despite a spill, was up to 4th place on the second Norton Villiers, confirming that the new bike was a force to be reckoned with.

Above, Freddie Mayes was flying on the Norton Villiers in the 250 Trophy race and led until the 5th lap (GF)

Alan Clough made his TV debut on a Husqvarna in the 250 Trophy race and was only narrowly beaten into 3rd place by his ex-teammate, Arthur Browning (MC)

Bryan Wade looks a bit apprehensive here, but he hit top form at Naish Hill and is caught on his way to taking the 250 Trophy race (MC)

A jubilant Wade held on to win his first Grandstand Trophy race, but all eyes were on the battle for 2nd, as Browning and Clough flashed across the line side-by-side, with Browning just getting the nod. Roberton brought Norton Villiers their first Grandstand Trophy points from 4th place, whilst Tom Leadbitter edged out Terry Challinor, who scored Sprite's first points in the Grandstand series, since Brian Nadin's effort at Wakefield three years earlier.

750 Trophy Race

The 750 Trophy race was like two races in one. At the head of things the 250 race-winner, Wade, was the Greeves in a BSA sandwich, with Vic Eastwood leading and John Banks in 3rd place, with a second trio consisting of Browning, Jeff Smith and Bickers a few yards adrift.

Eastwood, celebrated the birth of his first son, Scott, in style, by holding off the spirited attacks of Wade and Banks, the first three finishing in that order. But behind them there was a monumental scrap for 4th place, as the other three constantly traded places. Smith eventually prevailed ahead of Bickers, nursing a very sore shoulder, and Browning.

Surprisingly perhaps, Wade struggles to recall his most successful day's racing on Grandstand.

I don't remember much, but I really should have had both races. My brain must have been working that day, as I was happy with 2nd which was not like me!

However, Malcolm Carling's photo on the previous page, suggests that he still found time to entertain the TV viewers:

I twigged very early on, that if you got stuck in, then people watched and took photos and if you kept getting splashed over the papers it was good for the team and good

A superb Gordon Francis shot catches Wade and Vic Eastwood disputing the lead in the 750 Trophy race. John Banks (partially obscured by Eastwood), Ken Messenger (behind Banks), Robin Cox (18) Tom Leadbitter (27) and Jeff Smith (4) all give chase

History being made! In finishing 5th in the 750 Trophy race, Dave Bickers became the first rider to win both 250 and 750 Grandstand trophies in the same series (MC)

Below, 750 Trophy race winner, Eastwood, got a second win in the Four-stroke only race. The interested spectator in the background is none other than Dave Bickers (CB)

for winding other riders up too! Malcolm Carling and I worked well together, he always made himself visible out on the track, so you'd give it a bit extra for him.

The three points Bickers picked up for his courageous ride guaranteed him the Grandstand double and a unique place in the history of the series, as the only man to achieve this feat. Curiously, this would be the last time the great man would win a Grandstand Trophy, but his record in the series has no equal. The 'Coddenham Flyer' won 29 Grandstand races in the first four series and five out of the eight trophies awarded over the same period. Only Jeff Smith came close, with 24 wins and three trophies to his name.

Supporting Races

The final televised race of the day saw the West Wilts Club and the BBC experimenting with a new concept, in the form of a Handicap race. The go-ahead club also ran 'Two-stroke only' and 'Four-stroke only' races, won by Clough and Eastwood respectively. But it was the Handicap that the *Grandstand* viewers got to see with riders organised into five starting groups, setting off at intervals.

In an exciting race, group one rider, Leadbitter, was first to show, taking advantage of his early start. But it was Banks, surprisingly starting in group two, who proved the strongest, overhauling Leadbitter at half-race distance and holding off the flying Clough, who was really getting the hang of his 360 Husqvarna. Smith (group four), eventually squeezed out Leadbitter for 4th place, whilst Arthur Lampkin (group three) did just enough to beat Bickers, the first of the group five riders to finish.

Grandstand Trophy Race Results

250 Trophy	**750 Trophy**
1 B Wade (Greeves)	1 V Eastwood (494 BSA)
2 A Browning (Greeves)	2 B Wade (360 Greeves)
3 A Clough (Husqvarna)	3 J Banks (441 BSA)
4 A Roberton (Villiers Métisse)	4 J Smith (494 BSA)
5 T Leadbitter (Husqvarna)	5 D Bickers (400 CZ)
6 T Challinor (Husky Sprite)	6 A Browning (360 Greeves)

Man of the meeting, Bryan Wade, celebrates in style, with his father, Len (MC)

Round 8

Builth Wells, Breconshire, March 18, 1967

With a stunning backdrop, Dave Bickers races on to victory in the 250 Trophy race, with runner-up Alan Clough just creeping into the picture (MC)

Whilst the BBC *Grandstand* entourage was making its way to the mid-Wales market town of Builth Wells on the morning of Saturday 18th March 1967, news started to filter through of a shipping disaster off the coast of Cornwall. The *Torrey Canyon*, a Liberian registered oil tanker, had run aground on Pollard's Rock, between Lands End and the Isles of Scilly, spilling 119,328 tonnes of crude oil into the Atlantic and within days, beaches across the south-west of England, and even in northern France, were covered in a deathly black film.

Though no one knew it at the time, the catastrophe would have far-reaching consequences for Britain's wildlife and in the days to come newspapers, magazines and TV news would be dominated by images of stricken seabirds.

Back at Builth Wells, everybody was busily getting on with things in preparation for the final round of the series. With the silverware safely destined for the trophy cabinet of Dave Bickers' Suffolk home, it might have been expected that the racing at the final round of the series would be rather lacklustre, but nothing could have been further from the truth.

Clough, who challenged Bickers for the lead mid-race, was already looking completely at home on his 250 Husqvarna (MC)

250 Trophy Race

The 250 Trophy race saw Bickers soon take up his customary position at the head of the race, with Alan Clough and Arthur Browning in close attendance. However, Browning, who was already assured of second place in the series, saw his challenge disappear when his Greeves' engine temporarily seized, allowing teammate Bryan Wade to move up to 3rd place.

Meanwhile Clough, who had clearly mastered the different characteristics of his new Husqvarna, was all over the back wheel of Bickers and he even took the lead, briefly. But there was no stopping Bickers, who sped back to the front and did just enough to keep his former Greeves teammate at bay.

And what of the Greeves runners? Well, Wade finished 3rd, to consolidate fourth place in the series, Browning held on for 4th place, whilst Chris Horsfield and Scotsman Vic Allan, who scored his first Grandstand Trophy points, rounded off the top six.

750 Trophy Race

In the 750 Trophy race, second place in the series was still up for grabs, to be decided between Greeves' Browning and BSA's Vic Eastwood. However, the race proved to be more like a war of attrition, as one by one riders fell away. The BSA team were hit especially hard, as they lost the Lampkin brothers and Jeff Smith in rapid succession.

Then Clough, looking to build on his success in the 250 race, was struck in the eye by a flying clod of mud and had to abandon the race. There was more drama on the third lap,

Chris Horsfield, who always went well on the hilly Builth Wells circuit, sprang a surprise by taking the 360 Greeves to victory in the 750 Trophy (MC)

when Browning struck a straw bale, losing valuable time as he remounted and joined the fray. At the same time, Eastwood seized the opportunity to put some time into his rival.

One rider who managed to avoid all the madness was Horsfield, who had escaped the pack on his 360 Greeves. Compared with his performance in the previous series, Horsfield had been having a wretched time on the Greeves, but he proved to be more than an equal to the challenge in this, the final race of the series.

Bickers battled through to second place, but as the man with the chequered flag brought the series to a close, it was Horsfield who took a deserved victory. Behind Bickers, Eastwood finished 3rd to secure second place in the series, ahead of John Banks, whilst Browning recovered to salvage 5th place in the race and third in the series ahead of his Greeves teammate, Bryan Wade.

Though already a well-established rider in his native Scotland, Vic Allan was a new face to Grandstand viewers in 1967. At Builth Wells he scored his first points in the series with 6th place in the 250 Trophy race (MC)

Grandstand Trophy Race Results

250 Trophy
1 D Bickers (CZ)
2 A Clough (Husqvarna)
3 B Wade (Greeves)
4 A Browning (Greeves)
5 C Horsfield (Greeves)
6 V Allan (Greeves)

750 Trophy
1 C Horsfield (360 Greeves)
2 D Bickers (400 CZ)
3 V Eastwood (494 BSA)
4 J Banks (441 BSA)
5 A Browning (360 Greeves)
6 B Wade (360 Greeves)

1966-67 Grandstand Trophy Series Final Standings

250 Trophy:
1	D Bickers	8 8 8 8 8 8 0 8	56pts
2	A Browning	4 6 5 2 5 4 6 4	36pts
3	F Mayes	6 5 6 4 6 0 0 0	27pts
4	B Wade	3 0 0 5 4 0 8 5	25pts
5	A Clough	0 4 0 0 0 6 5 6	21pts
6	R Snoad	2 3 4 6 3 2 0 0	20pts

750 Trophy:
1	D Bickers	8 8 8 5 6 6 3 6	50pts
2	V Eastwood	5 4 2 8 0 5 8 5	37pts
3	A Browning	6 6 4 6 0 8 2 3	35pts
4	B Wade	0 0 6 2 3 3 6 2	22pts
5	J Banks	2 2 5 3 0 0 5 4	21pts
6=	C Horsfield	0 0 0 0 5 0 0 8	13pts
	D Nicoll	4 5 0 0 4 0 0 0	13pts

Dave Bickers may have dominated the televised meetings of 1966-67, but with young riders like Browning, Wade, Banks, Nicoll, Davis, Roberton and Allan rapidly emerging, the future looked bright for British motocross and also for the Grandstand Trophy.

1967-68
The Year Of Foot-and-Mouth

John Banks, West Stow Heath, 27th January, 1968 (BH)

Setting The Scene

After many years as a top-flight rider and having twice finished runner-up to Dave Bickers in the British championship, Alan Clough became the 250 British champion racing his Swedish Husqvarna. Clough also came close to a double, (250 and 500 champion) but eventually lost out in a three-way tussle with BSA factory riders Jeff Smith and Vic Eastwood. Clough won the final race of the series, but Smith, by finishing fourth, did enough to claim his ninth national title.

Bickers and Smith contested the 500 world championship again, with Bickers scoring his only GP wins in the Blue Riband event, in Sweden and in Luxembourg. However, neither could match the outstanding Paul Friedrichs, who registered his second world championship victory well clear of Smith, with Bickers 3rd in the final standings. Vic Eastwood was 8th and John Banks, who finished the season in good form, was 14th, one place ahead of privateer Keith Hickman on his Cheney BSA.

On The Move

By September 1967, reigning British champion Freddie Mayes, who had been riding for Norton Villiers, found himself on a bike which had been re-badged as an AJS. But a month later he had quit and joined the ranks of the privateers, racing a 250 twin-port CZ purchased from Dave Bickers. Fellow Norton Villiers man Andy Roberton, who had been the sensation of the 250 British GP at Halstead when he finished fifth overall in his maiden GP, also left and returned to a CZ.

Another star on the move was Bryan Goss, who apparently had replaced Mayes at AJS. He rode the Andover built two-stroke at a John Player Winternational meeting at Horton Common, Dorset, in late October, but by the time the Grandstand series got underway just a fortnight later, Goss was back on a Husqvarna and it was Malcolm Davis who was racing the AJS, along with top-Northern ace, Dick Clayton.

Following his GP heroics and subsequent selection for the *Motocross des Nations* team in September, Keith Hickman was offered a factory BSA in the autumn of 67, making his debut at the final round of the British championship at Builth Wells in October.

After a year on Greeves, Chris Horsfield returned to CZ, whilst some great performances at national level on his Comerford Greeves, saw Vic Allan rewarded with the use of a factory Greeves over the winter.

Into The 1967-68 Series

The summer of '67 was a happening time in Britain. In May, Francis Chichester completed his solo circumnavigation of the globe in 226 days, becoming the first yachtsman to achieve this feat and on 25th June, the world's first live satellite broadcast, *Our World*, overseen by the BBC in London, was viewed by an estimated 400 million people worldwide with The Beatles performing *All you Need is Love*, a song composed by John Lennon to mark the occasion, to close the two and a half hour epic.

The magnificent Queen Elizabeth 2 (better known as the QE2) was launched on Clydebank on 20th September, though it would be May 1969 before she would take her maiden voyage. The QE2 would, of course, go on to serve as the flagship of the Cunard Line until 2004, when it was replaced by the Queen Mary 2. As summer made way for autumn, two events occurred that would certainly have had an impact on Britain's troupe of motocross riders.

Travelling the country from end-to-end in the middle of winter, not to mention the cross-channel forays to lucrative continental meetings and criss-crossing Europe on the

GP trail, the riders needed some entertainment to brighten their trips and radio tended to be their favoured medium.

Remember, this was before the commercialisation of in-car cassette players and at that time radio listeners had been restricted to tuning in to the pirate radio stations of the day such as Radio Caroline, which broadcast from the North Sea. The introduction of the Marine Offences law in 1967 outlawed the Pirate stations and the BBC sought to take advantage of this situation when it launched BBC Radio 1, which went on air, along with BBC Radio 2, on 30th September 1967. Tony Blackburn, who had been head-hunted after making his name on Radio Caroline and Radio London, was the man spinning the discs and the first record to be played live on air was The Move's *Flowers in the Rain*.

Then on 9th October 1967, Barbara Castle, the Minister of Transport, introduced the very controversial breathalyser, a tool that allowed traffic police to apprehend suspected drink-drivers and submit them to a simple test, which would confirm whether or not they were over the newly imposed legal alcohol limit of 80mg of alcohol per 100ml of blood.

Now, I'm not saying that all of our scrambling heroes liked a drink, several such as Dave Bickers, were teetotallers but like any group of fit young men aged 18-35, many of them certainly liked their ale. The introduction of the new law led people nationwide to question whether to have that drink, knowing that they had to drive later. Statistics at the time show that there were 1,152 fewer deaths recorded on the road and 28,130 fewer slight injuries in the year following the introduction of the breathalyser.

However, the biggest news concerning the Grandstand series was the outbreak of foot-and-mouth disease, the first in the UK since 1953. The first confirmed cases were on a farm in Shropshire in late October and the disease soon spread very quickly. By November 18th, a ban was in place on the transportation of livestock and ten days later all horse racing was cancelled until further notice.

Off-road motorcycling was naturally affected in the same way, resulting in wholesale cancellations to the sporting programme. As a result, the Grandstand series of 1967-68 stood to be decimated.

Chris Horsfield tried this Kawasaki prototype in practice at Canada Heights, but found the machine unsuitable for the demands of top level motocross. He is pictured with former road-racer Terry Sheppard (foreground), who was responsible for the project (BH)

Round 1

Canada Heights, Kent, November 11, 1967

After going close on several occasions, Freddie Mayes finally got his Grandstand Trophy win in the opening race of the 250 series. Here he confidently flies his twin-port CZ (BH)

The meeting at Swanley went ahead as planned, but there then followed a hiatus of eleven weeks before racing resumed at West Stow Heath, Suffolk and this was the shortest Grandstand Trophy series on record, with just five rounds counting towards the trophies.

One man who was on peak form at Canada Heights was Freddie Mayes. After ten months riding and developing the Norton Villiers project bike, Mayes wanted a new challenge. The Norton Villiers, now badged as an AJS, had shown great potential, but Mayes was ultimately left frustrated after so many breakdowns. This was never more obvious than when he raced in the GPs. As British champion and the number one British rider on the 250 GP list, Norton Villiers naturally wanted him to race in the world championship, but Fred had had to endure a wretched time, travelling as far afield as Poland and Russia, with little to show for his efforts in terms of results.

In late 1966, Mayes bought himself a 250 twin-port CZ from Dave Bickers, who then offered him the use of his 360 bike, as he was taking a back seat on the TV scrambles scene and would only race in the second round at Bury St Edmunds in January 1967. First time out on the CZ, Mayes took 2nd place to Bickers in the 250 race at the John Player N°6 sponsored Winternational meeting, at West Stow Heath, near Bury St. Edmunds on October 22nd, and three weeks later he went to Canada Heights in confident mood.

Above, John Banks kicks up some dust on his way to an impressive win in the 750 Trophy race. Like Mayes, it was his first Grandstand Trophy success (BH)

Below, Jeff Smith, clearly enjoying his outing on the titanium framed 250 BSA, races to the runner-up spot in the 250 Trophy race (BH)

250 Trophy Race

A glorious autumn day greeted the riders and riding conditions were near perfect as the 250 Trophy race got underway. Mayes roared away up the hill to lead the field right from the start, with Arthur Browning, Husqvarna privateer Tom Leadbitter and Jeff Smith, in hot pursuit. Smith was flying on the lightweight 250 BSA (see p236) and had soon moved up to a comfortable second place, though he could make no impression on Mayes.

Browning took up station in 3rd place and Leadbitter was looking good for 4th spot. However, Bryan Goss, who had fallen on the opening lap was on a charge, taking his

Vic Eastwood, pictured as he passes the assembled BBC trucks in the paddock, was 2nd to teammate Banks in the 750 Trophy race and took the TV Invitation race (BH)

fellow Husqvarna man on the fifth lap. This seemed to unsettle Leadbitter, who fell a lap later taking out the hapless Bryan Wade in the process.

As the race entered the last lap, Goss demoted Browning, who then came under pressure from Mick Andrews, on his recently acquired factory Ossa. Andrews, who had battled through the field from a mid-pack position on the first lap, moved past AJS debutant, Malcolm Davis, as the race neared its conclusion and was visibly closing in on Browning at the flag.

So Mayes finally joined the elite group of Grandstand Trophy race winners, after previously finishing as runner-up in no less than five 250 Grandstand races.

After Canada Heights I was full of confidence in myself and from knowing that the CZ bikes I was riding were as good as anybody's.

However, Mayes would not get the opportunity to test his new-found confidence, as within a week the foot-and-mouth outbreak was wreaking havoc on the sporting scene.

750 Trophy Race

The 750 Trophy race produced plenty of action, right from the start. Several riders attempted to jump the start with the result that part of the start gate collapsed! For once, the race was restarted and when they got away this time, it was local man, Vic Eastwood, who led the charge. However, following a hotly disputed first lap, Arthur Lampkin led BSA teammates, John Banks and Alan Lampkin across the line, with Chris Horsfield, now racing a private CZ, next ahead of Eastwood on a fourth BSA.

With so much talk about the impact of the big two-strokes, the BSA team, under the guidance of Brian Martin, clearly wanted to stamp their authority on the 750 Trophy. In addition to those mentioned above, they also fielded Smith and new recruit, Keith Hickman, who had impressed the competition manager on the Cheney Victor on which he had represented Great Britain in the 1967 *Motocross des Nations*.

Veterans of many a TV race, Arthur Lampkin and Chris Horsfield, do battle in the 750 Trophy race. Lampkin finished 5th whilst Horsfield, back on a CZ, took 3rd place (BH)

At the front, another young rider was well on the way to his first Grandstand Trophy win, as John Banks forced his way past Lampkin and put some daylight between himself and the rest of the field. Banks, who would soon emerge as a top national and international rider, rode on to victory ahead of Eastwood, who had worked his way back into contention. Horsfield, prevented a BSA whitewash as Smith finally got the better of his old mate Lampkin, with new boy Hickman completing the top six.

Supporting Races

The TV Invitation saw Eastwood grab a well-deserved win after an intense battle with Lampkin, whilst Mayes, who had also won the 250 Invitation, rounded off a great day with third place on a 360 CZ, proving that he could also be a potential threat in the 750 class.

Grandstand Trophy Race Results

250 Trophy
1 F Mayes (CZ)
2 J Smith (BSA)
3 B Goss (Husqvarna)
4 A Browning (Greeves)
5 M Andrews (Ossa)
6 M Davis (AJS)

750 Trophy
1 J Banks (500 BSA)
2 V Eastwood (500 BSA)
3 C Horsfield (380 CZ)
4 J Smith (500 BSA)
5 A J Lampkin (500 BSA)
6 K Hickman (500 BSA)

Grandstand Trophy Series On Pause

In early January 1968 the BBC made the decision to run two 'behind closed doors' meetings to overcome the restrictions on movement caused by the foot-and-mouth.

Longleat Park

The first of these was held at Longleat Park, Wiltshire, home of the Marquess of Bath. The venue is better known today as a safari park, but in 1968 it was still in its infancy, having only opened to the public in 1966.

Jim Webb of the organising Frome Club remembers the event very well.

We were planning to run it at Asham Woods, but the farmer said that some of his neighbours were complaining, because they were worried about the foot-and-mouth. So I went to see Lord Bath, I worked as a farm manager on the Longleat Estate at the time, and he said, 'Well there's only one farmer and if he hasn't got his cows up there I'm not worried, as the deer don't get foot-and-mouth.' So that's what we did.

The foot-and-mouth wasn't very close anyway, so we put it on at Longleat Park in a bit of a hurry. I remember we went out to have a peep at the course with Brian Johnson, and Badger (Goss) brought along two new CZ's. Brian Johnson had one and I had the other one. So I'm riding it down the bottom of the track and of course the controls are the wrong way round (gear change on the left, brake pedal on the right) and I went straight through the paling with this brand-new bike. Badger only laughed!

The 'Longleat Lions' at play; Andy Roberton (2), Bryan Wade (16) and Bryan Goss (20). Goss tried a CZ for the day, but found it not to his taste and was soon back on his trusty Husqvarna (BH)

At Longleat Park, Vic Eastwood mauled his competitors, taking all three of the day's races (BH)

We could only invite riders from uninfected areas and there were no spectators allowed. When the riders arrived we had to disinfect the car tyres and the footwear and feet of anyone coming in, using an old stirrup pump.

Reporting in *MCN*, Gavin Trippe wrote that '30 riders from foot-and-mouth uninfected areas gathered together at the 'secret' Longleat Park course in Wiltshire.' He went on to describe the atmosphere - there were no spectators - as being 'eerie', with just the lions watching on from the neighbouring Safari Park!

Thanks to the organisational skills of Webb, his merry band of helpers, and the expertise of the BBC staff, the programme ran like clockwork as they ran off two 6-lap handicap races and a 6-lap Unlimited race in an hour and a quarter!

BSA's Vic Eastwood was the man of the meeting, winning all three races. Eastwood started both handicaps in the 'scratch' group, along with Dave Bickers and John Banks. He was simply unstoppable, getting the better of Bryan Wade in both handicaps with fellow BSA teamsters, Dave Nicoll and Banks, taking a 3rd place apiece.

To confirm his superiority on the day, Eastwood took the Unlimited by the proverbial 'country mile' with Banks edging Malcolm Davis, who turned in a very promising ride on the experimental 360 AJS. One man who was below par was Bryan Goss, who was trying a 360 CZ for the first time. However, he couldn't come to terms with the Czech bike and was soon back on his trusty Husqvarna.

Health and safety in action! Freddie Mayes looks on as his 250 CZ gets the stirrup pump treatment at the entrance to the Longleat Estate (BH)

Newport, South Wales

The following weekend the action moved to Newport, South Wales, where the format of the Longleat meeting was repeated; two handicap races and a scratch race to finish off. However, where the Frome Club had been blessed with good weather, this event's organising club, the Newport and Gwent, were cursed with truly atrocious conditions.

Riders faced a combination of freezing mud and icy patches on the Tredegar Fort circuit, but Dave Nicoll was in inspired form in the First Handicap. Starting from the second group he soon fought his way to the front and was never headed again, taking his first TV win since switching to BSA. Malcolm Davis chased hard on his 360 AJS, but was passed on the last lap by scratch man, Dave Bickers. Watching ACU official Harold Taylor remarked that Nicoll would start the next handicap from the back row!

The Second Handicap saw Bryan Goss, now back on his Husky following his brief dalliance with CZ, initially leading but a fall resulted in the carburettor flooding and his early retirement. Bickers also took a tumble and got tangled up in the ropes allowing Andy Roberton on a 250 CZ to take up the lead. The young Welshman was putting on a great show in his homeland, but he met his match in Vic Eastwood, who battled through the pack to snatch the win. Trials ace Tony Davis, elder brother of Malcolm, who rode several of the TV scrambles during this series, due to the huge number of trials that were cancelled, rode a 250 AJS to 6th place, but finished two laps down on Eastwood on the factory BSA!

The scratch race saw a vintage performance from Bickers, who would turn 30 the following week, as he simply rode away from everybody else, lapping the entire field bar Banks. Malcolm Davis took 3rd, Freddie Mayes on a 250 CZ was 4th, his best result of the day, whilst an inspired Roberton got the better of Nicoll in the battle for 5th place.

Tony Davis, pictured here racing wheel for wheel with Andy Roberton at Longleat, had a good day at Newport (BH)

Round 2
Bury St Edmunds, Suffolk, January 27, 1968

Two weeks after the South Wales mudbath, having been given the all-clear for racing to resume, the Grandstand Trophy series returned to our screens at the sandy West Stow Heath circuit near Bury St Edmunds, which proved to be ideally suited for television. This was not originally planned as a round of the series, but was hastily organised at the eleventh hour.

250 Trophy Race Cancelled

The organisers contacted riders on the Friday evening and although word spread quickly and there was a good turnout on race day, many factory bikes were still sitting in the competition shops, with Greeves most noticeably having no 250 models available for their factory riders. As a result, Bryan Cowgill, the head of the Outside Broadcast Unit, made an executive decision: the 250 race would have to be cancelled as there were riders holding points in the 250 series who didn't have bikes to ride.

750 Trophy Race

One man who had reason to be happy with the arrangements was local ace, John Banks, who lived just six miles from the circuit and regularly practised there; when he went to the startline for the 750 race he was determined to add to the eight points he had taken for his win in round one at Canada Heights.

Birmingham's Dave Smith helped bring Sprite plenty of publicity. A rapid start on his 360 saw him well placed in the 750 Trophy race and he rode on to a 6th place finish (BH)

The 750 Trophy race reached a thrilling climax, as Bryan Wade challenged local hero John Banks. The Bury St Edmunds man prevailed, to record back-to back wins in the series (BH)

A moment's relaxation between races as John Banks (seated) and Bryan Wade prepare to take Dave Bickers' FE 35 Ferguson tractor for a spin. Bickers had driven it to the circuit from his Coddenham home, some 25 miles away. He recalls: 'It was more frightening that any motocross race I ever did. Every time a lorry came past I'd nearly get blown off the road!' (BH)

The 750 Trophy race provided plenty of excitement, with Dave Bickers in his only Grandstand appearance of the series, racing just 25 miles away from his home, setting a stiff pace at the front shadowed by Banks and Greeves' Bryan Wade. These three eased clear of the pack and Bickers looked favourite to take the win until he overdid things and ran over his own foot in the deep sand! Wade found the Suffolk track to his liking and was giving Banks no quarter, as he constantly harried the local man.

As the race neared its end the two riders came together and Banks' footrest made contact with Wade's front wheel. Wade recalls:

John and I had some great battles, but generally he was never over hard with you and he usually gave you a bit of room. At West Stow we were both trying over hard and I was attempting to come down the inside of him on a very tight corner. It's a shame I couldn't flick him out of gear that would have been worth the spokes I lost.

Banks prevailed, Wade limped home in 2nd place and Jeff Smith, who had been involved in a first corner incident with Chris Horsfield, fought back and dramatically shot from 6th place to 3rd on the last lap. First to fall to the master was namesake Dave Smith, a promising youngster from Birmingham racing a new 360 Sprite, then came BSA teammate Keith Hickman and finally, within sight of the flag, Smith brushed aside a tiring Vic Allan.

Spare a thought for Vic Eastwood; second in the series before the race, he lost his petrol cap on the first lap and returned to the pits soaked in high octane petrol!

A 7-lap Invitation race saw Bickers race to the front again and this time he made no mistakes. However, it was quite like old times, as Jeff Smith lying 2nd gradually closed down the local rider. But Bickers knew Smith was coming and just had enough to hang on for his win despite a throbbing foot! Behind these two, Banks came through the field to take a well-earned 3rd spot ahead of Eastwood, whilst Allan, having an inspired day, finished ahead of the factory BSAs of Arthur Lampkin and Hickman.

In his only appearance in the 1967-68 Grandstand Trophy series, Dave Bickers showed that he'd lost none of his pace. Brian Holder was on hand to capture the moment, as Bickers grabs the lead on his way to victory in the TV Invitation race. In his wake are Alan Lampkin (19), Ray Jordan (35), Arthur Browning (38), Keith Hickman (17), Vic Allan (12), Jeff Smith (4), Dave Smith (36) and Arthur Lampkin (18)

Supporting Races

The meeting ended with another 8-lap Handicap race. Ray Jordan on another 360 Sprite led for the first four laps, though he was racing on borrowed time and was soon swallowed up by the baying pack. Hickman briefly took up the lead, but then yielded to the attacks of first Wade, then Eastwood. At the flag Wade held on for the win from a rapidly closing Eastwood, Hickman was safe in 3rd, Allan reversed the tables on Jeff Smith, and Jordan dug in to take 6th place.

One rider, who quietly used the meeting to become accustomed to his new 360 Husqvarna, was Andy Roberton. The young Welshman, who was rapidly making a name for himself, returned his CZs to Dave Bickers and raced the Brian Leask sponsored Husky for the first time. But although he didn't feature at the sharp end of the racing in Suffolk, it wouldn't be long before he made his mark on the Swedish bikes.

Grandstand Trophy Race Results

250 Trophy
Cancelled

750 Trophy
1 J Banks (500 BSA)
2 B Wade (360 Greeves)
3 J Smith (500 BSA)
4 V Allan (360 Greeves)
5 K Hickman (500 BSA)
6 D Smith (360 Sprite)

Jeff Smith battled through the field to finish 3rd in the 750 Trophy race. Here future Eastern Centre ace, Dave Cordle (the man with the flag), studies the master at work (BH)

Ray Jordan, on a second 360 Sprite, enjoying the limelight as he leads the TV Handicap (BH)

Round 3

Naish Hill, Wiltshire, February 10, 1968

By February 1968, things were returning to normal on the sporting scene, as the ban on horse racing was finally lifted after a break of two months, although some areas of the country were still affected.

The BBC Grandstand series returned to Naish Hill, Wiltshire, in mid-February, a setting that in a few brief years had become well-known to the BBC entourage and *Grandstand* viewers alike and there was a certain comfort and familiarity about the place for all concerned.

One feature at the Wiltshire circuit that readers may recall was an improvised 'tunnel' which had been added for this event. To this day, I can clearly remember Murray Walker commenting on Jeff Smith, as he raced his special lightweight BSA into the tunnel and out the other side.

On the personnel side, two riders were making their debuts on live television: first round 250 Trophy race-winner, Freddie Mayes, had been signed to race for the Spanish Montesa concern, whilst Chris Horsfield was contracted by AJS to race a 250, joining Malcolm Davis and Dick Clayton, who had started the season on a private 360 Husqvarna.

250 Trophy series leader, Freddie Mayes, made his Montesa debut at Naish Hill. Here he is seen getting a feel for the bike in practice (CB)

250 Trophy Race

At Naish Hill, Bryan Goss was really flying on the Husqvarna and led the 250 race from start to finish to record his first Grandstand Trophy win on the Swedish machine, all four of his previous victories having been on a Greeves. Behind him Jeff Smith broke clear of a group featuring Greeves men, Bryan Wade and Arthur Browning, and AJS debutant, Horsfield.

Smith really got the little BSA motoring well, but he could make little impression on Goss, who had a comfortable lead and eased right back in the closing stages. Wade broke clear of a tussle between Browning and Horsfield to finish 3rd, whilst Browning faded and Horsfield's AJS developed a misfire which saw him slip down the order and out of the points.

Meanwhile, Vic Allan, who was starting to establish himself of late, rode past into 4th, though he was passed in turn by Mayes, who was getting the feel of his new factory Montesa, and Browning held on for 6th place and the last of the points.

Bryan Goss on his way to his first Grandstand win on a Husqvarna in the 250 Trophy race (CB)

Poetry in motion; Vic Eastwood rode a flawless race in the 750 series leading from start to finish (CB)

750 Trophy Race

The 750 Trophy race saw series leader, John Banks, go missing early in the race with a badly slipping clutch, but teammate and closest rival, Vic Eastwood, made no mistakes, getting the drop on the competition at the start and leading from first lap to last. Behind him, two of the young lions of British motocross disputed 2nd spot, as Bryan Wade led Andy Roberton who was clearly getting the hang of his 360 Husqvarna after switching from CZ. Roberton pushed really hard, but it was the slightly more experienced Wade who prevailed to add 2nd place to his 3rd in the 250 race.

Further back, a battle was raging between the factory BSAs of Keith Hickman and Dave Nicoll, and Horsfield, who was racing a 380 CZ. Horsfield, who was determined to make up for his disappointment in the 250 race, shrugged off both BSAs, whilst Hickman led Nicoll home for 5th and 6th places.

Grandstand Trophy Race Results

250 Trophy 7
1 B Goss (Husqvarna)
2 J Smith (BSA)
3 B Wade (Greeves)
4 F Mayes (Montesa)
5 V Allan (Greeves)
6 A Browning (Greeves)

50 Trophy
1 V Eastwood (500 BSA)
2 B Wade (360 Greeves)
3 A Roberton (360 Husqvarna)
4 C Horsfield (380 CZ)
5 K Hickman (500 BSA)
6 D Nicoll (500 BSA)

Above left, the BBC cameramen are on hand to capture the action, as AJS teamsters Dick Clayton and Malcolm Davis emerge from Naish Hill's new 'tunnel' (CB)

Above right, on fine form, Jeff Smith finished 2nd on the little BSA for the second round in succession (CB)

Gloucestershire 'neighbours' Andy Roberton and Bryan Wade enjoyed their tussle at Naish Hill in the 750 Trophy race. Wade went on to finish as runner-up to Eastwood, with Roberton 3rd (CB)

Round 4

Kirkcaldy, Fife, March 2, 1968

For the first time in its history, the Grandstand Trophy ventured north of the border into Scotland for round four. The meeting was held at Kilrie Farm, near Kirkcaldy, a town situated on the Firth of Forth, to the north of Edinburgh, principally known at the time for its linoleum production. It was also the home to budding 20 year-old motocross star, Jimmy Aird, who in a few short years would go on to become one of the top riders on the national scene.

The riders were greeted by a sunny day, though the track was muddy and frozen in places and several of the leading riders would fall victim to the conditions. It was also a day that would see experience prevail over youthful exuberance, as the 'old guard' of British motocross returned to their winning ways.

250 Trophy Race

The 250 Trophy race that kicked things off provided plenty of entertainment for the viewers nationwide. Freddie Mayes on his factory Montesa led the charge, closely followed by Arthur Browning, local hero Aird, Malcolm Davis and Jeff Smith. Within a few corners though, Andy Roberton had rocketed into the lead on his Husqvarna, but his lead lasted less than a lap before he was on his ear! Roberton recalls,

The frozen ones (tracks) were the worst ones, it was like riding on concrete - absolutely lethal.

This left Mayes, who had won the opening round on a CZ, seemingly cruising to his second victory of the series, until he slid off and hit a post. Mayes was uninjured, but the

The start of the 250 Trophy race and Freddie Mayes (8) leads, from Arthur Browning (12), local lad Jimmy Aird (1), Malcolm Davis, Jeff Smith, Terry Challinor, Andy Roberton and Dick Clayton (PD)

Montesa's rear brake pedal had jammed, severely hampering his progress. Much to the delight of the partisan crowd, Aird then took up the running, but with double world champion Jeff Smith on his tail he panicked and became the third rider to fall whilst leading the race.

Smith made no such error in recording his first ever 250 Grandstand race win, whilst Aird recovered his composure to race on to a magnificent 2nd place. It was a case of mixed blessings for the AJS squad though; Malcolm Davis came home 3rd in front of Mayes, but in a dramatic last lap Dick Clayton's machine stopped dead and Chris Horsfield was passed for 5th spot by Browning, who had fallen no less than three times in the race!

750 Trophy Race

The question now was, could the 750 Trophy race match the excitement of the 250s? As the starter let the line go, we didn't have long to wait to find out. Vic Eastwood, in an almost carbon-copy of Roberton's ill-fated 250 start, led for the first 500 yards of the twisty Scottish circuit, building a healthy lead, before coming unstuck on one of the frozen patches and through flashed BSA teammate Lampkin, closely followed by Aird. Lampkin, who had been in television scrambles wilderness for some time, called on his vast experience and turned back the clock, as he raced to what would be his seventh and final Grandstand Trophy race win.

The young Scotsman took a comfortable 2nd place on his 360 CZ, but the man on the move was Eastwood, who made phenomenal progress in battling back from 14th at the close of the first lap, to claim an excellent 3rd at the flag. Malcolm Davis, on the much improved 360 AJS, finished 4th, bringing the Thruxton-based competition shop its first points in the 750 class, whilst series leader John Banks suffered a damaged exhaust in a first corner shunt, resulting in a lack of power and he could only bring his BSA home 5th, just in front of Smith.

Aird, the sensation of the meeting, recalls:

I can remember quite clearly coming down the hill in the 250 race and thinking 'Christ, I'm leading this.' But then I slipped off and had to fight back to get 2nd to Smithy. I remember passing Arthur (Browning) and Wadey on the way. In both races it was a matter of hanging on for grim death. It was a matter of just saying, 'I'm gonna do this.' There was no skill attached.

Jeff Smith came over to me in the paddock that day and said, 'I don't give advice to just anybody, but I'll give some advice to you. Pack your bags and go to Belgium!' I remember looking at him and just saying, 'How the hell would I get to Belgium?' I was only like 20 at the time and naturally, I stayed put! Many years later, I walked into a hotel in Perth, Australia, and Smithy was there sitting at the bar. He turned to me and said, 'I remember you, I once told you to go to Belgium!'

Whilst it was a day that young Jimmy Aird would always remember, for Bryan Wade it was definitely a day to forget. The young factory Greeves rider, who had been coming into excellent form, first fell in the 250 race, badly gashing a finger, then was unseated again in the 750s, breaking a wrist in the process.

A few corners later and Andy Roberton has grabbed the lead (PD)

Arthur Lampkin decided that the safest place to be in the 750 Trophy race was out front, which is where he stayed until the finish (PD)

Malcolm Davis followed up his 3rd place in the 250 Trophy race with a solid 4th in the 750 Trophy, to score AJS' first points on the 360 (PD)

Grandstand Trophy Race Results

250 Trophy
1 J Smith (BSA)
2 J Aird (CZ)
3 M Davis (AJS)
4 F Mayes (Montesa)
5 A Browning (Greeves)
6 C Horsfield (AJS)

750 Trophy
1 A J Lampkin (500 BSA)
2 J Aird (360 CZ)
3 V Eastwood (500 BSA)
4 M Davis (360 AJS)
5 J Banks (500 BSA)
6 J Smith (500 BSA)

So with one round left to play for, Jeff Smith would go to Caerleon two weeks later to try to secure a third Grandstand Trophy, but his first in the 250 class. However, it would not be easy for him, as following the cancellation of the 250 race at Bury St Edmunds, it had been decided that there would be two 250 races run in South Wales, both counting towards the Trophy series. Smith would have to call on all his experience as Freddie Mayes, Arthur Browning and Malcolm Davis could all still conceivably overhaul him.

In the 750 Trophy, BSA teamsters, John Banks and Vic Eastwood, were tied on 19 points apiece and the title seemed to be for them to decide in the final race. However, if they both failed to finish there was a remote possibility that Arthur Lampkin could draw level, but to do so, he would need to repeat his victory in Scotland.

Round 5

Caerleon, Monmouthshire, March 16, 1968

The final round of the abridged 1967-68 Grandstand Trophy series produced a real mixed bag of racing. There was plenty of drama in the 250 Trophy and some of the closest racing ever seen on television, whilst the 750 Trophy race that promised so much, couldn't have been more disappointing in terms of the battle for the trophy.

250 Trophy Race 1

The first televised event was the first 250 Trophy race and going to the line Jeff Smith knew that if he brought all his experience to bear and rode a calculated race, the trophy could be his. As the field got cleanly away, it was Smith's main challenger, Freddie Mayes, on the lightning-fast Montesa, who hit the front, determined to do all he could to take the series into a deciding race. However, he immediately came under pressure from Malcolm Davis, whose AJS was also showing an excellent turn of speed. Davis soon hit the front, with Mayes 2nd, but young Andy Roberton kept things interesting as he squeezed past Smith into 3rd place.

At the head of the race, Davis started to ease away from Mayes, but the Cambridgeshire rider knew that if he could keep Smith at bay, then the destination of the trophy would

Malcolm Davis ran away with the first 250 Trophy race at Caerleon and his 12-point haul on the day saw him leapfrog Arthur Browning and Freddie Mayes to finish as runner-up in the series. He is pictured here at the third round at Naish Hill (CB)

New 250 Grandstand Trophy holder, Jeff Smith, dominated the final race of the series to finish 17 points clear of Davis. Here he is leading Arthur Browning in the opening round at Canada Heights (BH)

only be decided in the final 250 race. However, it would appear that the pressure got to Mayes, as with the race nearing its close, he slid off the Montesa and his challenge was over. To cap things off, in his characteristic style, Smith eased past Roberton on the final lap to claim six points from 2nd place and his third Grandstand Trophy.

This was a bitter pill for Freddie Mayes to swallow:

The two months or so I had off from competitive racing (due to foot-and-mouth) did me no favours and when the 250 series started again I was not riding as confidently. The Montesa was very quick, but it didn't handle as well as the CZ. It was a little bit heavier as well and the front wheel had a tendency to slide away. Having said that, I should have won on it at Kirkaldy and been second in the first race at Caerleon, so no excuses!

At the flag, it was Davis from Smith and Roberton, who registered the best result yet by a Welshman, which was all the sweeter as he was racing on home soil. Behind this trio, Arthur Browning, who had suffered a terrible start, was finishing fast, though not fast enough to catch Alan Clough, who took 4th, or fellow Greeves man, Vic Allan, who added to his points tally with 5th place.

250 Trophy Race 2

The second 250 Trophy race proved to be a virtual victory procession for Smith, as he blasted out of the start and led from the first lap till the last. Behind him though, a tremendous scrap was building between Browning and Roberton. This remains one of Roberton's clearest memories from the Grandstand days:

I had a terrific scrap with Arthur Browning, we were going at it hammer and tongs. It was a hell of a race!

It would seem that the *MCN* correspondent, Gavin Trippe agreed, describing the duel as 'one of the most heart stopping scratches ever seen on TV'. At the flag, the Greeves man just got the verdict, whilst a tiring Jimmy Aird missed out on points, as Davis, Tom Leadbitter and Mayes all surged past in the closing laps.

750 Trophy Race

The 750 Trophy race promised so much, but was ultimately spoilt by a very ragged start, which left the main protagonists for the title, Banks and Eastwood, along with about half the field ensnared on the start line. Out of the chaos shot Arthur Browning, with Arthur Lampkin and Dick Clayton on the factory AJS snapping at his heels.

However, it was the youngest member of the BSA squad, Keith Hickman, revelling in the sticky going, who moved up to 2nd place and steadily reeled in Browning. Hickman recalls:

There'd been a bit of a false start and I was one of the lucky ones who got away. I remember passing Arthur Lampkin and following Arthur Browning on his Greeves. On the last lap I really pushed and caught Browning and as the BSA had a bit more go than the Greeves I slipped past him as we came onto the downhill stretch to the finish.

Hickman won his first BBC Grandstand race, and in the process leap-frogged Smith, who had been caught up in the startline *mêlée*, Wade and Lampkin, to finish third in the final standings. Banks could manage no better than 8th place at the flag, but despite

Keith Hickman rode a calculated race, closing down and passing Arthur Browning on the last lap to win the 750 Trophy race. Cecil Bailey caught him in action earlier in the series at Naish Hill in February

missing out on points he was the new Trophy winner, as Eastwood had been forced to retire with a burnt out clutch.

Dick Clayton was a happy man after the 750 race, as four and a half years after scoring his first points at Beeston where he suffered a big fall, he marked his long road from recovery with 4 points from third place.

Grandstand Trophy Race Results

250 Trophy Race 1
1 M Davis (AJS)
2 J Smith (BSA)
3 A Roberton (Husqvarna)
4 A Clough (Husqvarna)
5 V Allan (Greeves)
6 A Browning (Greeves)

250 Trophy Race 2
1 J Smith (BSA)
2 A Browning (Greeves)
3 A Roberton (Husqvarna)
4 M Davis (AJS)
5 T Leadbitter (Husqvarna)
6 F Mayes (Montesa)

750 Trophy
1 K Hickman (500 BSA)
2 A Browning (360 Greeves)
3 R Clayton (360 AJS)
4 A Roberton (360 Husqvarna)
5 A J Lampkin (500 BSA)
6 T Challinor (360 Sprite)

1967-68 Grandstand Trophy Series Final Standings

250 Trophy

1	J Smith (BSA)	6 8 8 6 8	36pts
2	M Davis (AJS)	2 0 5 8 4	19pts
3	F Mayes (CZ/Montesa)	8 4 4 0 2	18pts
4	A Browning (Greeves)	4 2 3 2 6	17pts
5	A Roberton (Husqvarna)	0 0 0 5 5	10pts
6	J Aird (CZ)	0 0 6 0 0	6pts

750 Trophy

1	J Banks (500 BSA)	8 8 0 3 0	19pts
2	V Eastwood (500 BSA)	6 0 8 5 0	19pts
3	K Hickman (500 BSA)	2 3 3 0 8	16pts
4	A J Lampkin (500 BSA)	3 0 0 8 3	14pts
5	B Wade (360 Greeves)	0 6 6 0 0	12pts
6	J Smith (500 BSA)	4 5 0 2 0	11pts

Despite failing to score at Caerleon, John Banks, pictured here at Naish Hill, succeeded Dave Bickers as the new 750 Grandstand Trophy holder (CB)

The Grandstand Trophy wins meant very different things to each of the victors. For Jeff Smith it was a great thrill, but also a tremendous achievement for himself and BSA (see p237).

For John Banks, who was beginning to emerge from the shadow of Smith, it had a very different significance. On receiving his BBC Grandstand Trophy at Caerleon, Banks told millions of watching BBC viewers how he hoped this would just be the beginning of things:

My ambitions are blunt and simple. I want to win a world title and do really well.

The close of the 1967-68 season heralded the end of an era for several of the key players in the Grandstand Trophy. After five series the producer, Brian Johnson was moving on to a job in the Science Features department, where he would initially direct *Tomorrow's World* before going on to write and direct *The Secret War* and produce *Test Pilot,* both of which were highly successful programmes.

Johnson was replaced by Richard Tilling, who would see the Grandstand Trophy series through to its conclusion before going on to succeed Bryan Cowgil as the studio producer for *Grandstand*.

It also marked Jeff Smith's last major trophy win and neither he, nor his arch rival, Dave Bickers, would add to their tally of Grandstand Trophies in the future. Instead a new group of hungry young riders was emerging from their shadows, led by the likes of John Banks and Malcolm Davis, who would both go on to be British champions in 1968.

Additionally there were riders such as Arthur Browning, Bryan Wade, Vic Allan, Andy Roberton, Jimmy Aird and Keith Hickman, who had all made their mark on this series and were looking for a slice of the action in the coming one.

At a time of change in the Grandstand Trophy series, the West Wilts Club's leading light, Ken Lywood (second from right) remained a constant. Here he is pictured with journalists (left to right) Gavin Trippe, Mike Bashford and Ralph Venables at the club's Naish Hill circuit in February

Jeff Smith's Lightweight Special

For the 1967-68 Grandstand series, two-time 500 Trophy winner, Jeff Smith, decided to channel his energy into winning the 250 class and with the blessing of BSA Competition manager, Brian Martin, he built up a super-lightweight 250.

> *I suggested to Brian that I collect together a pile of lightweight parts and build a 250 to run on battery and coil for the Grandstand Trophy. He was very enthusiastic and threw all of his considerable abilities into the project. In the end the bike weighed in at 199 lbs ready to race and was absolutely the most fun of all the machines I ever rode.*

Smith had been a regular on the 250 GP scene from 1960, when he was runner-up to Dave Bickers in the European championship, through till the end of the 1962 season where again he finished second, this time to Sweden's Torsten Hallman, who took the first of his four world titles. However, from 1963 onwards, he had focused exclusively on the 500 titles, winning back-to-back world championships in 1964 and 65 and taking six consecutive British championship wins.

Though he more often than not restricted his racing to the larger capacity 420, 440 and ultimately 494 BSAs, he always enjoyed the odd canter on a 250. In the Grandstand series, Smith first raced a 250 into the points at Builth Wells in January 1964, when he finished third behind Dave Bickers on the Husqvarna and Greeves' number one, Alan Clough.

Smith raced a two-fifty more regularly in 1964-65, making a nuisance of himself by scoring points in six rounds and taking the runner-up spot on three occasions. The first of these came at Tweseldown in December, when he split the factory Greeves of Alan Clough and John Griffiths. He would go on to finish the series in fifth place, just two points adrift of 250 specialist, Griffiths.

A proud looking Smith astride the titanium framed lightweight 250 complete with rear disc brake, pictured in the paddock at Canada Heights in November 1967. Smith's Grandstand debut on the 250 Barracuda-engined special resulted in a fine runner-up spot behind Freddie Mayes on a twin-port CZ (BH)

For the following series his name was being linked with a 250 special that ace bike builder Eric Cheney was preparing for him. A photo and article about the finished bike appeared in the *MCN* in the first week of December 1965, and it looked and sounded, on paper at least, like a winner. It was mooted that Smith would ride it in the Grandstand Trophy meeting at Lyng that weekend, however, that was destined not to be.

I do not remember what happened with the Cheney machine. It certainly looked a fine bike, but it fell between the cracks for some reason and I never did actually ride it.

However, he raced a 250 at most of the rounds in that series, scoring points in four of the eight rounds to finish seventh in the final standings. Over that winter, his best result came at Nantwich, where he finished third behind Bickers and rising star and fellow Birmingham resident, Arthur Browning. Curiously enough, Jerry Scott debuted the 250 Cheney BSA at the same meeting. Scott didn't figure in the points at Hatherton Hall, but would go on to take third place at Asham Woods in March, behind the factory Greeves of Bryan Goss and Freddie Mayes.

Smith was sidelined for much of the 1966-67 series through injury and it was only in the 1967-68 series that he really threw everything he had into the 250 Trophy.

Winning the 1967-68 250 BBC Grandstand trophy was like winning my first world championship. It was a wonderful feeling. I put maximum effort into that series.

As it turned out, this would be Jeff Smith's last major title and the fact that he won it against the odds made success all the sweeter:

By then the two-stroke was king and the 250 class was where the youngsters were. To win at 33, against the cream of the youngsters on a four-stroke was a lovely bonus. The trophy (a television camera in stainless steel) still has pride of place on our mantelpiece.

Nearing the end of the line; Smith's 250 photographed in the paddock, again at Canada Heights, but over two years later, in February 1970. Smith did not mount a challenge in the Grandstand series of 1969-70, but the development on the bike paid dividends in the 1970 250 British championship. Smith and the little BSA took a race win at the opening round at Nantwich in April and continued to finish every race they competed in, eventually finishing 3rd overall behind the AJSs of Malcolm Davis and Andy Roberton (BH)

1968-69
Going Into Orbit

Alan Clough, Clifton, 28th December, 1968 (MC)

Setting The Scene

On the domestic scene, Malcolm Davis won the first of his three 250 British championship titles racing for AJS. Malcolm had to overcome stiff opposition from Don Rickman, who made a concerted effort to win his first national title, and young Andy Roberton, who had a great season racing Husqvarna for Brian Leask.

Davis also raced the 250 GPs that season, but experienced a torrid time. He twice finished 4th overall, in Belgium and in Luxembourg, but fell heavily on the fast and treacherous Bilstein circuit in West Germany, knocking himself cold in the process.

Like Davis, Bryan Wade showed a lot of promise in his GP outings, finishing 7th overall in both the French and Dutch rounds. But again, like Davis, he crashed out of the West German GP breaking a wrist when he collided with a tree. After falling in the Swedish GP when seemingly set for victory, Wade finished an excellent 5th overall in his home GP at Dodington Park.

In the 500 British championship, John Banks, like Davis, was crowned champion for the first time. On the back of his BBC Grandstand and ITV World of Sport victories, Banks improved steadily over the summer to the surprise of many in the motocross world, finishing well clear of Vic Eastwood, who had switched to Husqvarna mid-season, and his BSA teammate, Dave Nicoll.

If Banks' improvement on the domestic front was a surprise, in Europe he was a sensation. After a steady start to the season, he slipped into top gear for the second half, winning the French and Dutch GPs outright and finishing as runner-up in Belgium and Switzerland. Over the season, Banks actually accrued more points than East Germany's Paul Friedrichs, but at that time a rider's seven best results counted from thirteen GPs, with Friedrichs scoring 42 points to Banks' 41 to complete his hat-trick of world titles.

On The Move

The biggest news in the 'transfer market' came out of the BSA camp. After three seasons together, Vic Eastwood and BSA had parted company rather acrimoniously. BSA competition manager, Brian Martin, had intimated that Eastwood was not a team player, whilst Eastwood had made it clear that for him it was about a team of one, and he was not prepared to go on with things as they were. In a candid column in the *MCN* of 17th April 1968, Eastwood reflected:

> *I re-signed with the promise of two new GP bikes. With only weeks to go to the first GP I only had a pile of bits. A month ago I got one engine. I opened my mouth to complain, it got in the press and that was me finished.*

Within days of leaving BSA, Eastwood had been snapped up by Husqavrna, with UK importer Brian Leask thrilled to supply him with the latest 250 and 360 models. Over the following months Eastwood would challenge for the 500 British championship, eventually finishing runner-up to Banks, would win his home GP at Farleigh Castle and would add the penultimate GP of the season in Luxembourg, to finish 6th in the world championship.

Many experts considered Eastwood a potential world champion in 1969 and he was keen to get in a good winter's training courtesy of the televised scrambles, so when the Grandstand series kicked off, he was in fine form armed with a 250 and a brand new 420 model.

Former British champion Freddie Mayes moved back to CZ, after a brief spell on a factory Montesa, whilst rising Scottish star, Jimmy Aird, moved in the opposite direction.

There was also plenty of activity at AJS, as Dick Clayton took up a factory ride with Greeves and Chris Horsfield moved on to race a Victor Métisse for the Rickman brothers. Meanwhile, Andy Roberton traded his Leask Husqvarna for a factory AJS ride, essentially returning to the team he had raced for previously, under the 'Norton Villiers' banner.

Into The 1968-69 Series

1968 will long be remembered for the student uprisings and protests that took place worldwide at a time of great civil unrest. In Britain things came to a head in March, when thousands of angry students descended on the US Embassy in Grosvenor Square to demonstrate their opposition to the war in Vietnam. The march ended in violence, as the Defence Secretary, the Secretary of State for Education and the Home Secretary were all attacked. In total, some 86 people were injured and the police made over 200 arrests.

The motorsport world was rocked on April 7th, when Formula One world champion, Jim Clark, was killed when his car left the track and ploughed into trees during a Formula Two race at Hockenheim. Clark, who was 32 years-old, was considered to be the 'King' of motor racing, with 25 Grand Prix victories and 33 pole positions, more than any other driver at that time.

Following floods in the South-West of England in July, the summer ended with the Great Flood of 1968, which mainly affected South-East England. A trough of lower pressure resulted in torrential rain and thunderstorms across the region on Sunday 15th September.

Whilst the BBC and ACU were no doubt finalising their plans for the upcoming Grandstand Moto-Cross series, the world was tuned in to the Olympic Games in Mexico. It will long be remembered for the Black Power salutes of the Afro- Amercian athletes, Tommy Smith and John Carlos, and also Bob Beamon's amazing leap of 8.90 meters (29 ft 2 1/2 in) in the long jump final, which to this day stands as the Olympic record. David Hemery was one of five gold-medal winners for Britain, in the 400m Hurdles.

A typical start with mud flying everywhere and Harold Taylor (on crutches at right of picture), literally, in the middle of things! Clifton, December 1968 (BH)

Round 1

Dodington Park, Glos, November 16, 1968

For the opening round of the 1968-69 Grandstand Trophy series, the BBC Outside Broadcast Unit paid its second visit to Dodington Park, a circuit that had hosted an excellent 250 British GP in August that year. Unluckiest man that day was definitely Malcolm Davis, who had been really flying on the factory AJS and led both races before ignition problems eliminated him.

1968 250 British Champion, Malcolm Davis, opened his Grandstand account with a win in the 250 Trophy race (CB)

250 Trophy Race

Davis would feature in the 250 Trophy race, but it was the young Scot Jimmy Aird, now racing a factory Montesa, who got the start. However, his race was soon run when he got horribly out of shape as he attempted to leap a ditch, landing awkwardly and breaking

Back on a CZ, Freddie Mayes raced to the runner-up spot in the 250 Trophy race (CB)

the frame of the Spanish bike. Into the lead raced Davis on the AJS, racing on what he considered to be the finest circuit in the country.

In the early stages the BSAs of Arthur Lampkin and Jeff Smith were well placed, but Lampkin was soon passed by both Freddie Mayes, now back on a CZ, and Eastwood, who had carved through the pack following a poor start to his TV debut on Husqvarna. Davis was to have no reliability issues this time out though and led to the finish, with Mayes 2nd and Eastwood finishing a commendable 3rd. Next came Lampkin, Dick Clayton, now a factory Greeves runner, and the latest teenage sensation, Richard Hughes, on another works Greeves, who scored his first Grandstand points.

One top Greeves runner missing from the opening rounds was Bryan Wade who was plying his trade Stateside, racing for Greeves in the Inter-AM series, where he would rub shoulders with the likes of Torsten Hallman and Joel Robert.

750 Trophy race

MCN reporter, Gavin Trippe, was thrilled by the 750 Trophy race, describing it as a 'cracker' and going on to add that it was:

a magnificent start to what looks like being one of the most open and intriguing contests in the fireside scrambling series which BBC introduced six winters ago.

Freddie Mayes got a flying start on his 380 CZ, but within half a lap Eastwood on his 420 Husqvarna had swept into the lead. However, Eastwood's lead was short lived, as he stalled the big Husky in a tight hairpin corner and slipped back to 7th place. Into the lead went Keith Hickman, the young factory BSA man from Cumnor, near Oxford, coping brilliantly with the tricky Dodington course. Hickman recalls:

Keith Hickman mastered the tricky Dodington Park off-cambers to pick up where he had left off in the previous series with a win in the 750 Trophy race (CB)

I remember Vic Eastwood and Dave Nicoll were going really well, but I slipped past Dave and I was away then. I went well on the fast grassy circuits and there was one particular section with a difficult off-camber and I was gaining time over everybody there.

Fellow BSA factory rider, Dave Nicoll, trailed Hickman, but where was the reigning Grandstand Trophy holder, John Banks? The answer was that he was struggling down field having problems getting the 500 BSA to grip on the grassy surface. He never found his rhythm during the race and would eventually finish out of the points in 7th place.

Eastwood was clearly the fastest man around the Gloucestershire track and after passing Dick Clayton for 6th place he wound on and passed first Arthur Browning, then Freddie Mayes in a pulsating final lap. At the flag, Eastwood was 3rd behind Hickman and Nicoll, but ahead of Mayes, Browning and Clayton.

Nicoll had enjoyed an upturn in form in the 1968 British championship, where he finished 3rd overall, the highlight being his double race win at Elsworth, Cambridgeshire.

In 1968 I had a full-500 factory bike and had adapted quite well by then and things went much better, so that was a big boost to my confidence.

This new self-belief would be reflected in some good rides in the Grandstand Trophy over the winter, though Nicoll's best days on the BSA still lay ahead.

Dick Clayton scored points in both 250 and 750 Trophy races on his TV debut for Greeves. Here he leads Jeff Smith in the 250 race (CB)

Supporting Races

The TV Invitation, which was recorded and run later in the *Grandstand* programme, was something of a four-stroke benefit. Banks initially followed Arthur Lampkin, but when his senior teammate made a mistake, he needed no invitation, sweeping past and holding the lead to the finish to make amends for his disappointing showing in the 750 Trophy. Hickman again showed his form, coming through to 2nd, with Chris Horsfield, now campaigning a Victor Métisse, taking 3rd ahead of the factory BSAs of Nicoll, Jeff Smith and Alan Lampkin.

Gavin Trippe concluded his race report by saying:

This was a thoroughly enjoyable two-hour meeting. Everything was conducive to top-class racing. The weather was fine, the course fast and dry, the starting system worked and the Bristol MCC organisation was good.

I'll bet the BBC and new moto cross producer Richard Tilling will be hoping this is the start of something good.

Grandstand Trophy Race Results

250 Trophy
1 M Davis (AJS)
2 F Mayes (CZ)
3 V Eastwood (Husqvarna)
4 A J Lampkin (BSA)
5 D Clayton (Greeves)
6 R Hughes (Greeves)

750 Trophy
1 K Hickman (500 BSA)
2 D Nicoll (500 BSA)
3 V Eastwood (420 Husqvarna)
4 F Mayes (380 CZ)
5 A Browning (380 Greeves)
6 D Clayton (380 Greeves)

Vic Eastwood showed blistering pace at Dodington, but a poor start in the 250 Trophy race and an error whilst leading the 750 Trophy race saw him finish both races in 3rd place. Here he is seen leaping the 420 Husqvarna (CB)

Round 2

Lyng, Norfolk, November 30, 1968

The second round of the series was run on the day that the Trade Descriptions Act came into force. The act was introduced to prevent manufacturers and traders from misleading the consumer. It makes you wonder how the Grandstand Trophy Moto Cross series would have been labelled!

November 30th also saw the Grandstand series return to the popular Cadders Hill circuit in Norfolk, after an absence of almost four years. Good weather and an excellent track greeted the riders, but a series of false starts blemished an otherwise excellent meeting.

250 Trophy Race

When the 250 Trophy race got underway following a false start, Vic Eastwood led the charge up the hill, whilst just a few yards behind him Freddie Mayes uncharacteristically looped his CZ and was run over by several passing riders, though luckily he escaped serious injury in the *mêlée*.

Vic Eastwood is perfectly poised as he leaps his Husqvarna uphill on his way to victory in the 250 Trophy race (MC)

As the race settled down, Eastwood led from Greeves' Dick Clayton, with the second Husqvarna of Alan Clough in close attendance. Then disaster struck the Wigan man, as the Greeves engine seized mid-race leaving the Husky pair of Eastwood and Clough well clear of the pack. Dodington Park winner, Malcolm Davis, was finding his feet and moved ahead of Browning, whilst his teammate, Andy Roberton, who had recently re-signed to AJS, was nicely placed in 5th spot.

The closing laps were enlivened by a tight three-way scrap. Roberton was snapping at Browning's heels, but in his effort to get past, he ignored the threat of Jeff Smith, who had charged up the order from 14th on the opening lap to snatch 5th from under the young Welshman's nose on the last lap.

Eastwood had won his first ever 250 Grandstand Trophy race, though he had previously tasted success on the 250 James in a BBC race at Naish Hill way back in February 1963 (see p27). Now could he record a double by adding the 750 Trophy race?

Malcolm Davis finished strongly in the 250 Trophy race, taking 3rd place and a share of the lead in the series with Eastwood (BH)

750 Trophy Race

Off the startline, two Greeves outstripped the pack to emerge at the head of the field, followed by two BSAs, as Browning led Clayton, Smith and John Banks. As he had shown in the 250 race, Clayton had the speed to worry the best, but a missed gear as he was preparing to pass Browning resulted in a fall and he slipped back down the field. An alert Banks took full advantage of the situation to slip past Smith and he too soon had his sights set on Browning.

At half-distance, Banks moved into the lead and eased away from Browning, but all eyes were on Eastwood who was storming through the field after he had been baulked when a rider had fallen in front of him going up the big hill. In the closing laps, Eastwood fought past both Smith and Browning to take an excellent 2nd place, whilst

Greeves teamsters Arthur Browning and Dick Clayton grabbed the lead in the 750 Trophy race on their 'Tubular' 380 Greeves (pre-production Griffons). Browning went on to finish 4th, as he had in the earlier 250 Trophy race (MC)

1968 500 British champion, John Banks, racing just 50 miles from his Bury St Edmunds home, had a comfortable win in the 750 Trophy race (BH)

Smith outmuscled Browning for 3rd. To complete the points scoring positions, Chris Horsfield on his Métisse edged Hickman on the factory BSA.

In battling back to 2nd spot, Eastwood had done enough to stand at the top of both Grandstand Trophy tables after two rounds, tied on points with Davis in the 250s, but a point clear of Hickman in the 750 class. But unbeknown to us all, disaster lay just around the corner for the popular rider from Kent.

Grandstand Trophy Race Results

250 Trophy
1 V Eastwood (Husqvarna)
2 A Clough (Husqvarna)
3 M Davis (AJS)
4 A Browning (Greeves)
5 J Smith (BSA)
6 A Roberton (AJS)

750 Trophy
1 J Banks (500 BSA)
2 V Eastwood (420 Husqvarna)
3 J Smith (500 BSA)
4 A Browning (380 Greeves)
5 C Horsfield (500 BSA Métisse)
6 K Hickman (500 BSA)

On Saturday December 14th, as he was competing in an ITV World of Sport meeting at Hawkstone Park, Eastwood fell heavily when he crashed into a tree, and suffered a compound fracture to his right leg. There had been many other spills on the day, with BSA teamsters Jeff Smith and Keith Hickman both victims of the treacherous conditions.

Chris Horsfield was at Hawkstone that day, but after riding the circuit in practice he decided not to compete and feels the meeting should have been called off:

It was so dangerous, so slippery, and you just didn't know what was rideable. It was black ice on rock, and I remember thinking, 'This is the first time in my life I'm going to call it a day. I'm not going to ride.' Vic took off at the start and was flying, but I saw his accident and saw him hit the tree.

Smith recalls a fall of his own and how quick thinking may have saved him from serious injury as he lay flat on his back in the middle of the track:

It was an incredibly frosty day and I went down hard along a fast straight. I ended up lying in the centre of the course on my back with my legs wide open and my head pointing in the direction of the race. I lay there and could not move, but I could hear the sound of oncoming machines! So as it was a frosty day I blew as large a column of condensing breath as I could into the air. It must have worked because they all missed me.

Smith escaped with a few cuts and bruises, but Eastwood's season lay in tatters as he lay in a hospital bed in the Royal Salop Infirmary in Shrewsbury, and sadly for all motocross fans, it would be 14 months before he would grace our racetracks again. Ironically, when he did return to action it was in an ITV World of Sport meeting at Castleford, Yorkshire, in February 1970.

A major draw in the paddock at Clifton was the 250 Cheney Suzuki. Here the merits of the machine are being discussed by Ken Sedgley, holding the bike, former BSA factory rider, John Harris (kneeling) and Jimmy Aird who was being linked with the bike at the time. However, it was Tom Leadbitter who raced the bike at Clifton and in several other TV meetings that winter) (BH)

Round 3

Clifton, Derbyshire, December 28, 1968

On December 21st, the Apollo 8 space mission began when it was launched from the Kennedy Space Center in Florida. This was by far the most ambitious mission in the Apollo Space Programme to date, as it was scheduled to include the first manned lunar orbit. The American astronauts, Frank Borman, James Lovell and William Anders spent Christmas 1968 orbiting the moon and making two live television broadcasts including photos of the Earthrise they had witnessed. Borman brought the transmission to a close with the following words:

And from the crew of Apollo 8, we close with good night, good luck, a Merry Christmas, and God bless all of you - all of you on the good Earth.

Whilst the Apollo crew had been broadcasting images to earth from a distance of 238,857 miles, three days later the BBC Outside Broadcast team boldly ventured some 150 miles north to Clifton in Derbyshire, for the third round of the series and the last before the New Year. Doubtlessly there was a lot of conversation in the paddock about the moon orbit, but when the dust settled over the hilly Clifton circuit, one man in particular was flying high, though one of the other stars had also attempted to go into orbit himself!

Alan Clough, from Poynton in Cheshire, who had been racing motocross for more than 10 years, had been competing in the Grandstand Trophy from the outset winning three 250 Trophy races and finishing as runner-up to Dave Bickers in the first two series. But after finishing 3rd in the 1965/66 series it seemed as if his TV star was waning and although he generally went well at Clifton, he had also suffered a major setback there, when he crashed whilst racing his works Dot in October 1960, and broke a thigh.

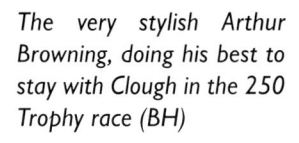

The very stylish Arthur Browning, doing his best to stay with Clough in the 250 Trophy race (BH)

The King of Clifton! Alan Clough was dominant in Derbyshire. Here he crests a hill on his way to victory in the 250 Trophy race (MC)

Top trials riders Alan Lampkin and Mick Andrews battled throughout the 250 Trophy race. Andrews, on the factory Ossa, took 4th, whilst Lampkin, trying Jeff Smith's 250, was 5th (BH)

Clough had been British champion after switching from Greeves to Husqvarna in 1967, but a serious knee injury picked up whilst racing in Belgium that season had hindered his form ever since, despite an operation at the season's close. However, Clough had shown some of his old form in the final round of the 1968 250 British championship at Hatherton Hall, Nantwich, where he won both races as the rain teemed down, and despite missing the opening Grandstand meeting at Dodington Park he had bounced back at Lyng, with second place to Eastwood, who was now on the sick list.

250 Trophy Race

The 250 Trophy race saw a great battle between the 1967 250 British champion, Clough, and the man who had succeeded him in 1968, Malcolm Davis, on his factory AJS. Following Vic Eastwood's crash at Hawkstone, Davis was sitting at the top of the Grandstand Trophy standings after two rounds and was very keen to extend his lead. He led in the early stages, but as Clough increasingly applied the pressure he crashed heavily, allowing the Husky rider and Arthur Browning to slip past.

Clough rode on to take a comfortable win from Browning, whilst a battered and bruised Davis limped across the line for 3rd. A second scrap between ace trials riders, Alan Lampkin and Mick Andrews, was eventually decided in favour of the local man, Andrews, who took his factory Ossa to 4th place ahead of Lampkin, who was enjoying an outing on Jeff Smith's ultra-lightweight BSA. To round-off the top six, Freddie Mayes, who had crashed out at Lyng, found himself in the points again.

Jeff Smith ended up as an interested spectator at Clifton. He had made the 35-mile trip to Derbyshire intent on racing, only to discover in practice that the shoulder he had damaged in his spill at Hawkstone Park was too sore for him to be competitive.

Vic Allan had his best result to date in the Grandstand Trophy, with 2nd behind the rampant Clough in the 750 Trophy race. Here he leads John Banks and Greeves teammate Malcolm Rathmell, who went on to score his first points from 6th place (BH)

750 Trophy Race

The start of the 750 Trophy race made good TV viewing, as first CZ runner, Jimmy Aird, caught his helmet on the rope and fell and then as the pack soared over the first jump, Dick Clayton collided with not one but two Lampkin brothers, Arthur and, future world trials champion, Martin, who took in a few BBC meetings that winter.

Amidst all this confusion, Greeves' rising star, Vic Allan, emerged in the lead, but after a few bends he had yielded to Clough, with Keith Hickman in 3rd place. But it proved not to be a good day for BSA. Defending 750 Trophy winner, John Banks, had been held up at the start, but was really flying through the field. He passed Hickman, who was struggling after losing a footrest, and set out after Allan, but his race was run when the ignition on the BSA died.

In the closing laps Browning demoted the stricken Hickman, who gamely held on for 4th place ahead of BSA teammate, Dave Nicoll. To complete the top six, Martin Lampkin's close friend and rival, Malcolm Rathmell, who had won an Invitation race at Lyng, continued his good run of form to score his first Grandstand points on his ageing 360 Greeves.

Factory BSA runner Keith Hickman was flying in the 750 Trophy race, but he did well to finish 4th after losing a footrest mid-race (MC)

Supporting Races

Clough, who after a barren spell of more than three years without a Grandstand Trophy win, took 250 and 750 wins on the same day, added a third victory in the Second Invitation. However, the man who set the Invitation races alight was Banks.

The East Anglian ace stormed to victory in the First Invitation after another poor start. Clough also suffered his only bad start of the day, but even he couldn't match Banks' blistering pace as he pulverised the opposition. Banks dramatically caught and passed Browning on the last lap of the six-lap dash with Allan third, whilst Clough worked his way up to 4th at the flag.

Clough made no mistakes in the last race of the day; the Second Invitation. He led from start to finish, though Banks was gaining rapidly on the Husky ace, until with just one corner left to go he spectacularly flew off the track, down a bank and came to rest in a ditch - an impressive flight, but not in NASA's league and with no time left for re-entry! Clough took the win unaware of the drama unfolding behind him, as Greeves teamsters Browning and Rathmell, who was enjoying his day's racing in Derbyshire, gratefully took 2nd and 3rd places respectively.

Man of the hour; Alan Clough (right) talking to Chris Horsfield back in the paddock (MC)

Grandstand Trophy Race Results

250 Trophy
1 A Clough (Husqvarna)
2 A Browning (Greeves)
3 M Davis (AJS)
4 M Andrews (Ossa)
5 A R C Lampkin (BSA)
6 F Mayes (CZ)

750 Trophy
1 A Clough (400 Husqvarna)
2 V Allan (380 Greeves)
3 A Browning (380 Greeves)
4 K Hickman (500 BSA)
5 D Nicoll (500 BSA)
6 M Rathmell (360 Greeves)

Round 4

Canada Heights, Kent, January 18, 1969

The first BBC meeting of the New Year brought two races that would have a great influence on the destination of the two trophies. It also saw Jeff Smith return from injury, Bryan Wade back from his US trip and Bryan Goss making a welcome return to the action following a long lay-off.

250 Trophy Race

The 250 Trophy race saw double-winner from Clifton, Alan Clough, blast off the line and get the jump on all his rivals. Wade soon joined him at the front though and the pair of them eased clear of the field, whilst behind them, Greeves teamsters Dick Clayton and Arthur Browning engaged in a race-long duel.

Clough and Wade battled it out, with the Nailsworth, Gloucestershire, based Yorkshireman briefly taking the lead, though he ultimately found himself outgunned by Clough's Husqvarna. Eventually, Clough drew clear of Wade to take his third consecutive

Who said the camera cannot lie? This camera is emblazoned with the BBC TV COLOUR logo, but former BBC producer, Brian Johnson, assures me that transmission would still have been in black and white at this time (BH)

Enjoying a purple patch of form, Alan Clough leads the field in the 250 Trophy race. Next up are Malcolm Rathmell (10), Bryan Wade (23), Arthur Browning (8), Bryan Goss (29) and Roger Snoad (25) (BH)

Grandstand Trophy race, Browning got the better of Clayton, and Goss led Smith home to complete the top six.

Malcolm Davis, who had led the series before the race, had gearbox problems on the AJS and finished outside the points in 8th place and ceded the series lead to Clough.

750 Trophy Race

Just as Clough had left his stamp on the 250 race, John Banks took complete control of the 750 Trophy race, leading off the line and then easing clear of the pursuing pack. For his part, Clough must have wished he had brought along his race-winning 400 of the previous meeting, rather than the 420 he was riding for the first time. Clough was out of sorts with the new engine, which had a lot more power, though a smaller power band, and he finished in a lowly 12th place.

In a race that was dominated by the BSA and Greeves riders, Clayton, inspired by his good showing in the 250 race, took up station in 2nd place on his 380 Greeves, ahead of the Lampkins, Arthur and Alan, who led Smith, Vic Allan, Browning and Wade. Clayton recalls:

> I had a good day out at Canada Heights, it was one of those tracks that I generally went well on.

With the first two riding comfortably within themselves, attention focused on the battle for 3rd. Arthur Lampkin, who was experiencing a dip in form, soon slipped downfield, but brother Alan held on to pip Allan for 3rd place, whilst Smith had a solid ride into 5th and Wade gave Browning the slip to claim the last points.

Wade, racing the pre-production 250 Greeves Griffon, pushed Clough hard in the opening laps, but had to settle for the runner-up spot (BH)

Supporting Races

A relative upset seemed to be on the cards in the TV Invitation when Smith looked set to cap his comeback with a win. However, after leading for three laps he was out when a titanium footrest bolt sheared. Through galloped Banks, previous 750 Trophy series leader Keith Hickman, looking to make amends for his spill in the 750 race, and Clough. Banks eventually ran out the winner, with Clough 2nd and Hickman 3rd in front of a Greeves trio of Wade, Allan and Browning.

With two rounds left to play for in the sixth series, Clough held a four-point lead over Davis in the 250 Trophy, whilst Banks had leap-frogged teammate Hickman to lead by a slender margin of two points in the 750s. However, both Clough and Banks had taken a major stride towards lifting the respective 250 and 750 trophies.

Jeff Smith looks on, as BSA Competition Shop mechanic, Norman Hanks, works on his bike. The interested party on the right of the photo is Smith's son, James (BH)

Dick Clayton always enjoyed racing at Canada Heights. Here he is pictured on his way to the runner-up spot in the 750 Trophy race (BH)

Grandstand Trophy Race Results

250 Trophy
1 A Clough (Husqvarna)
2 B Wade (Greeves)
3 A Browning (Greeves)
4 D Clayton (Greeves)
5 B Goss (Husqvarna)
6 J Smith (BSA)

750 Trophy
1 J Banks (BSA)
2 D Clayton (380 Greeves)
3 A R C Lampkin (BSA)
4 V Allan (380 Greeves)
5 J Smith (BSA)
6 B Wade (380 Greeves)

On 30th January 1969, the Beatles performed their last live 'concert', a seemingly impromptu affair that took place on the rooftop of Apple Records' Abbey Road recording studio. The band, along with American keyboard player, Billy Preston, played for 40 minutes before the police arrived and ordered them to stop playing.

Round 5

Caerleon, Monmouthshire, February 15, 1969

Alan Clough must have headed to South Wales in mid-February with one objective in mind - to win the 250 Grandstand Trophy race and put as much distance as possible between himself and his nearest challengers, Malcolm Davis and Arthur Browning. And with his recent run of form, you would have been brave to bet against that particular outcome.

250 Trophy Race

However, motocross, especially the winter variety, never really respected the form book and when the riders took to the line for the 250 Trophy race, there were 30 plus other riders there with their own objectives in mind. As the field got away, the first riders to show at the head of the race were the AJS pair of Davis and Andy Roberton. Bryan Goss was running 3rd, with Clough sandwiched by the Greeves of Vic Allan and Browning.

As Goss slipped downfield with too much air in his tyres, Allan made his move. First he split the AJS teamsters, then he moved ahead of Davis, as the leader's AJS developed a misfire. Clough also seemed to get the message, relegating Roberton to 4th and closing in on Davis. But then the problem with the AJS resolved itself and the last lap saw a dramatic climax to the race. Davis caught Allan and passed him for a narrow win, whilst teammate Roberton re-claimed 3rd place at Clough's expense. Bryan Wade finished strongly to claim 5th and Dick Clayton took the last points.

The last lap re-shuffle meant that Davis and Clough were now tied on points and that the winner of the Grandstand Trophy would be decided in the final round at Kirkcaldy in a month's time.

Vic Allan was in fine form and led the 250 Trophy race for several laps before yielding to Davis (MC)

Jeff Smith deep in conversation with Motorcycle News journalist, Mike Nicks (MC)

The AJS squad in the paddock at Soarbrook Farm, with left to right behind the bikes - Andy Roberton, Malcolm Davis and ace tuner, Fluff Brown (MC)

Having recaptured the lead in dramatic fashion from Vic Allan on the last lap, Malcolm Davis, resplendent in his best woolly jumper, heads for victory in the 250 Grandstand Trophy race (MC)

750 Trophy Race

The 750 Trophy race also had plenty of drama as Birmingham lad Dave Smith was a surprise leader on his 360 Husqvarna-engined Sprite. However, within a lap, Clough, racing the big Husky, had taken the lead of the race, though it would appear he hadn't taken control of it, as he then slipped off on a treacherous uphill section and lost the lead to John Banks.

At the same time, Keith Hickman and Dave Nicoll thundered their BSAs past Smith. Things got worse for the Sprite man when he too tumbled allowing his close friend, Browning, to move into 4th spot. Chris Horsfield on the BSA-Métisse followed Browning and almost pipped him at the flag, but the finishing order was Banks, Hickman, Nicoll, Browning and Horsfield, with the other Smith, Jeff, riding through to finish 6th.

Supporting Races

To round off an excellent afternoon's televised racing came the Invitation race. Bryan Goss, who had not featured in the 750 race, rocketed to the front on his new 400 Husqvarna, a bike he was to develop a real affection for. But right on Goss' rear wheel came Banks, closely followed by Hickman and Nicoll. The slippery conditions really seemed to suit the big BSAs and, in the space of three laps, all three had eased past the West Country ace.

However, there was still time for a few more position changes behind Banks before the chequered flag was readied. First, Nicoll brushed aside his teammate Hickman, who then also yielded to Vic Allan, who had forced his way up from 8th on the first lap. Hickman quickly regained his composure, though, and re-passed the Scotsman to seal BSA's second 1-2-3 of the day. Allan added 4th place on the 380 to his fine 2nd in the 250 Trophy race, whilst Goss stuck to his guns to hold off a fast-finishing Jeff Smith.

Above, John Banks, who was approaching the peak of his form, is seen on the way to his second win of the day in the Invitation race (MC)

Grandstand Trophy Race Results

250 Trophy
1 M Davis (AJS)
2 V Allan (Greeves)
3 A Roberton (AJS)
4 A Clough (Husqvarna)
5 B Wade (Greeves)
6 D Clayton (Greeves)

750 Trophy
1 J Banks (500 BSA)
2 K Hickman (500 BSA)
3 D Nicoll (500 BSA)
4 A Browning (380 Greeves)
5 C Horsfield (500 BSA Métisse)
6 J Smith (500 BSA)

With such good form of late, odds were high for Banks retaining the 750 Trophy at the final round in Scotland. However, if things went badly for him north of the border, he could still be caught by his teammate, Hickman.

A high-speed BSA train; Dave Nicoll leads teammates John Banks and Keith Hickman in the 750 Trophy race (MC)

Round 6
Kirkcaldy, Fife, March 15, 1969

A few days before the final round of the series at Kirkcaldy, the long awaited maiden flight of Concorde a joint aerospace project between Britain and France, took place. The prospect of a 'supersonic' airliner had really captured the nation's attention and on March 2nd, Concorde 001 took to the sky over Toulouse and just over a month later the first UK-built Concorde took off from RAF Fairford on April 9th.

Though the muddy conditions at Kilrie Farm on the outskirts of Kirkcaldy, would ensure that there would be no 'supersonic' performances, there was plenty of drama and some thrilling racing in store for the avid *Grandstand* viewers.

250 Trophy Race

Malcolm Davis and Alan Clough went to the line for the 250 Trophy race knowing that whoever finished first of the two would be champion, and as the field got away they experienced mixed fortunes. Davis slithered into the lead with Bryan Goss following, whilst Clough caught the peak of his helmet on the starter's rope which hindered his progress. However, the fortunes of the same riders were about to take another decisive turn.

At the head of the race, Davis had stretched away to a 50-yard lead, whilst Clough had recovered some ground and was in a gaggle of riders battling for 2nd spot. But on the third lap, as he was negotiating a tricky corner, Davis' AJS motor stopped dead and the Gloucestershire rider watched in agony as Clough and the rest of the field slipped past. Now it was simple; if Clough could finish in the points, he would be the new 250 Grandstand Trophy holder.

Alan Clough clinched the 250 Grandstand Trophy with 3rd place in Scotland. However, here is another picture of him enjoying his day in the sun at Clifton, earlier in the series (MC)

Arthur Browning took his second win of the day in the 750 Trophy race. Here he is pictured on the 380 Greeves leading Freddie Mayes at the opening round of the series at Dodington Park, where he finished 5th (CB)

Clough decided the safest place to be was out front, but at the same time he did not want to risk too much, so when Davis' teammate Andy Roberton challenged, he willingly yielded. However, the gods were really not in the AJS camp that day, as Roberton's AJS also failed less than a lap after he had taken the lead. At the time there was some suspicion in the paddock of foul play. However, the reason for the demise of the AJS machines was later put down to the team running the bikes on 2-star petrol rather than 4-star – a costly error all round!

Clough's former Greeves teammates, Arthur Browning and Bryan Wade, then took up the running, with Clough circulating safely in 3rd place. At the flag the order was the same, with Arthur Lampkin scoring some much needed points for 4th place ahead of Goss and Scottish champion, Willy Wallace on a Greeves.

Browning took the race win, his second in the Grandstand Trophy more than two years after his first at Cuerden Park on a 360, but it was Clough who received all the plaudits, as the winner of the 250 Grandstand Trophy. Clough also enjoyed support from a rather unlikely quarter:

Everybody loved the Grandstand series even people who didn't ride bikes. At that time, I knocked about with some of the Manchester United players, Nobby Stiles, Tony Dunne, Jimmy Ryan - we all went to a gym in Stretford - and Tony Dunne told me, 'We used to settle down and watch the scrambling on the TV before the match and we'd all be cheering you on.'

750 Trophy Race

The final 750 Trophy race looked as if it might produce a surprise winner. Vic Allan, racing in his native Scotland, had got a great start on his 380 Greeves and he led the race for the first four laps. However, things went pear-shaped for the four-time Scottish champion when he fell after being passed by teammate Browning on the last lap. A jubilant Browning rode on unchallenged to victory, to join a select band of riders who had won the two main TV races at a Grandstand Trophy round.

Veteran campaigner, Jeff Smith, came through to complete a 1-2 result for Birmingham, his best result of the series, ahead of his teammate and returning Trophy winner, Banks, who cruised into 3rd place. Alan Lampkin finished a fine 4th, whilst Wade came through to beat Hickman, who had never really been in the hunt for the win and, as a result, ceded 2nd place in the series to Browning.

Supporting Races

To celebrate his second Grandstand Trophy success, Banks went out and promptly stormed to victory in the TV Invitation. Browning initially set the pace again and must have been entertaining ideas of a TV triple, but Banks, with nothing at stake, really cut loose and brushed the Greeves man aside. And in a race solely disputed by the BSA and Greeves factory riders, Banks conquered Browning, Hickman won his battle with Allan and Alan Lampkin on a 500 defeated big brother, Arthur, who raced his 250.

Just as he had after winning his first Grandstand Trophy the previous year, Banks turned his thoughts to his season's principal objective, telling the waiting reporters, 'Now I can relax before the world championships start next month in Austria.'

John Banks successfully retained the 750 Grandstand Trophy, finishing 3rd behind Browning and his BSA teammate, Jeff Smith at Kirkcaldy. He is pictured looking in complete control as he heads for his first win of the series at Lyng, the previous November (BH)

Grandstand Trophy Race Results

250 Trophy
1 A Browning (Greeves)
2 B Wade (Greeves)
3 A Clough (Husqvarna)
4 A J Lampkin (BSA)
5 B Goss (Husqvarna)
6 W Wallace (Greeves)

750 Trophy
1 A Browning (380 Greeves)
2 J Smith (500 BSA)
3 J Banks (500 BSA)
4 A R C Lampkin (500 BSA)
5 B Wade (380 Greeves)
6 K Hickman (500 BSA)

1968-69 Grandstand Trophy Series Final Standings

250 Trophy

1	A Clough (Husqvarna)	0 6 8 8 4 5	31pts
2	M Davis (AJS)	8 5 5 0 8 0	26pts
3	A Browning (Greeves)	0 4 6 5 0 8	23pts
4	B Wade (Greeves)	0 0 0 6 3 6	15pts
5	V Eastwood (Husqvarna)	5 8 0 0 0 0	13pts
6	D Clayton (Greeves)	3 0 0 4 2 0	9pts

750 Trophy

1	J Banks (500 BSA)	0 8 0 8 8 5	29pts
2	A Browning (380 Greeves)	3 4 5 0 4 8	24pts
3	K Hickman (500 BSA)	8 2 4 0 6 2	22pts
4	J Smith (500 BSA)	0 5 0 3 2 6	16pts
5	D Nicoll (500 BSA)	6 0 3 0 5 0	14pts
6	V Eastwood (420 Husqvarna)	5 6 0 0 0 0	11pts

1969-70
The End Of An Era

Dave Nicoll, Naish Hill, 29th November, 1969 (BH)

Setting The Scene

Bryan Wade took the first of his five British championship wins in the 250 class in 1969, following a sensational ride in the final round of the series at Tirley in August, where he answered his critics and handled all the pressure. Going into the last race Wade was level on points with Malcolm Davis, who stormed the start, but Wade bided his time and passed Davis mid-race to ease away to a comfortable race win and the title.

Sadly, Wade didn't contest the 250 GPs in 1969, with teammates Arthur Browning and Vic Allan representing Greeves at selected rounds. AJS also fielded two riders, initially Malcolm Davis and Andy Roberton, though Jimmy Aird would replace Davis from May onwards following Davis' dismissal (see below).

John Banks was in awesome form in the 500 British championship, racking up nine wins from ten races and finishing with more than double the points total of runner-up Vic Allan, who enjoyed by far his best British championship form to date.

With a better run of luck, Banks may well have been celebrating world championship success too. Runner-up spots in the season opener in Austria and Holland gave way to back-to-back GP wins in Czechoslovakia and Russia. This elevated Banks to the top of the rankings, and another 2nd to Roger de Coster in Belgium kept him on track for a world title. But the BSA was found wanting in the run in, and Banks narrowly missed out for the second year in succession as Swede, Bengt Aberg, on a factory Husqvarna overhauled him in the final GP in Switzerland.

On The Move

For the second season running, the AJS camp was making the news. In May they sacked their top rider, Malcolm Davis, amid claims that he wasn't making enough effort. This was difficult to comprehend, as the AJS had proved to be far from reliable, especially in the GPs. Davis switched to CZ, with bikes supplied by Dave Bickers, but in November he sprung a surprise by returning to the fold at AJS.

Meawhile, Jimmy Aird, who never felt fully at home on the Andover-built machines despite a season of doing the GPs, moved in the opposite direction, switching back to CZs whilst West Country ace, Rob Taylor, got his break with a factory AJS ride after racing Husqvarna earlier in the year.

To fill the void left by Davis, Bickers tempted his former Greeves teammate Alan Clough, who had been experiencing a lean spell on his trusty Husqvarnas, to ride for CZ.

Other News

When the 1969-70 Grandstand series took off, Andy Roberton, who had shown well in the 250 GPs, found himself touring the US promoting the AJS marque in the Inter-Am series with fellow rider Bengt Arne Bonn, a Swedish national champion, and AJS engineer Peter Inchley.

Into The 1969-70 Series

The whole world had been seized by the events of 20th July, 1969, when the crew of Apollo 11, Neil Armstrong, Buzz Aldrin and Michael Collins, landed on the moon. The following day Neil Armstrong became the first man to set foot on the moon, and the world watched on as he delivered the famous line, *'That's one small step for man, one giant step for mankind.'*

Taking a similar 'step' of faith, on 5th October 1969 the BBC launched one of its most ambitious comedy shows to date, when *Monty Python's Flying Circus* was screened for the first time. Though highly controversial at the time, and not expected to survive beyond its first season, the show would go on to be a huge success with four series being shown from 1969 through to 1974.

The Grandstand Trophy series, which was going into its seventh season, proved to be as competitive as the very first, the 250 contest being the most open yet, with each of the six rounds producing a different winner. In the 750 category, riders such as Dave Nicoll, Bryan Goss and Vic Allan would emerge to challenge John Banks, who was looking to score a hat-trick of Grandstand Trophy wins. Consistency would prove to be a big factor in both series, with the overall winner and runner-up in each case scoring points at all six rounds.

Winner of the opening 250 race of the series at Naish Hill, was Arthur Browning. Here he holds a narrow lead over Jeff Smith, before the two Birmingham riders had a coming together (BH)

Round 1

Naish Hill, Wiltshire, November 29, 1969

Bright, sunny weather greeted the riders for the first round of the series, as racing returned to the tight, twisty Wiltshire circuit for the fourth time in the Grandstand series, though the surface was icy in places and there were plenty of tumbles during the day's racing.

250 Trophy Race

The 250 Trophy race kicked things off, a race that would cause a few surprises as several lesser known riders managed to get amongst the points. Arthur Browning soon established himself at the head of the race, but teammate Dick Clayton was looking sharp, as he moved up to challenge for the lead. But his effort was short lived, as the Greeves oiled up a plug and his race was over.

Behind Browning, Jeff Smith was enjoying a tussle with Malcolm Davis, who was making his first public appearance on an AJS after recently re-signing to the Andover based factory. Smith seemed to have the upper hand, but as he moved up to challenge Browning, the two Birmingham men made contact and Smith went into the ropes. This left Browning in a winning position whilst Smith recovered, but not before Davis had ridden past for 2nd place.

However, it was not to be Smith's day, as the little BSA let him down when a battery wire broke. 250 British champion, Bryan Wade, also went out after a clash

Back on an AJS, Malcolm Davis was in the thick of the 250 action at Naish Hill. Here he leads surprise package, 21 year-old Gerald Winsor, who had a terrific race on his 250 Husqvarna. Davis finished 2nd and Winsor 3rd (BH)

with another rider wiped out his rear brake. In all the confusion, Gerald Winsor, a 21 year-old postman from Devon racing a private Husqvarna, rode through to an excellent 3rd place at the flag, closely followed by factory AJS man, Rob Taylor. Bryan Goss was 5th after getting the better of fellow West-Country man, Vic Vaughan, who was enjoying a successful outing on his privately-owned 250 BSA.

750 Trophy Race

Browning also featured prominently in the 750 Trophy race, but it was BSA factory runner Dave Nicoll, who had scaled new heights in the summer when he won the Luxembourg GP at Ettelbruck, who gated fastest. Conditions couldn't have been much more different for Nicoll, but he held a short lead over a group that contained the Greeves of Clayton, Browning and Wade, and his BSA teammate, John Banks.

Banks, the reigning 750 Trophy holder, quickly moved past Wade and Browning, but he tangled with Clayton and, unbeknown to him, ripped his front brake cable off. This caused plenty of entertainment for the TV viewers, when he dived downhill and only realised the problem when he went to grab a handful of front brake! Dragging his feet on the ground helped slow the BSA, but he still fell and re-entered the race back in 5th place again.

As the race entered the final lap, Clayton and Browning were pushing Nicoll, who had been forced to reduce his pace as he experienced cramp in his forearms. But then disaster struck the ill-fated Clayton, when the Greeves' gearbox seized up, leaving Browning to chase Nicoll to the line. Wade took a comfortable 3rd place, whilst Banks was grateful to salvage some points from 4th, ahead of Smith and Malcolm Davis on the 360 AJS.

Dave Nicoll opened his Grandstand account with a storming win in the 750 Trophy race, just holding on to beat the inspired Browning (BH)

Supporting Races

Banks showed his form in the TV Invitation though, racing to a start-to-finish win. Behind him Clayton finally brought the Greeves home, though he had to settle for 3rd place when Smith passed him on the last lap. The hapless Clayton would eventually win the 750 Invitation ahead of Taylor and Brian Atkinson on his Tom Kirby sponsored BSA Métisse, but by that time the TV equipment had been stowed away and the Outside Broadcast Unit was making its way back to Shepherd's Bush.

So with one round down, Browning and Nicoll, who had recorded his first Grandstand Trophy win after several minor TV wins, had established themselves as Trophy contenders.

Grandstand Trophy Race Results

250 Trophy
1 A Browning (Greeves)
2 M Davis (AJS)
3 G Winsor (Husqvarna)
4 R Taylor (AJS)
5 B Goss (Husqvarna)
6 V Vaughan (BSA)

750 Trophy
1 D Nicoll (500 BSA)
2 A Browning (380 Greeves)
3 B Wade (380 Greeves)
4 J Banks (500 BSA)
5 J Smith (500 BSA)
6 M Davis (360 AJS)

The unluckiest man on the day was Greeves factory runner, Dick Clayton. Mechanical problems denied him in both Trophy races, but he got some consolation from winning the 750 Invitation (BH)

250 British champion, Bryan Wade, enjoying himself in the sun at Naish Hill, where he finished 3rd in the 750 Trophy race (BH)

Round 2

Caerleon, Monmouthshire, December 27, 1969

The last Grandstand Trophy round of the 1960s saw the cast of this long-running BBC series racing in a familiar setting, this being the seventh time that the BBC Outside Broadcast crew had made the 280-mile round trip to the South Wales venue. However, one of the stars of the day's racing had put in a good few extra miles to make it there for the start.

Kirkcaldy resident, Jimmy Aird, regularly the most travelled rider in the paddock, registered a round-trip approaching 900 miles to perform in front of the BBC cameras in South Wales, but on this occasion it would prove well worth the effort.

250 Trophy Race

The 250 Trophy race epitomised the Grandstand Trophy series with racing taking place on a muddy circuit and thrills and spills aplenty. With Jeff Smith away racing in New Zealand, John Banks was given the opportunity to deputise on Smith's lightweight 250. Despite having a few extra pounds in the saddle, the Barracuda-engined special rocketed Banks to the front of the field, though a missed gear quickly undid all the good work. As the race settled, it was the unfancied Aird, back on a CZ after a brief spell on a factory Montesa, who led the field.

The young Scotsman seemed to be riding within himself as he led the Greeves of Bryan Wade and Arthur Browning, who had spent Christmas in bed with flu. But Aird then appeared to have blown his chance of TV glory when he slipped off the CZ and allowed Wade to take up the running. However, undaunted he rapidly remounted and had the last laugh, when Wade also took a tumble and effectively handed the race back to him.

From there on, Aird made no mistakes, taking the flag to become the first Scotsman to win a Grandstand Trophy race. Behind him Dick Clayton on his factory Greeves battled

Dave Nicoll, sending up a wave of mud and slush, led the 750 Trophy race from start to finish, just as he had at Naish Hill (RD)

Jimmy Aird finds himself down, but not out, in the 250 Trophy race. Bryan Wade, here seen slithering past his prone rival, inherited the lead from the Scotsman, but also slid off to hand the win back to Aird (RD)

through to 2nd place ahead of teammate Browning, and Bryan Goss won a private battle with the AJS works riders, Rob Taylor and Malcolm Davis.

Aird remembers his moment of TV glory very clearly:

They brought me two factory CZs over for the Newport meeting. The 250 had an oil pump and so it ran on straight petrol, not mix. The Czech mechanic told me, 'All you have to do is keep the throttle open and just change gear.' The bike was so fast and it was the sort of track that suited me, quite grassy and with big wide corners, and I won the first ever colour television race on that bike, even though I didn't ride very well.

750 Trophy Race

Banks had got into trouble in the 250 race, when the handlebars came loose as he rode through a gully. The resulting fall relegated the BSA man to last place and led to an early retirement, but his main objective was to win the 750 Trophy race. However, once again his hopes were dashed, this time ironically by a poor start.

When the race got away, Dave Nicoll, as he had in the previous round, got the best start, brushing aside Browning, and soon putting some distance between himself and the baying pack. Browning fell on the first lap and with a jammed rear brake his race was run, but another Greeves runner, Vic Allan, fresh from a successful trip to the USA for the Inter-AM series, then took up the chase.

Banks was working his way through the field and on lap three he passed Goss and factory Sprite man, Dave Smith, who was enjoying a good run of form. When Banks caught Allan there was a brief but explosive duel between the two, which was resolved in favour of the East Anglian, who then attempted to close down his teammate. But the clock ultimately defeated Banks and Nicoll took his second consecutive 750 race win. Allan finished clear of Goss, with Smith holding off Bryan Wade who claimed the last of the points.

Supporting Races

Just as he had done at Naish Hill the previous month, Banks finally got things right in the TV Invitation race. However, as the riders flew up the hill from the start, it was Allan who emerged as the race leader, closely followed by Banks, Nicoll and 250 winner, Aird, out on a super potent 420. But a slip on one of the uphill stretches saw Allan not only lose the lead to Banks, but also drop him down to 9th place. Banks rode on to a comfortable win, whilst Nicoll and Aird traded places several times, with the Essex man eventually coming out on top, as Aird wrestled with the big CZ.

Grandstand Trophy Race Results

250 Trophy
1 J Aird (CZ)
2 D Clayton (Greeves)
3 A Browning (Greeves)
4 B Goss (Husqvarna)
5 R Taylor (AJS)
6 M Davis (AJS)

750 Trophy
1 D Nicoll (500 BSA)
2 J Banks (500 BSA)
3 V Allan (380 Greeves)
4 B Goss (400 Husqvarna)
5 D Smith (400 Sprite)
6 B Wade (380 Greeves)

Ray Daniel captures a contented BSA camp in the Caerleon paddock after the 750 Trophy race. Competition Shop Manager, Brian Martin (with pipe), talks with his charges, John Banks (left), Dave Nicoll (centre) and Keith Hickman (obscured by Martin)

Just four days after John Banks had won the TV Invitation race at Caerleon, a Mike Nicks profile of Britain's top motocross star appeared in *MCN*, with Banks talking candidly about his dislike for the winter scrambles:

> *When I get back from six months of world championship racing on the continent, I want to forget about scrambling for a while. But I can't, because riders like Bryan Wade and Andy Roberton are waiting for me, hoping for the chance to beat me.*

The relaxation that he seeks doesn't come in winter, mainly because BSA insist that he rides their machines in the winter television meetings. And Banks hates these damp, dreary brawls in slush and snow.

> *To the public we must look like circus clowns when we have to struggle through rain and mud. I dread waking up on a Saturday morning and finding ice and snow on the ground, because a fall on a frozen track could cost me a world title.*

> *Television racing will cut three years out of Vic Eastwood's career* (he added, referring to the complicated leg injuries that Eastwood - then tipped as a future world champion - received in an ITV World of Sport meeting the previous December.)

Ironically, it was a TV event that would rob Banks of the best part of a season, when he tried to ride through an injury picked up at the opening round of the 1970 British championship at Elsworth. With an ITV World of Sport trophy on the line, Banks opted to race at Morestead Farm near Winchester, where he won the title but aggravated his knee in the process and after a couple of abortive comebacks, he eventually had to have surgery. As a result, he yielded his British crown and failed to mount a challenge for the world championship.

The above comments suggest that Banks was a somewhat reluctant hero as, like it or not, he was one of the biggest stars of the TV events and television coverage had made him a household name in the UK. However, it came as no surprise that, at the first BBC TV meeting of the new decade at the Salvation Army Fields at Hadleigh, Essex, he was in the thick of the action as usual.

Round 3
Hadleigh, Essex, January 3, 1970

This was a meeting that Murray Walker remembers all too well, not for the racing, or the weather, but for the fact that he very nearly didn't make his appointment in the BBC commentary box.

My wife, Elizabeth, had made all the arrangements and told me that she'd got us a room in a beautiful old hotel in a quaint little place called Lavenham. Having rested well, I woke up, as I always did on a Saturday morning at 6 o'clock, and I thought to myself, 'I'm in Suffolk.' So, I turned to my wife and said, 'Come on, wake up, we're in the wrong place. We're supposed to be in Hadleigh!' So she said, 'What do you mean? It's about ten miles from here!' And I said, 'What, Hadleigh in Essex?' to which she countered, 'You didn't say anything about Essex!' (Hadleigh, Suffolk, is, as Elizabeth Walker had supposed, about 10 miles distant, whereas Hadleigh, Essex, is some 55 miles away and required a drive of a good 90 minutes).

At that time one of my clients in the advertising agency was General Motors and we had a Vauxhall Ventora. It had a 3.3 litre Bedford truck engine in it and the advertising slogan for the car was, 'Vauxhall Ventora, the lazy fireball'. Well, that morning it was a very energetic fireball on the way to Hadleigh, Essex, I can tell you, and we arrived there with about 15 minutes to spare before the first race!

TV viewers were treated to a great battle in the 250 Trophy race between Bryan Goss and John Banks, who was racing Jeff Smith's lightweight BSA (BH)

250 Trophy Race

The race in question was the 250 Trophy race, which saw Malcolm Dearn on his Greeves lead the race to the first corner, shadowed by John Banks, having another outing on Jeff Smith's 250 'Titan', Bryan Goss, Alan Clough and Malcolm Davis. However, Dearn's moment in the limelight was short lived, as the Greeves' engine seized up on the first lap.

When the field sped across the line to start its second lap, Goss had established himself as the race leader with Banks 2nd ahead of Clough, who was now campaigning a CZ, and similarly mounted Caerleon winner, Aird. Goss seemed to be in control of things, but Banks remained menacingly close throughout the race.

Then, as the race entered its last lap, Goss was temporarily slowed by a backmarker in sight of the finish and Banks seized his chance, sweeping past dramatically to win by inches at the line. Aird held on to 3rd place to score some more valuable points, whilst Vic Allan took 4th ahead of Davis and Bryan Wade, who came through the field from a poor start.

Banks got the verdict, after passing Goss when he slowed to pass a backmarker (BH)

750 Trophy Race

Following his wins at Naish Hill and Caerleon, BSA factory rider Dave Nicoll was looking at the prospect of notching up a hat-trick of wins in the 750 Trophy race, something that hadn't been done in either category since Dave Bickers' dominance of the 1966-67 series. However, fast-gating Bryan Goss was the man who led the field away, no doubt still smarting from his defeat in the 250 race.

Goss led for the opening three laps, but was ominously shadowed by the factory BSAs of Nicoll and Banks, who both passed him in rapid succession as his big-Husqvarna began to lose power. Nicoll, who had recently celebrated the birth of his third son, Robert, raced on to complete a memorable hat-trick of wins ahead of Banks, whilst Arthur Browning, who had struggled to 7th in the 250 race, finished 3rd ahead of Greeves teammate, Allan, with Davis just holding off fellow AJS factory runner Andy Roberton to complete the point scoring positions.

Nicoll, who was brimming with confidence at that time recalls:

Caerleon 250 Trophy race winner, Jimmy Aird, found himself in the points again at Hadleigh, from 3rd place (BH)

> *BSA was the biggest, and the best team to be in and I fitted in well. I'd grown in confidence over the summer, travelling to most of the GP's with John Banks and Keith Hickman, who were close friends. I also had a good relationship with Brian Martin and the competition shop staff at Small Heath.*

In August 1969, Nicoll's career had scaled new heights, when he won the Luxembourg 500 GP at Ettelbruck, standing atop the podium flanked by the then world champion, Paul Friedrichs and the future world champion, Bengt Aberg.

> *Over the winter of 1969-70 I was at my best and I went to those early races knowing I should win. My confidence was high and I remember powering underneath Bryan Goss on an adverse bend at Hadleigh. However, at the latter rounds I remember thinking 'I must finish and collect points', as I was feeling the pressure.*

Though he could see his grip on the 750 Grandstand trophy slipping, Banks topped off a largely successful day's racing by taking the Invitation race. Allan made the early running with Goss, before Banks seized control and raced on to record his second win of the day. Behind him, Allan fell on a downhill stretch leaving Goss in a comfortable second place, whilst Davis improved to 3rd ahead of Browning and Dearn, and Clough rode his big CZ into 6th place.

Having a laugh! Dave Nicoll concluded a hat-trick of wins in the 750 Trophy series, proving to be too strong for his teammate, and at that time double British champion, John Banks (BH)

Vic Allan (9) leads out of the first corner in the Invitation race, with Bryan Goss, Jimmy Aird (11 directly behind Allan), Malcolm Dearn (26) and John Banks (3) all snapping at his heels. Banks went on to take the race win, with Goss 2nd and Dearn 5th (BH)

With the series at its mid-point, there was a fascinating three-way tie in the 250 class, with Aird, Browning and Goss on 13 points apiece, whilst in the 750 class Nicoll, on 24 points, was eight clear of Banks on 16, with Allan third on 9.

Grandstand Trophy Race Results

250 Trophy
1 J Banks (BSA)
2 B Goss (Husqvarna)
3 J Aird (CZ)
4 V Allan (Greeves)
5 M Davis (AJS)
6 B Wade (Greeves)

750 Trophy
1 D Nicoll (500 BSA)
2 J Banks (500 BSA)
3 A Browning (380 Greeves)
4 V Allan (380 Greeves)
5 M Davis (360 AJS)
6 A Roberton (360 AJS)

Greeves teamsters Arthur Browning and Vic Allan, who were both enjoying good form, finished 3rd and 4th behind the factory BSAs in the 750 Trophy race (BH)

1970 ushered in a new era in air travel, as Boeing's 747 'Jumbo jet', which had made its maiden flight in February 1969, made its first commercial trans-Atlantic flight, leaving New York's JFK airport on 22nd January and arriving at Heathrow on 23rd. The plane, with seating capacity for a staggering 452 passengers, featured spiral staircases which took passengers to the first-class section of the plane and a bar and lounge where they could sip their Martini cocktails - so seventies!

By then the transport for many motocross riders had also evolved, though in most cases not so glamorously as for air travellers. By the early 70s, the old vans and pick-up trucks that were so basic were disappearing, to be replaced by comfortable cars that could tow a trailer with two bikes all day at the national speed limit. An expanding network of motorways also meant that travelling to meetings was a lot quicker and far more comfortable than it had been when the Grandstand series had begun back in 1963.

Round 4
Canada Heights, Kent, February 28, 1970

Eight weeks passed between the Hadleigh meeting and round four at Canada Heights, though the riders had been far from idle during that time. In addition to the Tweseldown Winter series that several of the BBC regulars raced in, there had been two ITV World of Sport meetings; at Hawkstone Park on January 10th and Castleford on February 21st, where Vic Eastwood had made a very welcome return to racing.

Whilst Dave Nicoll was seemingly running away with the 750 BBC Grandstand Trophy, Eastwood, his former teammate at Matchless, had been through a long and arduous recuperation following his accident at Hawkstone Park in December 1968. Nicoll, who had travelled to his first GPs in company with Vic and his father, told me:

> Vic was always very focused, he had a good sense of humour, but took his racing very seriously. In the early days Vic and his father were a close team, very much like Kurt and myself. When his wife Ann came on the scene she took over as second in the team. Vic's determination to overcome the serious leg injury was amazing; he altered the footrest positions to compensate for the lack of knee movement. However, I'm convinced that his injury stopped him reaching his full potential.

The 250 Trophy remained somewhat of a lottery at this stage, but the form book indicated that John Banks was the red-hot favourite to win the 750 Trophy race, the Bury St Edmunds man having won all six of the televised races at the ITV meetings. But others were on form, including Grandstand Trophy leader, Nicoll, Greeves' Vic Allan, who was challenging Banks in the ITV series, and Bryan Goss, who had won three finals at a meeting at Yarley, Somerset in early February, on his 400 Husqvarna. As it turned out, the meeting was all about one man.

250 Trophy Race

The 250 Trophy race got the meeting off to a cracking start. Goss gated fastest, but he was hotly pursued by Malcolm Davis and Allan. However, before the first lap was run Davis was

In unstoppable form at Canada Heights, Bryan Goss has a healthy lead over Vic Allan in the 250 Trophy race, with a string of riders following in their wake (BH)

Vic Eastwood is back! After a long convalescence following his accident at Hawkstone Park in December 1968, Eastwood made a very welcome return to the TV screens in 1970 (BH)

out of the running after taking a spill. Goss was setting a hectic pace at the front of the race and only Allan could stay remotely close. Behind them Davis fell for a second time after he had recovered well enough to challenge Browning for 3rd place.

At the sharp end, Allan stuck to his task and steadily closed down Goss in the closing laps. At the line it was a virtual photo-finish, but Goss just held on to take the win, Browning held off Banks, who couldn't match the turn of speed he'd shown in the previous round and Davis won a duel with Jimmy Aird for 6th spot.

750 Trophy Race

Goss made another blistering start in the 750 Trophy race to lead Vic Allan and Tom Leadbitter into the first corner. However, Rob Taylor soon moved up to 2nd place, with John Banks hot on his heels. Banks was pushing hard and by the end of the second lap he had inherited 2nd when the chain on Taylor's factory AJS broke.

In spite of Dave Nicoll's amazing start to the season, reigning champion Banks wasn't about to give up on the Grandstand Trophy. However, he may have been in too much of a hurry to catch Goss, as he slid off the big BSA a lap later, allowing a high-speed train, consisting of Allan, Nicoll, Hickman, who was making a return to racing after a three-month absence, and Andy Roberton, to race through.

Double-winner Goss leads the charge in the 750 Trophy race and was never headed. In close attendance are Vic Allan, with tartan strip on his helmet, Alan Clough (3), Tom Leadbitter (13), Arthur Browning (9), John Banks (partially obscured by Allan) and the AJS pair of Malcolm Davis (19) and Andy Roberton (18) (BH)

Vic Allan had a great day out on the Essex coast, taking the runner-up spot to Goss in both the 250 and 750 Trophy races. Here Brian Holder catches him motoring on aboard the factory 380 Greeves

Out front, Goss rode on to his second win of the day and this time there was nothing Allan, or even the previously peerless Nicoll, could do about it. Goss took the eight points, with Allan 2nd and Nicoll 3rd, whilst Banks fought back to salvage 4th place ahead of Hickman and Bryan Wade.

Supporting Races

To round off what was arguably Goss' finest afternoon on TV, he went out and won the TV Invitation race at a canter, from John Banks. Allan was the best of the Greeves men again, ahead of Browning and Wade and BSA's Hickman took 6th place at the flag. According to *MCN* reporter Mike Nicks, Husqvarna importer Brian Leask invited Goss back to his nearby home at Crawley to watch the racing on television, and I'm sure he would have loved every minute of it! Goss, who would go on to become 500 British Champion in 1970, still remembers how his season kicked off:

Once I started to go well, I was so confident. You can always tell when you're going well, you go out and win races and it's like you aren't really trying. Everything was going brilliantly and I was really starting to enjoy the 400 Husky.

By virtue of his double win, Goss moved into the lead in the 250 Trophy standings for the first time, with a three-point lead over Browning, whilst Nicoll, despite losing his iron-grip on the 750 Trophy, moved another point ahead of his nearest challenger, Banks, with just two rounds still to play for.

Reigning 750 Grandstand Trophy holder, John Banks, is in a big hurry to catch Bryan Goss and gets a bit out of shape (BH)

Grandstand Trophy Race Results

250 Trophy
1 B Goss (Husqvarna)
2 V Allan (Greeves)
3 A Browning (Greeves)
4 J Banks (BSA)
5 M Davis (AJS)
6 J Aird (CZ)

750 Trophy
1 B Goss (400 Husqvarna)
2 V Allan (380 Greeves)
3 D Nicoll (500 BSA)
4 J Banks (500 BSA)
5 K Hickman (500 BSA)
6 B Wade (380 Greeves)

The BBC Pulls The Plug

In early March, the BBC dropped a bombshell when it announced that it was to pull the plug on the Grandstand Moto-Cross series, just a month before the last round at Dodington Park. It would appear that this came as quite a shock, even to the ACU and its liaison officer with the BBC, Harold Taylor.

It seems that at the time it was felt that the format had become rather outmoded and that the presentation of the sport on TV was in need of a facelift. However, Bryan Cowgill, the BBC's Head of Sport, told the motorcycle press:

There is no question of our abandoning coverage of motorcycle sport in Grandstand. On the contrary, we shall be looking hard at new ways and means of improving it.

MCN's Mike Nicks, writing in his weekly *Moto Cross Talk* column, suggested that the way forward for the BBC might be to target major international events, which no doubt would have pleased John Banks and Britain's other GP runners.

However, this news hit the ACU and the organising clubs hard and many of the riders were also disappointed by the decision. Within days of hearing the news, Malcolm Davis had launched a campaign to try to save the series and he told Nicks,

I'm going to write myself and tell them (the BBC) *how much we enjoy the series and how they present it. Dave Nicoll, Bryan Goss and Andy Roberton are among other riders who said they'd do the same.*

During the winter of 1969-70, the BBC also started broadcasting rallycross on a regular basis, when the Thames Estuary Automobile Club helped them televise a series of events from Lydden Hill, Kent. This, like the motocross series, appeared on *Grandstand* with Murray Walker providing the commentary. Ironically, ABC Television had again paved the way for this new sport when they first broadcast an event, also from Lydden, on 4th February 1967, which was shown on the *World of Sport* programme.

Walker cannot recall anyone at the BBC explaining why the Grandstand Moto-Cross series was coming to an end and recalls:

It was an osmotic process, as scrambles and rallycross overlapped for a short while, but I think one of the reasons for the switch was that scrambling had been grossly over exposed on television. You must remember that in the early days we were on TV weekend after weekend.

Walker makes a very good observation here, as from 1968 onwards, in addition to the Grandstand Trophy series, ITV had also been running their own World of Sport Motocross series. Over the winter of 1968-69 there was a full quota of TV meetings with each channel running a six-round series. Below is the schedule for that winter:

October	12th	ITV Cuerden park, Lancs	January	18th	BBC Canada Heights, Kent
November	2nd	ITV Scarborough, Yorks		25th	ITV Castleford, Yorks
	16th	BBC Dodington, Glos	February	15th	BBC Caerleon, Mons
	30th	BBC Lyng, Norfolk		22nd	ITV Brill, Bucks
December:	14th	ITV Hawkstone Park, Salop	March	15th	BBC Kirkcaldy, Fife
	21st	BBC Clifton, Derbys		29th	ITV Morestead Down, Hants

With such a busy schedule it is not difficult to imagine how the average armchair sports fan, not wholly interested in off-road motorcycle racing, may have become a little disenchanted with the sport. What do they say about too much of a good thing?

Round 5

Frome, Somerset, March 14, 1970

With round five being staged at the Asham Woods track, just 20 miles away from Bryan Goss' home in Bradford Abbas, the Dorset man was the red-hot favourite to carry on where he had left off in the previous round at Canada Heights. However, in motorcycle racing, as we've already seen, nothing is ever guaranteed and despite two good performances in the Trophy races, Goss would not be the star of the show.

That honour went to Scotland's Vic Allan, a young rider who had been steadily growing in status since his move south of the border in 1967. For Allan, the Grandstand Trophy race success must have been like waiting for a bus; you wait and wait then two come along at the same time! On what would turn out to be a truly inspired weekend for the Scot, he would become the sixth and final rider to win both the 250 and 750 Grandstand Trophy races on the same day.

250 Trophy Race

The 250 Trophy race saw Allan get a flyer from the start, as he out-dragged Goss to the first corner. As Vic recently recounted:

I got away first and I just kept my head down.

A quick sideways glance confirms that Vic Allan has his first Grandstand Trophy win in the bag in the 250 race, reversing the result from Hadleigh with victory over Bryan Goss (CB)

It would appear that this was literally true.

I dipped my head under the elastic tape and away I went, 'cause I knew they weren't gonna call it back!

Behind the leading pair, Bryan Wade briefly led Malcolm Davis, before the trophy contender slipped past to chase the leaders, whilst John Banks and Jimmy Aird slipped out of contention when they tangled on the opening lap. Worse was in store for Arthur Browning, whose Greeves gave up the ghost early in the race, which effectively ended his hopes of claiming a Grandstand Trophy.

Goss knew that with Browning out, a win in front of his loyal fans in Somerset would be enough to see him claim the trophy. However, Goss had to concern himself more with staying ahead of Davis, which played into Allan's hands. The Scotsman did just enough to stay clear of Goss, with Davis 3rd. Andy Roberton on a second AJS burst through to snatch 4th place from Wade, whilst Ray Jordan on the factory Sprite just managed to stay clear of a rampaging Banks, to claim his first Grandstand Trophy points.

Goss never relented in his pursuit of Allan, but he had to remain vigilant with Malcolm Davis never too far away in 3rd place (CB)

750 Trophy Race

For Dave Nicoll, the objective in the 750 Trophy race was simple; finish in front of John Banks and the trophy would be his. At the start it looked as if Allan and Goss would have the duel that had never really materialised in the 250 contest. But on the opening lap, Goss was hit in the face by a clod of earth and rapidly slipped back down the field.

With Goss floundering, Nicoll burst into 2nd place followed by teammate Banks, who was desperate to finish ahead of the Essex man. But Nicoll stuck doggedly to his game plan, holding off his BSA teammate to win his first major trophy at the age of 25.

I remember winning the series at Leighton, with all the press taking photos of me with the trophy, but what we hadn't realised at the time, was that it was to be the last series.

Further down the field, from 11th on the opening lap, Roberton staged a spirited recovery, battling through to snatch 4th at the flag, beating the third BSA of Keith Hickman and Goss, who had also caught his second wind. But Allan was the hero of the day as he raced to his second TV win.

I'd been riding in America in the Inter-AM series and I'd got some good results, including 4th overall at Carlsbad. (Behind the Swedes, Arne Kring, Bengt Aberg and Ake Jonsson, who dominated the series.) That series really brought me on and I was really pumped up when I came back.

With two televised race wins under his belt, Allan was hoping to add a third and emulate Goss' exploits at the previous round. However, a fall at the first corner put paid to that particular dream and Banks, closely followed by Goss, raced clear of the field to finish in that order ahead of Nicoll, Roberton, who scored his third 4th place from three races, Hickman and young Malcolm Ballard from Hooe, near Hastings.

Somebody who remembers Vic's TV success very clearly is his older brother Robbie:

As it was a Saturday, I was down in Aberdeen at the fish market, having dropped off a lorry load of herrings and that's quite a rough part of Aberdeen. I knew I didn't have time to go home and catch the Grandstand races and this guy said, 'Don't you worry about that, we'll go across to the pub, they've got a TV there.' So we went into this pub, which was full of fisherman watching the horse-racing, and the bloke I was with

In the early stages of the 750 Trophy race, double-winner Allan, leads Goss (hidden behind Allan) and the BSAs of Keith Hickman and Dave Nicoll (CB)

just marched up and changed it to the motocross. So then all hell breaks loose and this guy says, 'Hey, this laddie's brother is racing motorbikes on the TV, and just as he said that, thank Christ, the race starts and Vic is out front. Well by the end of the race, we had everyone in the pub shouting 'Come on, Vic, lad!' I thought I was gonna be in a right old punch up, but it all worked out good in the end!

Supporting Races

For the record, Allan got his third win in the non-televised Invitation from Goss, whilst for Roberton it must have felt like a serious case of *déjà vu*, as he finished 4th - for the fourth time on the day!

But Allan didn't settle for that. Later that same day, he caught a ferry to Holland and, despite getting just a few laps of practice, raced to overall victory the following day in the traditional international curtain-raiser at the St. Anthonis. This stunned a lot of people in motocross circles, but, as he had shown racing in the US, he was a rider with great strength and stamina who would go on to make history when he won both 250 and 500 British championships four years later.

So with the final round of the series to come a fortnight later at Dodington Park, the destiny of the 250 Grandstand Trophy was very much in the hands of Bryan Goss. Only Malcolm Davis could overhaul him and to do so he would have to win with Goss finishing 6th or lower. Whatever happened, in true TV drama tradition, the stage was set for a grand finale.

Back in the paddock after the 750 Trophy race and John Banks (right) is the first to congratulate Dave Nicoll on winning the Grandstand Trophy. In finishing ahead of Banks, Nicoll put himself in an unassailable position with one round of the series remaining (CB)

Andy Roberton was 'Mr Consistency' at Asham Woods, finishing 4th in no less than four races. Here he turns on the style on the 370 AJS (CB)

Grandstand Trophy Race Results

250 Trophy
1 V Allan (Greeves)
2 B Goss (Husqvarna)
3 M Davis (AJS)
4 A Roberton (AJS)
5 B Wade (Greeves)
6 R Jordan (Sprite)

750 Trophy
1 V Allan (380 Greeves)
2 D Nicoll (500 BSA)
3 J Banks (500 BSA)
4 A Roberton (370 AJS)
5 K Hickman (500 BSA)
6 B Goss (400 Husqvarna)

Round 6

Dodington Park, Glos, March 28, 1970

On the day that the Grandstand Trophy series came to an end, Simon and Garfunkel's *Bridge Over Troubled Water* had just reached number one in the UK singles chart. Sadly, though, for Britain's armchair scrambles fans there was no 'bridge' for the Grandstand series, though ITV were quite happy to continue with their World of Sport series.

There can have been fewer circuits more worthy of staging the final 'episode' after more than six years of broadcasting than Dodington Park. The rolling grassland circuit, near the magnificently titled village of Old Sodbury, had been home to the 250 British Motocross GP in 1968 and 69 and was one of the finest motocross venues ever used in Britain.

Supporting Race

Before the televised races took place, the organising Bristol Club included a Supporting Invitation race to help settle the nerves, a race that Bryan Goss, riding his 400 Husqvarna, seized control of and won comfortably from Vic Allan, after John Banks had taken another tumble in his attempts to stay with Goss.

250 Trophy Race

So, when the 250 Trophy race got underway, series leader Goss was the hot favourite to add another eight points to his tally from a win. But it was his chief rival, local man Malcolm Davis, racing on his favourite circuit and being cheered on by his legions of supporters, who took the lead and just eased away from the entire field.

While Davis drew further ahead at the front of the field, his AJS teammates, Andy Roberton and Rob Taylor were also flying and a 1-2-3 for the Andover factory looked like a possibility in the early laps. Behind Taylor came the Greeves duo of Arthur Browning and Dick Clayton with Goss sandwiched between John Banks and Jeff Smith, on their lightweight BSAs, in 7th place and out of the points.

Cecil Bailey was on hand to capture the action, as Andy Roberton gets the works AJS out front at the start of the 250 Trophy race. Left to right behind him are John Banks (14), eventual winner Malcolm Davis (6), Jimmy Aird (20), Rob Taylor (18), Freddie Mayes (12), Randy Owen (5) and Bryan Goss, obscured by Vic Eastwood (7)

A very determined Malcolm Davis forcing on to victory and although he was not destined to win a Grandstand Trophy he would go on to lift his second British championship on AJS later that year (CB)

At this stage Goss must have feared that he was about to blow his last chance at winning a coveted Grandstand trophy:

When I got to Dodington for the final round, I thought to myself, 'You've got to win this, it'll be your last chance to get one of these trophies.' I was so worried in the race; I couldn't get out the gate at the start and I was so afraid I'd fall off. There was a muddy ditch that we had to cross and I'd jumped into it on the big bike, but on the 250 I wouldn't risk it and just rode through. Nothing was going right and I saw Malcolm was out front and he was flying on the AJS.

With the clock running down, Clayton had moved up to 3rd place behind Roberton, with Browning in tow. But then Goss got a lucky break, when Taylor tangled with Banks and both riders hit the deck. Suddenly Goss was up to fifth place and if he could hang on till the end of the race he'd take the trophy:

I couldn't believe it when I saw Banksy and Taylor go down, but I still had a race on my hands, with Clayton and Browning in front of me on the Greeves and Smithy just behind me buzzing that little BSA of his.

As it turned out Goss didn't have to worry too much about Smith, as the veteran campaigner pulled out of the contest on the last lap in protest at the very ragged start that he had fallen victim to. This allowed Freddie Mayes, a 'friendly rival' of Goss', into 6th to ride shotgun for the Dorset man to the flag.

It was a fitting end to the Grandstand Trophy series, that one of its most ardent supporters from its inception in October 1963 was there to receive the 250 Trophy. Goss had twice finished 3rd overall in the 250 Trophy, but he hit a purple patch of form in the year that he would turn 30, and within six months he would add the 500 British championship to his already impressive list of achievements.

750 Trophy Race

However, there were still races to be run and TV viewers to entertain and for Goss there was no time to rest on his laurels, as he had to switch bikes and ride to the line for the very last Grandstand Trophy race. At the start it was the two Vics, Allan and Eastwood, who raced clear, followed by Goss and Browning. However, within a lap Goss had passed Eastwood and race leader Allan's Greeves had died on him and with it his hopes for overhauling Banks in the series. Browning and Eastwood then tangled, with the unfortunate Husky rider going into the ropes.

All this left Goss, unwittingly, in the clear and he rode on to register his seventh Grandstand Trophy race win and draw level with Alan Clough, Vic Eastwood and Arthur Lampkin. He was unchallenged for the rest of the race and with all the pressure off, he was able to just savour the moment and have some fun on his bike.

Behind Goss there was a monumental four-cornered battle for second place to keep the armchair viewers on the edge of their seats, with the new 750 Trophy holder Nicoll, leading Bryan Wade, Clayton and Banks. Wade momentarily moved up to 2nd, but then fell in a mudhole and when Nicoll came under increasing pressure from Clayton and Banks, he sensibly yielded. In the closing laps Clayton did just enough to quell the attacks of Banks to claim 2nd place, with Nicoll holding on for 4th place ahead of the CZ pair of Hereford based Randy Owen, scoring his first Grandstand points, and Jimmy Aird.

When Freddie Mayes won his British championship in 1966, Bryan Goss had played his part by beating Dave Bickers in the final round. At Dodington Park, Mayes, seen here leading his good friend Goss, returned the favour by chaperoning him to 5th place and the three points he needed to secure the 250 Grandstand Trophy (CB)

Greeves' Dick Clayton, saved his best ride of the Grandstand series for the last ever Trophy race. The popular rider from Wigan won a thrilling three-way battle with John Banks and the new 750 Grandstand Trophy holder, Dave Nicoll (CB)

Left, a fine Ray Daniel photo captures Vic Allan, John Banks and Bryan Goss exiting the mud splash at Dodington in close formation in the opening Invitation race

With the pressure of the 250 race removed, Goss was in scintillating form for the remainder of the meeting, winning the two remaining finals. Here he is pictured savouring his ride on the 400 Husky as he heads for victory in the 750 Grandstand Trophy (CB)

Supporting Race

To complete one of the best day's racing of his long career, Goss went out and won the TV Invitation, his third win of the day, though no doubt the points gained from the 250 race brought him the most pleasure. Banks was the only rider to challenge Goss, but on this kind of form, even the British champion had to settle for second best. A long way behind the leading pair, Keith Hickman, who had been plagued by mechanical problems in the previous races, took 3rd place ahead of the AJS' of Davis and Taylor, with Terry Challinor 6th on his factory Sprite. What was Goss' overriding memory on such an historic day?

I remember that when they gave out the trophies at Dodington, we had to stand up on a trailer and I said to Dave Nicoll (6ft 3ins to Bryan's 5ft 6ins), 'You'd better stand down that end, because of the slope!'

Grandstand Trophy Race Results

250 Trophy
1 M Davis (AJS)
2 A Roberton (AJS)
3 D Clayton (Greeves)
4 A Browning (Greeves)
5 B Goss (Husqvarna)
6 F Mayes (CZ)

750 Trophy
1 B Goss (400 Husqvarna)
2 D Clayton (380 Greeves)
3 J Banks (500 BSA)
4 D Nicoll (500 BSA)
5 R Owen (360 CZ)
6 J Aird (360 CZ)

1969-70 Grandstand Trophy Series Final Standings

250 Trophy

1	B Goss (Husqvarna)	3 4 6 8 6 3	30pts
2	M Davis (AJS)	6 2 3 3 5 8	27pts
3	A Browning (Greeves)	8 5 0 5 0 4	22pts
4	V Allan (Greeves)	0 0 4 6 8 0	18pts
5	J Aird (CZ)	0 8 5 2 0 0	15pts
6	J Banks (BSA)	0 0 8 4 0 0	12pts

750 Trophy

1	D Nicoll (500 BSA)	8 8 8 5 6 3	38pts
2	J Banks (500 BSA)	4 6 6 4 5 5	30pts
3	V Allan (380 Greeves)	0 5 4 6 8 0	23pts
4	B Goss (400 Husqvarna)	0 4 0 8 2 8	22pts
5	A Browning (380 Greeves)	6 0 5 0 0 0	11pts
6	B Wade (380 Greeves)	5 2 0 2 0 0	9pts

The presentation that marked the end of an era. Left to right, Greeves Competition Shop manager, Bill Brooker, with the 250 Manufacturers Trophy, 750 Grandstand Trophy winner, Dave Nicoll, 250 Grandstand Trophy winner, Bryan Goss, and the ever present Harold Taylor (CB)

PROGRAMME 1/-

BRISTOL MOTOR CYCLE CLUB
WESSEX CENTRE

B.B.C. TELEVISION MOTO-CROSS (6th ROUND)

AT

DODINGTON PARK
OLD SODBURY

SATURDAY 28th MARCH 1970

The programme for the final round of the BBC Grandstand Trophy series. It is interesting to note that the programme cost double the price of that for the opening round of the inaugural series at Hawkstone Park in October 1963 (see p39) despite being of a far more austere design

International Racing

Following the presence of the Swedes, Torsten Hallman and Rolf Tibblin, at a snowbound Beaulieu Old Park, in January 1963, the BBC had been itching to stage televised International racing. So it was, that following the successful conclusion of the inaugural Grandstand Trophy series, the BBC broadcast a three-way International Team Relay from Muswell Hill Farm, Brill, on Saturday 28th March 1964.

Britain took on strong teams from Belgium and Sweden, but despite the presence of such stellar motocross personalities as world champions Hallman (250) and Tibblin (500), and the outrageously talented Belgian teenager, Joel Robert, the racing as a spectacle was a huge disappointment.

Essentially it was the race format that was flawed. Each nation had a three-man team, with just three riders taking to the startline. The race itself became very processional, once Robert's CZ died on the exit from Brill's famous water splash. Dave Bickers, built a huge lead over Hallman, which Arthur Lampkin and Jeff Smith subsequently built on and at the flag, Smith was 36 seconds clear of Tibblin.

The win may have been good for the morale of the British trio, but for TV viewers, it paled in comparison to the regular Grandstand Trophy series. Peter Howdle, reporting in the MCN, referred to it as an 'International TV Flop' adding that 'As a spectacle it was a dead loss.'

The riders line up for the main event, the International Relay Race. Murray Walker and Harold Taylor look on far left (MC)

The soviet quartet. Left to right, Gunnar Draugs, Yuri Ageyev, Igor Grigoriev and Victor Arbekov, with their team coach, the 'little man from the KGB' and ACU official, Harold Taylor (BH)

Cancelled Czechs

The next scheduled BBC International was for October 23rd 1965, at Farleigh Castle, a GB v Czechoslovakia match race, which had to be cancelled at the last minute. In its place a 'Four Corners' meeting was hastily arranged and duly televised. The unlikely hero was the Eastern team's Andy Lee, who was in superb form on his Matchless Métisse winning both Team races. But it was the all-star Northern team of Jeff Smith, Arthur Lampkin, Alan Clough and John Griffiths, that claimed the team event.

Welcome Comrades!

The following month a team from the USSR made the long trip to Canada Heights in Kent, and by this time, the ACU and the BBC now had a more entertaining format; two International races, with the host nation and the visitors putting out a four-man team in each race.

Marge Clarke, the secretary of the Sidcup and District MCC, was a young woman in her late teens at the time. "My mum was heavily involved in organising the TV meetings and my job was to help out any way I could. When the Russians came over they drove all the way in these funny little cars that kept breaking down and they turned up with a little man from the KGB, who went everywhere with them."

Run in particularly muddy conditions, the event played into the hands of the home riders. Dave Bickers dominated both races ably supported by Chris Horsfield, Alan Clough and Bryan Goss. Of the Soviet squad, only the recently crowned 250 world champion, Victor Arbekov, challenged Bickers. He led race two for the opening three laps and the USSR team took the race victory, but the Brits hung on to record a narrow victory over the two legs.

Successful Format

Over the next eighteen months or so, this format was adopted for a series of international team races that followed. These included match races against Belgium and Czechoslovakia.

GB v Belgium, , January 1966. Man of the meeting, Joel Robert, won all four of the day's main races (BH)

GB v Belgium, Nantwich, November 1966. Winner of the first Team race, Arthur Browning, leads Joel Robert (MC)

GB v Czechoslovakia, Ripon, February 1966. Petr Dobry showed his class, winning both Team races in difficult conditions (MC)

GB v Czechoslovakia, Clifton, January, 1967. Bryan Wade fully justified his selection for the GB team, taking two 3rd place finishes in the Team races (BH)

Man of the meeting, Olle Pettersson, leads Torsten Hallman and Dave Bickers at Canada Heights, October 1966 (BH)

Turning back the clock; Arthur Lampkin leads Torsten Hallman. The two had first met on the GP trail back in 1960 (BH)

Marauding Vikings

In October 1966 the Sidcup Club hosted another TV match race, this time against a very strong quartet of Swedes; 250 world champion, Hallman, being joined by Tibblin, Olle Pettersson and Jan Johansson.

Factory BSA man Vic Eastwood, racing on his home patch, took the first International race ahead of Johansson on his 360 Lindstrom and Pettersson on a 250 Husqvarna. With Dave Bickers and Bryan Goss heading Tibblin and Hallman, and Arthur Lampkin finishing 8th, the two teams were all level on 18 points with the second race set to decide things.

At the start things were evenly matched, with the outstanding Pettersson leading. Eastwood was flying again until he lost his chain and Bickers went out when his CZ oiled a plug. At the finish, Goss was the only home rider to challenge the Swedes, finishing 3rd ahead of Tibblin and Johansson, as Sweden comfortably won the match.

On this occasion, three men were to make a strong impression on young Marge Clarke, though for very different reasons. "Harold Taylor turned up in his beautiful Daimler Dart sports car, to take me to welcome the Swedes at their hotel. When we got there, I remember trying to communicate with one of the riders in my pigeon French, only to discover it was Arthur Lampkin! Rolf Tibblin was so funny, he'd recently had an operation on his knee and at any opportunity he'd hitch up the leg of his leathers to show us his scars."

Despite the added glamour of such events, the Internationals never really caught the general publics' eye, probably because the field was reduced to just eight riders, which often made the races very processional.

Bold plans for the future

In February 1968, a Czech 'delegation' visited Castleford, Yorkshire, for an ITV World of Sport meeting, to gain first-hand experience of how the sport was televised in Britain. Ludek Kutil, who was responsible for motor sport coverage on Czech TV, told MCN's Gavin Trippe that he would write to the BBC suggesting a four-meeting winter TV series, with events to be held in England, Belgium, Sweden and Czechoslovakia and to be televised on Eurovision. With a field of 16-20 riders, this would definitely have been a more exciting proposition, though sadly nothing ever came of it.

Sidecar Motocross
Into the Lion's Den

Sidecar scrambling had featured in the very first televised meeting at Beenham, back in December 1954, and it found an audience via the ITV events televised by channels such as ABC and Southern in the late 1950s and early 1960s. The BBC also included it in the meeting they televised from Beaulieu in January 1963, but it wasn't until January 1965 that they would appear on the schedule during the Grandstand series.

Sadly, the timing could not have been worse, as the sidecar boys took their bow on screen at the meeting that took place in arguably the worst ever conditions during the lifetime of the Grandstand Trophy series.

1964-65

The meeting in question, at Palmer's Farm, Heightington, was run in truly atrocious conditions, which prompted Peter Howdle, reporting in the *MCN*, to refer to it as the 'Grandstand Mudlark'. Howdle went on to say it was:

The first sidecar race to be televised during the Grandstand Trophy series was at Bewdley, Worcestershire, in January 1965. Here, veteran driver Bill Turner, with Derek Forbes in the chair, plots a course through a sea of mud (MC)

Bill Turner again. Here holding a slim lead over Bob Norman and Brian Reid on the 650 EGB – a Triumph-powered outfit sponsored by the Eastern Gas Board! (BH)

a meeting that was more of a gamble than a scramble. Gamble? Ask the sidecar boys! After ploughing a grassland course into a sea of mud, their BBC-TV debut was the greatest lark of the lot.

The sidecar riders found it virtually impossible to climb the final steep hill on the circuit, their outfits getting well and truly bogged down in the glutinous mud. As a result, tow ropes were issued to marshals and soon brought into use. Only four crews made it to the finish, with future multi-British champion Nick Thompson narrowly defeating Dave Treleaven, with Dave Elvidge next ahead of John Turner.

Despite such an inauspicious entrance, the sidecar boys were in action again at the following round at Canada Heights five weeks later, where thankfully the weather and riding conditions were more conducive to sidecar motocross. The race winner was Rufus Rose from Wimbourne, Dorset with his brother, Tiger, in the chair. Earlier in the meeting, Tiger's place had been filled by Murray Walker, who was taken out for a lap of the track in the sidecar. It would seem that Murray was always up for a challenge!

Although the race at Canada Heights had painted sidecar racing in a more favourable light, this branch of the sport would have very limited exposure on the Grandstand series. A sidecar race was included in the penultimate round of the 1964-65 series at Bulford Camp, Wiltshire in March 1965, but the race, won by the Price brothers, Roy and Stan, was not televised. The Price brothers would go on to take their place in sidecar scrambling history, however, by becoming the first winners of the ACU Sidecar Driver's Star later that year.

1965-66

Sidecar racing was included for two rounds of the 1965-66 series, with vastly contrasting fortunes. Conditions at the sixth round at Jewels Hill, Kent in February 1966, were so bad that the sidecar race had to be abandoned after just one lap. Again, the balance was redressed at the final round of the series at Muswell Hill Farm, Brill, the following month, when a fiercely competitive race graced the TV screens. The race was won by Dave Treleaven and his passenger Ken Canfield, from John Turner and Mick Meredith, with the larger than life Dennis 'Wacker' Westwood and Monty Hughes finishing third after leading the race till two-thirds distance.

Winner Treleaven, who was equally at home racing on the continent, remembers this well:

I followed Wacker Westwood and I worked out where I could get up enough speed to overtake him. On one corner his line was the same every lap, so I made my move and just squeezed by and I made sure he didn't get back past again, because he was a hard old boy to beat!

Treleaven also recalls a moment of kindness from Murray Walker.

After the race he said to me, 'Go over to that double-decker bus, that's our canteen and tell them I said you've got to have a decent meal.' and that's what it was like in those days.

This meeting showed sidecar racing at its best, with three quite different outfits filling the first three positions. Treleaven favoured a 500 BSA Gold Star outfit, which was obviously lighter, though not as powerful as his rivals' machines. Turner raced a 650 Triumph outfit, built by his father Bill, who also raced at this meeting, and Westwood rode a 'Wackman' powered by a 650 Norton twin.

Successful as the Brill race had been, it would be the last to grace the screens during the Grandstand series, as the BBC and the ACU took the decision to focus exclusively on the 250 and, the new for 1966-67, 750 solo series in the future.

Race winners at Brill, Dave Treleaven and Ken Canfield, on their BSA Gold Star-engined outfit (BH)

All Good Things...

John Banks powers his 500 BSA through the mud at a snowy, Asham Woods in January 1971. Note the BBC cameraman perched high atop a flat-bed crane (CB)

All good things, so we're told, must come to an end and I think most of the people who were involved in the Grandstand Trophy Moto-Cross series would agree that, on balance, it was a good thing.

On these pages many of the riders have voiced dislike for the winter scrambles meetings, but as Jeff Smith told us, he received a hero's welcome when he walked through the gates of the BSA factory at Armoury Road of a Monday morning. And didn't Dave Bickers speak about how he always enjoyed spending a weekend in the company of his friends and rivals?

For others, such as Arthur Lampkin, it was simply a case of being a good professional. Arthur, who lest we forget was once referred to as 'Mr Television', told me:

I rode for BSA and I rode where they told me to. They wanted me winning TV races because it sold bikes.

It was good for BBC personnel too. Murray Walker is proud to say that motorcycles were his first love and in the BBC documentary *Life in the Fast Lane* which chronicled his life, he stated that his time providing the commentary for the TV meetings, 'was the key that unlocked my career'. And what a career he had!

In a similar vein, Brian Johnson's sterling work on Grandstand served as a springboard to an illustrious career with the BBC, but Johnson looks back on the time he spent producing the motocross meetings with great affection.

"At that time I was producing all sorts of programmes for the BBC and I could have been doing a Promenade Concert or Come Dancing, but I always looked forward to doing the motocross because, a) it was good television, and b) because all the guys were so friendly."

Around the time that the BBC and the ACU got together to finalise plans for the Grandstand Trophy series, a group of four relatively unknown musicians were recording their first album at EMI studios in London. A few months later they were 'sweeping the nation' with their unique brand of pop music and a day after the opening round of the inaugural series at Hawkstone Park they appeared on *Sunday Night at the London Palladium*. That band, of course, was The Beatles and it is a strange coincidence, but within a month of the announcement that the BBC and the ACU could not agree on a way forward for the series, the Fab Four had announced that due to artistic differences, they would be disbanding. It would appear that both the BBC Grandstand Trophy series and the Beatles had reached the end of the *Long and Winding Road*.

However, *Grandstand* was still alive and kicking and, as previously mentioned, the BBC, with Murray Walker once again in the commentary box, had switched its attention to rallycross, another fast, exciting and, (with the advent of colour broadcasts) a colourful sport, which again I

Rather fortuitously, race winners at the New Year's Moto Cross at Frome, Bryan Wade (250) and John Banks (500), were awarded Grandstand Trophies. I say this, as Wade and Banks raced a total of 15 minutes each to win their trophies, whilst Dave Bickers and Jeff Smith had to contest 12 rounds to win theirs in the first Grandstand series in 1963-64 (CB)

remember watching as a youngster, though, for me, it never had quite the same appeal as motocross.

In the months that followed, the BBC did televise a few meetings though there was never any suggestion that it was a series. Indeed the first of these, broadcast from a very wintry Asham Woods, Frome, on 2nd January 1971, saw race winners Bryan Wade (250) and John Banks (500) awarded Grandstand Trophies for just 15 minutes plus one lap of hard graft. Bryan Wade recalls:

Malcolm Davis handed it to me. We were really going for it in the race and fortunately for me, Malcolm over-cooked it going up the hill and came over backwards.

Vic Allan then took up the running but Wade proved to be too strong.

I was delighted to get the trophy; I thought I'd missed the boat!

The next month, an international meeting from Dodington Park hit our screens and although not many overseas riders attended - the entry was decimated by a GPO strike which prevented invitations getting through - the presence of the factory Suzuki riders, Joel Robert, Sylvain Geboers and Roger De Coster, was a huge lift for the organisers. However, on the

Dave Bickers made a welcome return to the TV screens for the February meeting at Dodington Park. Here Cecil Bailey captures him leading BSA ace, Keith Hickman

The Suzuki trio of Joel Robert, Sylvain Geboers and Roger De Coster were expected to dominate the meeting, but the BSA boys had the last laugh. Here overall winner Dave Nicoll prepares to sweep past Geboers (CB)

day, it was the BSA squad that came out on top - how ironic that within a few months the BSA competition shop would close, whilst Suzuki went on to a string of world championships.

For the time being though, on a treacherously slippery surface, the 500cc four-strokes found more grip than the high-revving two-strokes and John Banks and Dave Nicoll did the winning, ably supported by Jeff Smith and new recruits, Andy Roberton and Vic Allan. Nicoll took the Norton Villiers Trophy from Banks, the two riders separated by less than a second after 30 minutes racing, with Roberton third overall. Maybe this was the new formula the BBC was looking for, though for top ranked GP riders, I can't imagine a mid-winter's mudbath was high on their list of priorities.

On a personal level, the Grandstand Trophy series was unquestionably a good thing as it set in motion a chain of events. Had I not watched the early meetings and tried to emulate the stars on my Triang scooter, maybe my father wouldn't have taken the family along to watch its first scramble. Had I not been to that meeting, maybe I would never have developed an interest in off-road riding. Had I not … you get the picture! The fact is I did watch it and it certainly provided the spark that would lead me to become an off-road motorcycling fanatic and a keen, if not hugely talented, trials rider in my youth.

It is my hope that in reading this book many others will have been reminded of a wonderful period, not just in motocross, but also in their own lives, when for a few brief years we could tune-in to watch our motocross heroes racing, seemingly, week in and week out. Sadly, words and photos will have to suffice, as with the notable exception of that truly unique Invitation race from Canada Heights, described earlier, the remaining footage is buried deep in the vaults of the BBC archives.

Returning to my opening comment, the jury could be out all day on whether the Grandstand Trophy series was a good thing or not, especially if said jury consists of ex-riders and BBC technicians and cameramen! Suffice it to say,

It was the best of times, it was the worst of times.

Grandstand Trophy Winners

Series	250		500	
1963/64	Dave Bickers	Husqvarna / Greeves	Jeff Smith	BSA
1964/65	Dave Bickers	Greeves	Chris Horsfield	Matchless
1965/66	Dave Bickers	Greeves / CZ	Jeff Smith	BSA

	250		750	
1966/67	Dave Bickers	CZ	Dave Bickers	CZ
1967/68	Jeff Smith	BSA	John Banks	BSA
1968/69	Alan Clough	Husqvarna	John Banks	BSA
1969/70	Bryan Goss	Husqvarna	Dave Nicoll	BSA

Grandstand Trophy Race Winners

	63/64	64/65	65/66	66/67	67/68	68/69	69/70	Total
Dave Bickers	10	7	2	10	-	-	-	29
Jeff Smith	10	5	6	-	3	-	-	24
Alan Clough	-	3	1	-	-	3	-	7
Vic Eastwood	1	2	-	2	1	1	-	7
Bryan Goss	1	1	2	-*	-	-	3	7
Arthur Lampkin	2	3	-	1	1	-	-	7
John Banks	-	-	-	-	2	3	1	6
Chris Horsfield	-	1	3	1	-	-	-	5
Arthur Browning	-	-	-	1	-	2	1	4
Malcolm Davis	-	-	-	-	1	2	1	4
Dave Nicoll	-	-	-	-	-	-	3	3
Vic Allan	-	-	-	-	-	-	2	2
Keith Hickman	-	-	-	-	1	1	-	2
Jerry Scott	-	1	1	-	-	-	-	2
Jimmy Aird	-	-	-	-	-	-	1	1
Alan Lampkin	-	-	1	-	-	-	-	1
Andy Lee	-	1	-	-	-	-	-	1
Freddie Mayes	-	-	-	-	1	-	-	1
Bryan Wade	-	-	-	1	-	-	-	1
Races run	24	24	16	16	10	12	12	114

* Goss was later stripped of his win at Naish Hill and the win awarded to the original runner-up, Jeff Smith

There were a total of 19 race winners over 7 seasons (this does not include winners of the televised Invitation races).

Riders' Index

Key to Indexes

Riders in CAPITALS
These riders appeared in most races between 1963 and 1970. and therefore on most pages. Photos of them appear very frequently throughout the book.

Riders / entries in bold
These riders appear frequently in the page range shown. Bold page ranges indicate they include photos of the rider. Place names of the tracks are also shown in bold in the Main index

Page Numbers in bold
Indicates a photo relating to the term indexed.

Aberg, Bengt	265, 275, 285
Ageyev, Yuri	295
Aim, Jim	15, 16, 24, 92, **95**, **148**, 149, 150, 178
Aird, Jimmy	**227-292**
Allan, Vic	**206-303**
Andrews, Bernie	**14**, 60, 61
Andrews, Mick	104, 125, 126, 127, 145, 146, 213, 214, **251**, 253
Arbekov, Victor	136, **295**
Archer, Les	**6**, 8, 11, 100
Atkinson, Brian	269
Atkinson, Eric	10
Avery, John	**5**
Ballard, Malcolm	285
BANKS, JOHN	
Barugh, Bill	11
Bentham, Frank	10
Beresford, Gordon	67
BICKERS, DAVE	
Blakeway, Gordon	13
Bonn, Bengt Arne	265
Bowers, Mick	138, 139
Browning, Arthur	**105-296**
Burton, John	**13-168**
Canfield, Ken	**300**
Challinor, Terry	176, 202, 203, **227**, 233, 299
Cheney, Eric	11, 102, 126, 136, 152, 160, 168, **170**, **187**
Cheshire, Terry	10
Clayton, Dick	51-291
Clayton, John	15-16, 63, 64
CLOUGH, ALAN	
Cook, Tony	71, 74
Covell, Ken	**70**
Cox, Robin	**202**
Cox, Terry	98, 99
Crooks, Norman	13
Curtis, Brian	27
Curtis, Dave	36, **55**, 56, 57, 58, 132
Darrieulat, Frank	14
DAVIS, MALCOLM	
Davis, Tony	103, **217**,
de Coster, Roger	265, 302, 303
Dearn, Malcolm	275, **277**
Dobry, Petr	**296**
Done, John	**36-185**
Draper, John	6, 28
Draugs, Gunnar	**295**
EASTWOOD, VIC	
Ellis, Scott	19
Elvidge, Dave	113, 119, 299
England, Ivor	168
Fairburn, Ron	13
Forbes, Derek	298
Francis, Gordon	21
Friedrichs, Paul	135, 173, 209, 239, 275
Geboers, Sylvain	302, **303**
Giles, John	**6-158**
GOSS, BRYAN	
Greer, Ernie	41-119
Griffiths, John	**13-103**
Grigoriev, Igor	**295**
Gwynne, Bill	24, 43, 44, 54, 55, 64, **67**, 68, **70**, 197
Hallman, Torsten	**18**, 24, **25**, 26, 27, 34, 83, 35, 236, 242, **294**, **297**
Harris, John	**13-248**
Harrison, Colin	147, 150
Heanes, Ken	168
Hickman, Keith	**102-243**
Hodge, George	121, 123
Hole, Peter	129
HORSFIELD, CHRIS	
Hubbard, Jack	16
Hughes, Monty	300
Hughes, Richard	242, 244
Jackson, Billy	**54-159**
Johansson, Gunnar	133
Johnasson, Jan	297
Johnson, Joe	21, 27, **28**, 30, **98**, 99, 102, 105, 117
Jonsson, Ake	285
Jordan, Ray	**221**, **222**, 285, 287
Jordon, Rob	vi, 161
King, Geoff	14, 24
Kring, Arne	285
Lamper, Pat	47, 48, 51, 52, 98, 99, 100, 103, 156,
Lampkin, Alan	**60-263**
LAMPKIN, ARTHUR	
Lampkin, Martin	13, 149, 253
Langston, Ron	10
Leadbitter, Tom	149, 150, 198, **202**, 203, 212, 213, 232, 233, 248, **280**
Lee, Andy	**23-295**
Lewis, John	**70**, 139, **156**
Louis, John	**15**
Lundin, Sten	35, 133, 169
Manns, Bob	**6**
Matthews, Jack	27, 154, **156**
MAYES, FREDDIE	
Meredith, Mick	300
Messenger, Ken	**28**, 202
Miller, Sammy	19, 103
Nadin, Brian	71, 74, 88, 92, 94, **96**, 102, 141, 142, 202
Neve, Len	54
Nex, Phil	5
Nicholson, Bill	xi
NICOLL, DAVE	
Nilsson, Bill	133
Norman, Bob	166, **299**
Owen, Randy	113, 114, 147, **148**, 150, **288**, 290, 291
Peach, Mike	87, 88, 92, 116, 129, 131
Pease, John	16
Peplow, Roy	92, 154, 156
Pettersson, Olle	**297**
Povey, Bryan	19
Preston, Dickie	13, 121, 123
Price, Roy	299
Price, Stan	299
Rathmell, Malcolm	**252**, 253, 255
Reid, Brian	299
Rickman, Derek	**5-239**
Rickman, Don	vi, **9-239**
Robert, Joel	71, 83, 108, 135, 136, 242, **294**, **296**, 303
Roberton, Andy	**191-303**

305

Robertson, Ken	16	Smith, Dave	**218**, 220, **221**, 259, 272		135, 136, 173, 294, 297
Robinson, Colin	**15**	**SMITH, JEFF**		Timms, Jim	16, **28**
Robinson, Tim	**15**	Smith, Pete	47, **90**	Treleaven, Dave	113, 166, 299, 300
Rose, Rufus	16, 119, 299	**Snoad, Roger**	**98-255**	Turner, Bill	6, **7**, 113, 166, **298**, **299**, 300
Rose, Tiger	299	Stocker, Jack	6, **7**	Turner, Cyril	6
Sadler, Bob	166	Stonebridge, Brian	xi, **4**, **5**, 8, 10, 11, 12,	Turner, John	113, 166, 299, 300
Scott, Jerry	**43-163**		35, 77, 100	Vaughan, Vic	268, 269
Sedgley, Ken	57, 58, 176, 177, **248**	Taft, Paul	11	**Wade, Bryan**	**139-302**
Selling, Frits	100	Taft, Peter	11, 12	Walker, Brian	149, 150
Sharp, Bryan	14, 168	Tate, Maurice	13	Wallace, Willy	262
Sharp, Triss	16, 168	Tate, Ron	13	Ward, Geoff	xi, 5, 11, 36
Sharp, 'Pop'	168, 169	Taylor, Rob	265, 268, 269, 271, 272, 280,	Westwood, Dennis	166, 300
Sheehan, Jim	10		**288**, 289, 291	Wilkins, Frank	14
Silvester, Terry	13, 57, 58, 60, 61, 67, 70,	Teuwissen, Jef	135	Winsor, Gerald	**267**, 268, 269
	73, **74**, 77, 80	Thompson, Nick	113, 119, 299	Wraith, Peter	19
Sleeman, Terry	**70**	Tibblin, Rolf	18, 24, **25**, 27, 35, 83, 84,		

Main Index

ABC Television	xi, 7, 8-17, 33, 36, 120,	BBC Grandstand Team Trophy	23, 24	British Grand Prix	5, 34, 151, 202, 239
	283, 298	BBC Shepherd's Bush	30, 269	Bredbury *(Stockport)*	12
Aberfan disaster	174	BBC Television Centre	164	Brooker, Bill	**152**, 173, **292**
Accrington	16	BBC Television Team Trial	19	Brown, Fluff	258
ACU (Auto Cycle Union)	5	BBC West Region *(Bristol)*	16, 19, 22	**Builth Wells**	**44**, 48, 68-70, 136-139,
ACU Benevolent Fund	10	Beamon, Bob	240		204-207, 209, 236
ACU Scrambles Drivers' Star	5, 8, 36,	Beatles	38, 160, 209, 257, 301	**Bulford Camp**	124-127, 169, 299
	43, 83, 131, 135, 169	Beaulieu, Lord Montague	14, 16, 24, **25**,	**Bury St Edmunds**	**208**, 211, 212,
ACU Sidecar Drivers' Star	299		26, 27, 294, 298		218-222
Adamson, John *(Bowman)*	69	Beenham, Church Woods	5, 19, 168, 298	Cadders Hill, *see Lyng*	
Aim, Sue	95	**Beeston**	49-52, 77, 233	Cadwell Park	173, 174
Aldrin, Buzz *(astronaut)*	249	Beeston Castle	49	**Caerleon**	xi, 2, 8, **30**, 32, 56-58, 59, 77,
Allan, Robbie	285-6	**Belmont**	143-146, 152		100-103, 133, 147-150, 151, 152,
Apollo	8, 249	Bentley Springs *(Wakefield)*	10, 11		170, **174**, 175-177, 229,
Apollo 11 *(Moon landing)*	265	**Bewdley**	112-114,115, **298**		230-235, 258-260, 270-272,
Apple Records *(Abbey Road studio)*	257	**Biggin Hill**	157-159, 299		273, 275, 283
Armoury Road *(BSA Factory)*	48, 83, 301	Black, Cilla	77	Camberley & District MCC	5
Armstrong, Neil	265	Blackburn, Tony	210	Campbell, Donald (Bluebird)	194
All You Need Is Love	209	Boeing 747 'Jumbo Jet'	277	**Canada Heights**	115-119, 121, 139,
Anders, William *(astronaut)*	249	Borman, Frank *(astronaut)*	143, 249		174, **210**, 211-214, 218, **231**,
Andrews, Eammon	10	Bracebridge Street *(Norton factory)*	132		**236**, **237**, 254-257, 278-282,
Anglia TV	16, 23	Brands Hatch	151		283, 284, 295, **296**, 299, 303
Armchair Theatre	10	Brian Stonebridge Memorial	35	Carling, Malcolm	iv, 131, 202, 203
Asham Woods, *see Frome*		*Bridge over Troubled Water*	288	Carlos, John	240
Avengers	10	**Brill**	iv, v, 1, 81, 164-167, 283,	Carter, Albert	24
Avon Tyres	20, 21, 59		294, 300	Carter, Chris	**43**, 49, 57, 70, 92, 106, 107,
Bannister, Roger	7	Bristol MCC	244, 288		145, 146, 147, 150
Bantam, BSA	163	British Championships	35, 170, 173, 209,	Castle, Barbara *(Transport Minister)*	146, 210
Barlow, Lionel	158		236, 239, 265, 273, 286,	Castleford	248, 278, 283, 297
Bate, Cuth	182		289, 290	Chaplin, Barry	22
Baxter, Raymond	6	British Experts Trial	100, 103	Chaplin, Roger	22, 23,

Chaplin, Tony *(Chas)*	22	Frome & D MC & LCC	160, 215, 217,	Lavery, Chris	25
Chattaway, Christopher	7	Foot-and-mouth disease	32, 208, 210, 213,	Leask, Brian	119, 221, 239, 281
Cheltenham Home Guard Motor			215, 216, 232	Leeds United	8
Cycle and Light Car Club	28	Fox, Paul	20	Leighton, *see* Frome	
Cheney, Eric	11, 55, 83, 102, 126, 136,	Fraser, Tom *(Transport Minister)*	146	Lennon, John	160, 209
	152, 160, 168, 169, **170**, 176,	Garston Farm *see* East Meon		Lewis, Philip	23
	187, 237, **248**	Gemini VII	143	*Life in the Fast Lane*	301
Chichester, Francis (Sir)	209	Glastonbury (1965 250 GP)	**151**	Light, Bob	152
Churchill, Winston (Sir)	112	Goldie *(the Golden Eagle)*	123	Likely Lads, the	104
Clark, Jim	8, 240	Goss, Neville	14, 16, 24	Little Norton, *see* Yeovil	
Clarke, Marge	295, 297	Grand Nationals	v, **5**, 34, 35, 45, 78,	*Long and Winding Road, The*	301
Clift, Aly	87		83, 135, 169, 173,	**Longleat Park**	83, 215-216
Clifton	12, **14**, **60**, 65-67, 81, **84**,	Great Flood	240	Lovell, James *(astronaut)*	143, 249
	85-88, **132**, 151, 199, **238**,	Greeves, Bert	71	Lower Hill, *see* Prestbury	
	240, **248**, 249-253, 254, 261,	**Hadleigh**	135, 169, 273, 274-277,	Lundin, Sten	35, 133, 169
	283, **296**,		278, 284	Lydden Hill	283
Coleman, David	20	Hailwood, Mike	**21**	**Lyng**	8, 140-142, 237, 245-247,
Collins, Michael	265	Hankom Bottom, *see* Winchester			251, 253, **263**, 283
Come Dancing	301	Hanks, Norman	**257**	Lywood, Ken	19, 20, 22, 45, **235**
Concorde	261	Hatherton Hall, *see* Nantwich		Manchester United	262
Cortina, Ford	163	**Hawkstone Park**	vi, 29, 30, 34, **35**, **38**,	Manx Norton	xi
Cotswold Scramble	135		39-44, 128, 131, 132, 135, 151,	Marquess of Bath	215
Cross-in-Hand, *see* Crowborough			168, **169**, 170, 173, 182-185,	Marsland Gander, Leonard	6, 7
Crowborough	128-131, **170**		186, 247, 251, 278, 279, 283,	Martin, Brian	48, 66, 83, 168, 179, 213,
Cook, Peter	100		293, 301		236, 239, **272**, 275
Coombes, John	71	Heath, Jack *(Pacemaker)*	60, 67	Matthews, Stanley	7
Cooper, Bob	132	Hedlund, Nils	84	Maybug Scramble	45, 170, 171
Cowgill, Bryan	19, 20, 22, 30, 218, 283	Hemery, David	240	McGregor, John	23
Cuerden Park	iv, 76, 78-81, 195-199,	Herringfleet Hills, *see* Somerleyton		McGuire, Barry	151
	200, 262, 283	Herriot, Maurice	89	McLaughlin, Brian	43
Daily Telegraph	6	**High Hoyland**	12, 71-74, **75**, 108	*MCN*, *see Motor Cycle News*	
Daleks	59	Hopkirk, Paddy	8	*Mi Amigo* (Radio ship)	210
Dimmock, Peter	19, 20, 30	Howdle, Peter	**165**, 294, 298	Moore, Bobby	194
Dodington Park	v, 178-181, 239,	Hutchinson, Colin	171	Moore, Dudley	100
	241-244, 246, 251, **262**, 283,	Hutton Conyers, *see* Ripon		Mobile/hand held cameras	30, 48, 54, **96**
	286, 288-293, **302**, **303**	Hutton, Len	7	*Monty Python's Flying Circus*	265
Draper's Farm, *see* Prestbury		Independent Television (ITV)	5, 8, 10, 14,	Motocross des Nations	iv, 19, 22, 170,
Dr Who	52		16, 19, 30, 36, 38, 108, 163,		209, 213
Dunne, Tony	262		239, 247, 248, 273, 278, 283,	*Motor Cycle*	6, **39**
Dykes, Jim	20, 21		288, 297, 298	*Motor Cycle News*	iv, v, 43, 48, 49, 64, 70,
East Chickerell *(Weymouth)*	14	Inchley, Peter	265		87, 92, 106, 111, 131, 136, 145,
East Meon	**172**, 190-194	Inter-AM series	242, 265, 272, 285		147, 150, 152, 158, 165, 170,
Eastwood, Scott	202	International racing	294-297		175, 191, 216, 232, 237, 239,
Ellis, Scott	19	*It's Not Unusual*	124		242, 273, 281, 283, 294,
Elsworth	35	Jackpot Scramble	135		297, 298
Eve of Destruction	151	Jewels Hill, *see* Biggin Hill		Mr Television	8, 12-13, **39**, 301
Farleigh Castle	19, 45-48, 83, 170, 173,	John Player Winternational	209, 212	Muswell Hill Farm, *see* Brill	
	239, 295	Johnson, Brian	19, 21, 22, 24, 30, 41,	**Naish Hill**	19, **20**, 22, 27, **28**, **36**, 45,
Farnsfield	12		49, 174, 175, 187, 215, 235,		59-61, 200-203, 223-226, **230**,
FIM	28, 89, 173		254, 301		**232**, **234**, **235**, 246, **264**, **266**,
FIM 750 *Coupe d' Europe*	173	Kennedy, John (President)	53		267-269, 270, 272, 275, 304
Final Score	20	Kilrie Farm *see* Kirkcaldy		**Nantwich**	2, 12, 83, 93-96, 97, 98,
Flowers in the Rain	210	Kirby, Tom	92, 269		152-156, 158, 181, 185, 237,
Forsyte Saga	195	**Kirkcaldy** (also Kilrie Farm)	8, 227-229,		251, **296**
Francis, Gordon	v, 21		258, 261-263, 270, 283	**Newport** *(see also* Caerleon)	56, 217, 271
Frome	97 99, 105, **134**, 152, 160-163,	Kuril, Ludek	297	Nicks, Mike	**258**, 273, 281, 283
	166, 170, **171**, 215, 217,	Kyffin, Roger	**65**, 67	Nicoll, Robert	275
	237, 284-287, 301, **302**	Larkstoke, (Warks)	12, 34, 35, **36**, 135	North Hants Motor Cycle Club	63

North v South Scramble	151, 168-171	Smith James	**257**
Norton Villiers Trophy	303	Smith, Tommy	240
Not only ... but also	100	Soarbrook Farm, see Caerleon	
Oh Boy!	10	**Somerleyton**	iv, **82**, 89-92
Olympic Games	84, 89, 240,	Southampton & DMCC	14, 24
Our World	209	Southern Scott Scramble	5
Pacemaker	**60**, 67	Southern TV	8, **9**, 14, 53, 298
Palmer's Farm, see Bewdley		South Reading MCC	6
Patchquick Trophy	170	Spanish GP	83
Parkinson, Denis	xi, **10**, 11, 14, 16, 71	*Sports Personality of the Year*	20
Pinhard Prize, the	23	*Sports Special*	20
Polanka, Sten	136	*Sportsview*	20
Portsdown Hill (Hants)	14	SSAFA	10
Prestbury	28, **29**	Steed, Donald	**15**, 16, 23
Preston, Billy	257	Stewart, Jackie (Sir)	119
Preston Cobb, Derry	100, 129, 136, 193	Strakonice, Czechoslovakia (CZ factory)	71
Queen Elizabeth 2	209	Stiles, Nobby	262
Race programmes	**39, 167, 293**	Student uprisings	240
Radio Caroline (pirate radio)	151, 210	Sudbury MCC	15, 16, 22
Radio London	210	*Sunday Night at the London Palladium*	38, 301
Radio 1 and 2	210	Surtees, John	8
Rallycross	xii, 283, 301	Swanley, see Canada Heights	
Ramsey, Alf (Sir)	194	Swarfega	**124, 167**
Rediffusion	10	*Tale of Two Cities, A*	2
Retford *(Bevercotes)*	12	Taylor, Harold	5, 19, 22, 36, **43**, 45, 49,
Ringinglow *(Sheffield)*	12		89, 217, **240**, 283, **292**,
Ripon	12, 120-123, 159, 296		**294, 295**, 297
Royal Enfield Project Bike	**44**	*Test Pilot*	235
Ryan, Jimmy	262	Thames Estuary Automobile Club	283
Saffire, see Kyffin, Roger		Thundersley *(Greeves factory)*	150
Scott, Claude	83	Tilling, Richard	235, 244
Scott Trial	154	*Tomorrow's World*	235
Scottish Six Day Trial	60, 154	*Top of the Pops*	62
Secret War	235	Torrey Canyon	205
Sheperd's Bush	269	Trippe, Gavin	175, 191, 216, 232, **235**,
Sheppard, Terry	**210**		242, 244, 297
Shrubland Park	22, 35	Trophee des Nations	19, 36
Sidecar racing	6, 7, 10, 14, 16, 31, 112, 113,	Tunstall (Staffs)	12, **17**
	114, 119, 157, 166, 298-300	**Tweseldown**	iv, v, x, 43, 60, 62-64,
Slazanger	10		104-107, 132, **133**, 186-189,
Small Heath *(BSA Factory)*	66, 108, 113, 275		236, 278
Smith, Irene	89		

Tweseldown Winter series	278
Twist *(cartoonist)*	15
Tye Farm, Gt Cornard	15, 16, 22, **23**
Tynan, Kenneth *(BBC 3)*	135
Tyne Tees Television	12
Vale-Onslow *(MC dealers)*	80, 81
Venables, Ralph	21, 43, 64, 111, **235**
Ventora, Vauxhall	274
Viney, Hugh	133
Wade, Len	**203**
Wakefield *(see also* High Hoyland)	10, 11, 12, 71, **74**, 108
Walker, Elizabeth	**11**, 274
Walker, Graham	7
Walker, Murray	xi, 3, 7, **11**, **18**, 19, **21**, 23, **25**, 27, 28, 36, **48**, **54**, 95, 116, 118, 119, **133**, **147**, **165**, 171, **174**, **187**, 199, 223, 274, 283, **294**, 299, 300, 301
Wallace, Edgar (Alderman)	9
Webb, Jim	215, 216
Weeks, Alec	21, 22
Welling, Bob	23
Wessex National	45
Westleton	75-77
West Stow Heath, see Bury St Edmunds	
Westward Television	12
West Wilts Motor Club	19, 20, 22, 27, 45, 59, 203
Weymouth and South Dorset MCC	14
Whitehouse, Mary	135
Wigg, Peter	22
Winchester	v, 8, 14, 27, **29**, **37**, 44, 53-55, 63, 273
World Cup (1966)	164, 168, 194
World of Sport	8, 10, 239, 247, 248, 273, 278, 283, 288, 297
Yarley	278
Yeo Vale Motor Cycling Club	108
Yeovil	108-111, **112**, **113**
YouTube	119